Asian Culture and Psychotherapy

Asian Culture and Psychotherapy

Implications for East and West

Edited by

Wen-Shing Tseng,

Suk Choo Chang,

and

Masahisa Nishizono

University of Hawai'i Press
Honolulu

10 09 08 07 06 05   6 5 4 3 2 1

Library of Congress Cataloging-in-Publication Data
Asian culture and psychotherapy : implications for East and West / edited by
Wen-Shing Tseng, Suk Choo Chang, Masahisa Nishizono.
p. cm.
Includes bibliographical references and index.
ISBN 0-8248-2854-2 (hardcover : alk. paper) —
ISBN 0-8248-2133-5 (pbk. : alk. paper)
1. Psychotherapy—Asia. 2. Psychology—Asia. 3. Cultural psychiatry—Asia.
4. Psychiatry, Transcultural—Asia. 5. Asians—Psychology. 6. Buddhism and
psychoanalysis. I. Tseng, Wen-Shing. II. Chang, Suk Choo. III. Nishizono,
Masahisa.
RC451.A72A85   2005
616.89'14'0095—dc22

2004021955

University of Hawai'i Press books are printed on acid-free
paper and meet the guidelines for permanence and durability
of the Council on Library Resources.
Designed by Tseng Information Systems, Inc.
Printed by The Maple-Vail Book Manufacturing Group

Contents

Preface

The idea for this book began to take shape while we were attending the Cultural Psychiatry Conference organized by the Transcultural Psychiatric Section of the World Psychiatric Association held in Rome, Italy, in 1998. During the conference, the many stimulating presentations and discussions on the relationship between culture and psychotherapy suggested a need for a further, in-depth, comprehensive inquiry. Sharing common Asian backgrounds, we felt that it would be a good idea to start with culture and psychotherapy in Asia. Our purpose in doing so was to refine our understanding of why and how the common, universal matrixes of the human mind become shaped in such a way that they contribute to the Asian mind and take on "Asian" patterns of personality, feeling and thinking, and psychopathology, and, consequently, approaches to healing. Examining Asian experiences and perspectives will enable us to better compare them with those of the West, thereby learning from and complementing each other and leading to a more wholesome approach to healing.

The idea took even better shape during the Second Pan Asia-Pacific Conference for Mental Health organized by the Chinese Association for Mental Health in Beijing, China, in 1999, when the list of chapter authors was made and the goal and framework of the book project were clarified. We then approached the University of Hawai'i Press, which was receptive to the idea, and the project was launched.

However, there were difficulties. Even though all the chapter authors were experts in their chosen topics in their native environments and in their own languages, for them to conceptualize and express certain cultural and psychological issues in English posed formidable problems. Foremost among them was that discussing basic Asian cultural and psychological values in English was like explaining non-Euclidean space using the corollaries of Euclidean geometry. Fortunately, we, as editors, were fluent in most of the authors' languages and had considerable experiences in Western, in particular, American, modes of thinking. In addition, we were able to work cooperatively with the contributors to develop this important work.

The contents of this book have been carefully planned and organized, and edited in close collaboration with the chapter authors to maintain the book's integrality. Although all the chapters address the same overall issue, overlapping is minimized, and cross-references are indicated, as necessary. Because many non-English terms are used, a glossary is attached at the end of book for the readers' reference. Following the contemporary world trend, Chinese terms are spelled according to the pinyin system, and any other spelling used previously, such as the Wade-Giles system and pronunciations in Japanese or Korean, are indicated in the glossary, with brief explanations. Diacritical marks (macrons for Japanese words and breves for Korean words) are indicated.

We are very grateful to Patricia Crosby, executive editor at University of Hawai'i Press, for her vision and interest in our project. Her academic interest in and familiarity with Asian cultures made our work much easier and afforded us valuable advice. We are also grateful to Masako Ikeda in the editorial department for her useful assistance in completing the project. Many thanks also go to Kathy Luter Reimers for her experienced English editorial work to improve the manuscripts written by the Asian authors. Our appreciation extends to Ok-Young Chang, M.A., for working on the breves for Korean words and Christine Yoshida for her assistance in reference checking and indexing.

It is with profound sadness that we inform our readers that Dr. Keigo Okonogi, the author of chapter 4 on the subject of the Ajase complex, passed away while we were in the final stages of preparing the book for publication. Dr. Okonogi was a professor and former president of the Kodera Foundation for Psychoanalytic Study in Tokyo. According to his widow, Dr. Eiko Okonogi, in spite of suffering intensely from terminal cancer for two years, Dr. Okonogi continued his work and published a few books on psychoanalysis and the history of his own work. His devotion to academic work and his attitude toward life are greatly admired and respected.

Finally, we would like to thank all of the chapter authors and coauthors, who have worked with us since the beginning of this project in a cooperative, scholarly, and persistent way. Among the valuable rewards that we have gained in our work as editors have been the new knowledge and insight contributed by each chapter author. They have helped us expand our knowledge tremendously and have greatly increased our comprehension of Asian culture, way of thinking, psychology, behavior, and problems, and, most important, the Asian way of healing the mind. They have further provided us with a better balance in the knowledge and experiences we have gained from contemporary (Western) psychotherapy. We hope that this book will be useful to all scholars, clinicians, and students of behavior and social science who are interested in culture and mental health and eager to expand their understanding of the differences and similarities in the human mind and the art of healing in the East and West.

Wen-Shing Tseng
Suk Choo Chang
Masahisa Nishizono

CHAPTER 1

Asian Culture and Psychotherapy: An Overview

Wen-Shing Tseng, Suk Choo Chang, and Masahisa Nishizono

This book is about Asian culture and psychotherapy. It looks at Asian culture as it relates to traditional Eastern approaches to healing, on the one hand, and to modern psychotherapy, which is largely of Western origin, on the other. One of the essential functions of a culture is to provide ways to relieve the suffering of its people. Since the forms of suffering are inevitably related to cultural patterns, the methods of healing also follow the culture's characteristic values and beliefs. The main focus of this book, therefore, is Asian culture and its relation to, and influence on, psychotherapy. It examines the similarities and differences between the diverse cultures of the East and the West and their implications for the application of psychotherapy. The book is based on the fundamental assumption that, beyond universally observed factors, culture is a significant variable and has a direct impact on the theory and practice of psychotherapy—the healing of the mind.

Scholars of behavioral science have defined culture in various ways. After analyzing hundreds of definitions of and statements about culture, American anthropologists Kroeber and Kluckhohn (1952) suggested the following formulation: "Culture consists of patterns, explicit and implicit, of and for behavior acquired and transmitted by symbols, constituting the distinctive achievement of human groups, including their embodiments in artifacts; the essential core of culture consists of traditional ideas and especially their attached values; culture systems may, on the one hand, be considered as products of action, on the other as conditioning elements of further action."

Based on these concepts, this book will examine Asian culture and how its ideas, beliefs, and values, as reflected in common sayings, legends, myths, dramas, philosophical thoughts, religions, and so on, directly or indirectly influence the psychotherapy performed in Asia. It will not merely seek to identify the unique issues relating to the theory and practice of psychotherapy in Asia but also examine how cultures pattern their common, basic, biological, and psychological matrixes into two contrasting types that we call "East" and "West."

Asian Culture

In order to discuss Asian culture, it is necessary to first clarify what we mean by Asia. For the sake of convenience, we use the term "Asia" broadly to refer to the regions around the Asian continent. Customarily, this is regarded as the "East" by Westerners, in contrast to the "West," which, from an Asian perspective, largely includes Western Europe and North America. These conventional definitions are used here to stress the differences that may exist in the world, not only geographically, but also socially and culturally.

From a geographic perspective, this book will concentrate more on East Asia, which includes China, Japan, and Korea. The societies of Southeast Asia, such as Thailand, Indonesia, and India, are included only occasionally. This is simply because, although Southeast Asia and East Asia share common basic values, the authors of this book are more familiar with, and have greater access to, East Asian traditions.

We are aware that within any society there are usually heterogeneous subcultures associated with differences related to socioeconomic, geographic, religious, or minority ethnic factors. Society is subject to cultural changes over time, as well, particularly when it is exposed to other cultures. Therefore, overgeneralization about any cultural group needs to be carefully avoided. However, for the sake of comparison, we will simply address the culture of any society as if it is a homogeneous one, and refer to Asia, or the East and the West, at a gross conceptual level.

The Study of Asian Culture and Mental Health

Although it is a difficult task, it is necessary to identify the overall "Asian culture" to be elaborated in this book. A review of literature reveals numerous publications that focus on the cultural systems of different societies, such as Chinese culture, Japanese culture, Korean culture, and so on, but few that deal comprehensively, in an integrative manner, with Asian culture as a whole.

Numerous publications regarding the psychology and mental health of Asian people have appeared in the past several decades. For example, there was a series of books that addressed culture and mental health in Asia and the Pacific (Lebra 1972, 1974, 1976; Caudill and Lin 1969). Some works are specifically concerned with the Japanese (Doi 1973, 2001; Lebra and Lebra 1974) or the Chinese (Bond 1986, 1991; F. L. K. Hsu 1953; Lin, Tseng, and Yeh 1995; Tseng and Wu 1985). Several publications focus on Asian-Americans (E. Lee 1997; Lee and Zane 1998; Sue and Morishima 1982), while others focus more specifically, from a cultural perspective, on psychotherapy for Asians (Cheng, Cheung, and Chen 1993; Cheng, Baxter, and Cheung 1995; Korean Academy of Psychotherapists 1995; Nishizono and Yamamoto 1988; Tseng 1997). These publications have provided useful knowledge regarding the culture, psychology, mental health, and healing of the minds of Asian people.

Common Threads Found in Asian Cultures

A few issues must first be clarified. Culture, like all other phenomena, can be better understood in relation to and comparison with what is already familiar to the observer, provided that he or she takes a comparative perspective. In doing this, some people dwell on the popular, folk level, others on the philosophical, intellectual level, and still others on the deviant, fringe level (Tseng 1997, 5–6). With this in mind, several themes have been commonly recognized as characteristic of Asian culture, and are summarized as follows.

Harmony with Nature

Scholars (Kluckhohn 1951) have pointed out that, for the sake of comparison, there are several frameworks that can be used to analyze the value systems of people in a certain cultural group. These include their orientations toward time, activity, the nature of human beings, the relationship between humans and nature, and interpersonal relations. With regard to the relationship between humans and nature, including such concepts as conquering, obedience, and harmony, it can be said that harmony with nature is strongly emphasized in Asian culture. This attitude toward nature, it has been speculated, is related to the traditional means of livelihood in Asia, namely, agriculture (Wright 1953). Chinese Daoist philosophy reflects this view.

Tradition and Continuity

Another dimension that can be utilized for comparison is orientation toward time, namely, past, present, and future. Spiegel (1988) has pointed out that, in contrast to the American emphasis on the future and the present, with less concern for the past, the Asian orientation toward time is generally in the order of past, present, and future. This view needs some clarification and adjustment. For instance, even though Asian people have a high regard for tradition and the past, as illustrated in the customs of ancestor worship and citing traditional thought, they are also very concerned with the future, emphasizing, for example, lasting marriages and the care and education of their offspring. Thus, the Asian orientation toward time is varied, depending on the issues addressed, and should not simply be generalized as primarily toward the past.

Synthetic Integration of Differences

From cognitive as well as attitudinal points of view, people in Asia tend to have a relatively high tolerance for variety, and easily accept differences in a synthetic manner, without a sense of conflict. For instance, Westerners may be amazed to learn that, in Asian societies, people allow the coexistence of different religions within a family, such as a father who is agnostic, a mother who is Buddhist, and children who are Christian or something else. Even one person may observe more than one religion for various occasions, as in Japan, where he or she may have a traditional Shinto wedding and a Buddhist funeral. This is in contrast to the Western, monotheistic tradition. It is not a problem for Asians to respect things that are old and traditional and, at the same time, value things that are new and modern.

Importance of Family

Valuing the family is another common thread observed among most Asian people. Close ties among family members are always emphasized, and the importance of filial piety is stressed. Close mother-child relationships are accepted and practiced, and become the basis for dependent-indulging love (*amae,* in Japanese) in adult social relationships (Doi 1973). This idealization of harmony, togetherness, and family also produces characteristically complex conflicts (J. Hsu 1995). Nevertheless, the family is regarded as the primary source of support and the basic unit of society. This concept is illustrated by the existence of a law in some Asian societies that requires children to care for their elderly parents or face legal punishment. Also, the most serious thing that can happen in a person's life is to be disowned by his or her parents, thus losing his or her family ties.

Vertical Relations

In interpersonal relations, vertical relations override horizontal relations. This emphasis has various ramifications, including a greater respect for authority and a moral sense of responsibility toward elders, parents, and higher officials. Again, many fail in the discharge of their culturally endowed obligations, and their failure breeds unwarranted fear, timidity, and distrust.

As a result of this emphasis on a hierarchical social system, people tend to respect the parental figures within a family and the authority figures within institutions and society in general. Obedience is stressed in parent-child relations and, by extension, in authority-subordinate relations. With the movement toward democracy, the emphasis on vertical relations is gradually fading; instead, horizontal relations, such as those between husband and wife and among colleagues, are receiving greater emphasis.

Interpersonal Relationships

Although interpersonal relationships are important aspects in all our lives, they are of relatively more concern for Asian people. It has been pointed out that, in contrast to individually oriented Westerners, Easterners are more situation oriented (F. L. K. Hsu 1953). This means that, instead of taking the perspective of the "self" and asserting one's rights, benefits, and boundaries, Asians are enculturated since childhood to be concerned with others' opinions and how they will be regarded and received by others. From this concern there developed a culture concerned with "face," which is more or less shame oriented, rather than guilt oriented. The basic, underlying assumption is that a person cannot survive without others and cannot exist outside the group.

Harmonious Resolution

An extension of the concern for others in interpersonal relationships is the emphasis on the harmonious resolution of problems. People are encouraged to bend, to endure, to tolerate, to comply, and not to stand out, rather than to fight, to challenge, or to defy. It is important for clinicians to know in therapy with their clients that seeking harmonious solutions is more valued than confrontation. It should be explained that this does not result in a fatalistic or passive end. A person has the basic right to defend himself or herself and even challenge an authority figure if he or she is seriously harmed by others or mistreated by an authority. What is important is determining in what situations harmonious solutions are aimed for, before reaching a point of no return. Thus, many variations exist for the same individual, within the same society, and among different societies in Asia. Therefore, careful judgment and application are necessary, beyond the general patterns that have been described.

Needless to say, all cultures are different from each other, as are all individuals. Therefore, each culture must be seen in its own light, in its difference and uniqueness from others. At the same time, however, we need to recognize what is common behind and beneath unceasing social changes and inexhaustible surface variations among cultures. What we want to know is what makes the societies of Southeast Asia, and those of Northeast Asia, "Asian" (or "Eastern"). What, if any, is the central, organizing principle, the logic of the societies, that makes them "Asian"? In answering these questions, our implicit control and reference point is the "Euro-American" (or "Western") model. Our fundamental assumption is that all cultures that are durable and widespread must meet the needs and aspirations of human beings. How do Asian traditions meet them, for better or for worse? How do they relate to the experiences, perspectives, and logic of the West? Finally, how can the wisdom of cultures accumulated separately for thousands of years, having now met, be integrated?

Culture and Psychotherapy

The importance of the influence of cultural factors on the practice of psychotherapy began to attract the attention and concern of scholars and clinicians in the early 1960s. This was reflected by the study of indigenous healing practices, with comparisons to contemporary, formal psychotherapy (Frank 1961; Kakar 1982; Torrey 1986; Tseng and McDermott 1975); the investigation of culturally specific psychotherapies (Jilek 1982; Lebra 1976); the examination of intercultural psychotherapy (Hsu and Tseng 1972; Tseng and Hsu 1979); and transcultural psychotherapy, or counseling across cultures (Marsella and Pederson 1981; Pedersen, Lonner, and Dragun 1976). Topics relating to "culture and psychotherapy" have been dealt with in countless publications (Abel and Metraux 1974; Tseng and Streltzer 2001). The term "transcultural" psychotherapy, or "cross-cultural" psychotherapy, stresses the importance of crossing the cultural barrier that exists between the therapist and the patient. "Intercultural" psychotherapy indicates that the cultural backgrounds of both the patient and the therapist are going to interact through the process of therapy, and, therefore, the "intercultural," "interactional" process is emphasized. Even though these terms have slightly different connotations and implications, they all highlight the significant impact of cultural processes on the practice of psychological therapy.

Along with the human rights movement and the concern for ethnic minorities, as well as increased cultural contact through migration, foreign travel, and the expansion of information networks, a greater awareness of the cultural differences among people of diverse backgrounds has developed. From a clinical perspective, it has become almost a matter of common sense to most clinicians that psychotherapy needs to be culturally sensitive, relevant, oriented, and responsive. Recently, the term "cultural competence" has become popular, and cultural competence is required in clinical work in addition to basic clinical competence.

Even though it is necessary to approach the effect of culture on psychotherapy from multiple perspectives, namely, technical, theoretical, and philosophical dimensions (Tseng 1995), when approaches to "culture and psychotherapy" are reviewed, it is found that most concentrate on the technical adjustments needed for culturally suitable psychotherapy. These include raising cultural sensitivity, overcoming language barriers, adjusting therapist-patient relations, promoting cultural understanding, increasing cultural empathy, and so on.

However, few scholars or clinicians have examined culture and psychotherapy from theoretical or philosophical levels. It is a salient fact that the contemporary, formal mode of psychotherapy has been derived mainly from the West. The theories for understanding human nature that comprise the foundation of the clinical practice of therapy, such as those of human behavior, personality, psychological development, defense mechanisms or coping patterns, psychopathology, and the optimal resolution of problems, are based primarily on the clinical experiences and research of Western scholars and clinicians with Western European and Northern American patients. To what extent these Western-derived theories are universal and can be applied to people of other cultures, particularly in the East, is a challenging issue awaiting vigorous exploration.

Although the practice of psychoanalysis no longer prevails in contemporary Western societies, some psychoanalytic theories are still considered useful for understanding the nature of human psychology. In contrast to other schools of psychotherapy, such as cognitive or behavior therapy, psychoanalytic-oriented psychotherapy focuses on the dynamic nature of human nature and is more useful for examining the cultural aspects of depth psychology. However, the psychoanalytic theory concerning human psychology is a product of the West. Determining the extent to which it can be applied to people in the East, and in what ways it needs modification, revision, or expansion, are challenges waiting for us.

Actually, some scholars and clinicians have started to tackle these issues from theoretical perspectives (Tseng 2001, 779–794). For example, F. L. K. Hsu (1973) has challenged the concept of the self and personality as defined by Western scholars. He has pointed out, for instance, that the boundaries of the ego are basically different between the people of the East and the West. Ego boundaries are much more prominent and clear for people in a culture that emphasizes the importance of the "individual." Ego boundaries are relatively blurred and fused with other people (particularly immediate, close family members) in a culture that is situation oriented. S. C. Chang (1988) holds a similar view.

Among theories of personal development, it has been pointed out that, although Eric Erikson's (1950) concept of psychosocial development is useful, there is a need for cultural modification regarding the themes or tasks that are identified and stressed in each developmental stage. Also, the pace of development between different stages may be different from culture to culture, being faster in certain stages, more delayed in others (Tseng 2001, 788–790). Obviously, the theory requires cultural adjustments.

It has been thought that the psychosexual development theory proposed by Sigmund Freud, which is concerned with the development of basic biological drives and instincts, is universally applicable. However, some scholars and clinicians have indicated the need for cultural modification and expansion of the theory (Chang 1998). This is particularly true with respect to the Oedipus complex observed in the phallic stage of development. For instance, how a paternal figure is involved in a parent-child triangular conflict may change in different family systems (Malinowski 1927), and the intensity of and culturally sanctioned solutions for the complex will vary (Tseng and Hsu 1972). Even entirely different emotional complexes, such as the Ajase (Okonogi 1978) and the Ganesha (Kakar and Ross 1987), are recognized in certain cultural backgrounds, in addition to the Oedipus complex. These issues are dealt with in detail in chapter 4, by Okonogi, and chapter 5, by Kakar. It seems that, with regard to the basic universal of child-parent relations, the child-father relationship develops as the primary framework in certain cultures, the child-mother relationship in others. If this is the case, the causes, implications, and consequences (including psychotherapeutic approaches) of such divergent and contrasting developments require a great deal more study.

It needs to be pointed out that these theories have been developed primarily to help clinicians understand and interpret their patients' behavior. Very few scholars have attempted to deal directly with the cultural perspectives of the therapy itself. This is a challenging subject for future exploration.

The philosophical dimensions of the effect of culture on psychotherapy have been revealed by a few scholars and clinicians, emphasizing the importance of the philosophical views that influence the process, direction, and results of psychotherapy. For instance, Varma (1982) has reported that the practice of psychotherapy is extremely difficult in India, primarily because of the fundamental philosophical views and attitudes of the people. According to Varma, they have a fatalistic view of life, believing that their present suffering is the result of sins committed in earlier incarnations. It is difficult for psychotherapy, which aims at the resolution of problems in life, to flourish in such a belief system. Thus, it is clear that basic philosophical concepts and attitudes have a direct, significant impact on psychotherapy. This subject has rarely been elaborated by scholars in the past, and awaits further exploration.

Scope and Goal of This Book

From the discussions above, it is clear that there is a great need to examine culture and psychotherapy at the theoretical and philosophical levels, beyond their technical or practical dimensions. The goal of this book is to conduct such a theoretical exploration, at least from the Asian perspective, with the hope that it will open the door to more culturally relevant and competent psychotherapy.

Examining Personality and Psychopathology and Their Relationship to Therapy

Psychotherapy seeks to understand and, thereby, help to resolve, a patient's predicaments and sufferings. In doing so, it is necessary to study not only the patient's symptoms and psychopathology, but, even more basically in the Asian context, the personality and its disorders. This is because, from a traditional Asian perspective (especially Confucian), symptoms are signs, the tip of the iceberg, or an epiphenomenon of the underlying, or overarching, personality. To achieve the book's goal, section 1 addresses personality and psychopathology, on which the psychotherapist should focus before undertaking psychotherapy for a patient from any culture.

In chapter 2, Cheung and colleagues focus on the issue of personality in China. After a long-term evaluation of the Chinese personality, they developed an indigenous personality instrument for the Chinese. They first reviewed the obstacles to measuring the Chinese with a Western-derived instrument, and ascertained the need to design an instrument designed especially for the Chinese, by focusing on the culturally unique dimensions of Chinese behavior patterns and personality formation. After a massive survey and measurement of personalities in the normal Chinese population, they pointed out that there is a different personality profile for Chinese and American people (Cheung et al. 1996). Somatization has been identified as an important aspect of Chinese psychopathology. Interpersonal relatedness is an important personality dimension in the interdependent Chinese culture. Further, a unique coping mechanism, "passive-rationalization" (called the "Ah-Q" spirit, the mentality of dealing with problems in the manner of a dramatic figure, Ah-Q, in a novel written by well-known writer Lu Xun), is commonly recognized and needs to be measured as a unique Chinese personality trait. These results point to the existence of culturally characteristic personality traits, which need to be considered from a mental-health perspective to determine what constitutes a normal, healthy personality in the East and how to provide psychotherapy for people with that profile. The lessons learned from the development of a personality inventory that includes cultural considerations have set the tone for the following chapters in this book.

In chapter 3, Nishizono, based on his experiences as a psychotherapist, reviews the cultural changes that have occurred in Japan from traditional times through the Meiji era, before and after World War II, and the present. Through insightful observation, he describes the vicissitudes of psycho-pathology that have occurred in association with three stages of cultural change in Japan. He points out that the practice of psychotherapy is not static, but dynamic, responding to changes in lifestyle, psychopathology, and the social need for the latter.

In particular, he explains that, although people continue to stress the importance of traditional values to maintain harmony with others and with nature, they are also being asked to follow a trend toward modernization and establish their individualized selves. Consequently, in recent years, dynamic psychotherapy, which focuses on the care of the individual at the intrapsychic level, has been gathering more interest among young psychiatrists and clinical psychologists. This phenomenon corresponds to the increased concern with the individual in psychotherapy, in accordance with the cultural changes occurring in contemporary Japanese society. It is found that dynamic psychotherapy is useful for certain psychopathologies that are becoming more prevalent in contemporary Japanese life, such as borderline personality disorder and eating disorders, problems that had limited treatment results from the descriptive-oriented psychiatric care that existed in the past.

Theoretical Exploration Centering on Parent-Child Relations

Immediately after the elaboration of personality and psychopathology, section 2 explores the theoretical exploration of Asian psychology, with particular focus on parent-child relations. Psychotherapy, especially psychoanalytically oriented therapy, emphasizes the importance of early-childhood experience. The parent-child relationship in early life not only molds personality formation, but shapes inherent psychological problems in adulthood. This is the core and source of emotional complexes. Therefore, it is important and relevant to examine parent-child emotional relationships and complexes from a cross-cultural perspective. This examination is attempted through an analysis of Asian mythology, folklore, and other cultural products, such as children's stories and plays, to which people refer in daily life. It is believed that such cultural products can reveal the basic psychology of a culture at a deep emotional level, through more primary processes and less inhibited expressions.

In Western psychoanalysis, the Oedipus complex, or the parent-child triangular conflict and resolution, is considered a basic developmental stage through which each child must go. Scholars in the past considered the complex universal. However, this section illustrates that the classic Oedipus complex derived from Greek mythology is only one type of parent-child complex that occurs and needs to be resolved. There are other interpersonal emotional complexes rooted in parent-child issues, as illustrated by the Ajase complex, which involves the mother and son, rather than the father and son (chapter 4); the parent-child conflicts described in the Ganesha complex, in which the son is defeated by the father, rather than conquering him (chapter 5); and the prohibition against a man looking at a woman, which derives from the mother-child relationship (chapter 6). Parent-child complexes with different forms and solutions are compared cross-culturally through cultural products, such as fairy tales and plays, in Asian and Southeast Asian societies and the West (chapter 7). They illustrate how different people, based on their cultures, experience and deal with basic parent-child relations in various, diverse ways, rather than in the one, classic way described in Greek mythology.

More specifically, in chapter 4, Okonogi describes the Ajase complex, the unique emotional complex between mother and son found in Japan, which is not well known to Western scholars. The complex borrows from a legendary Indian story about Prince Ajatasatru, who had murderous desires toward his own mother for what she had done to him. Okonogi pointed out that this mother-son complex is pre-Oedipal and does not involve the father figure or sexual matters. It is entirely different from the Western Oedipus complex, which involves a triangular relational complex among the parents and the child in the phallic stage (Okonogi 1978, 1979).

In chapter 5, based on psychoanalytical experiences and insights from India, Kakar indicates that certain forms of the maternal-feminine may be more central in Indian myths and psyche than in their Western counterparts. In the story of Devi, the omnipotence and sexual energy of the goddess, expressed in the imagery of her dancing and riding naked, exhausting even the most powerful male to abject submission and ultimately death, leaves the image of the goddess as man-woman. Further, Kakar elaborates on the importance of the mother-son relationship with the story of Ganesha—the most popular and adored Hindu god, a son of the powerful goddess Devi. The story reflects a Hindu mother's expectation that her son will arrange his life around her and see her as the center of the universe, an expectation that Kakar (1978) refers to as the Ganesha complex.

Following this, in chapter 6, Kitayama elaborates on mother-child relations through an analysis of Japanese mythology and folktales centering on the taboo against a man's looking at a woman. He indicates that, because of the close emotional relationship between mother and son, the man (as a son) has difficulty viewing the "ugly" side of women (his spouse —often resulting from exogamy with a nonhuman female) beyond the idealized mother-figure. He points out that the prohibition against looking is a taboo set up for man against woman, due to the early (oral) stage of fixation with and idealization of the mother (Kitayama 1985).

Finally, in chapter 7, Tseng and his colleagues examine the Oedipus complex as it is revealed in Asian cultural products. They disclose that the nature and intensity of the Oedipus complex in Asian societies is carefully and subtly described, rather than presented explicitly. In addition, the way in which the parent-child conflict is resolved is often different in the East. The child is always defeated by parental authority, an appropriate solution for intergenerational conflict in Eastern societies, which emphasize parental authority figures. These findings point out that the nature and pattern of personal development is greatly subject to the cultural environment in which an individual grows up (K. I. Kim 1978; Tseng and Hsu 1972).

Based on this theoretical exploration of parent-child relations, the therapist is encouraged to understand the human emotions and complexes relating to early childhood experiences in a broad sense, with consideration of cultural perspectives. Based on this kind of cross-cultural comprehension and insight, more proper assessment, understanding, and care of patients can be delivered in clinical service, particularly centering on the issues of parent-child relationships. This is true for all culturally diverse patients, whether Eastern or Western.

Reviewing Traditional Thought and Philosophy
as the Backbone of Therapy

In section 3, traditional thoughts and philosophies of Asian origin are examined, that is, the systems of thought and philosophical ideas and attitudes that have long been held by Asian people and have formed the core of guidance in their thinking, behavior, and reactions to life. In order to carry out culturally oriented psychotherapy, a therapist cannot ignore the importance of these traditional thoughts and philosophies, which directly or indirectly influence the patient's mind, emotions, and behavior.

The thoughts and behavior of Asian people have been heavily influenced by three traditions—Confucianism, Daoism, and Buddhism—in a compound and complementary way. These philosophies are elaborated in chapters 8, 9, and 10 of this section. Clearly, they are not in themselves psychotherapies, intending to heal a person's troubled mind. However, they do contribute to understanding human nature, guiding people in their thinking and behavior, suggesting ways to face and deal with psychological problems and seek good mental health.

In chapter 8, Yan examines the essence of Confucian thought. He points out that Confucianism emphasizes the fundamental benevolence, rather than evil, of human nature and teaches that the goal of life is to cultivate this nature and develop one's potential, rather than to conquer the external world, and to maintain proper human relations in society. From mental health and psychotherapeutic perspectives, he indicates that Confucian thought advocates benevolent empathy toward others (including patients), seeking harmony as the principle of interpersonal relations and following the golden mean in dealing with problems. Basically, the Confucian school believed that every person had the potential to achieve maturity and that self-cultivation was the means to achieve it.

Young and colleagues, in chapter 9, describe the basic views of Lao-zi, the originator of the Daoist school of thought in ancient China, which, in subtle, unofficial ways, influenced the philosophical attitudes of people through many centuries, influencing Chinese Buddhism, traditional medicine, and so on. They indicate that Daoism views the person as a tiny part of nature and that a person's goal is to follow the way of life that exists in the universe. Lao-zi's view of the world is characterized by the Concept of Opposites, with the existence of two poles in every matter; the way to deal with life is, paradoxically, to follow the virtue of not-contending, or doing nothing. Lao-zi helped us see the nature of our lives from an entirely different perspective and offered a paradoxical way of coping with problems. Young and colleagues also report their clinical experiences conducting a Chinese style of cognitive therapy by utilizing Daoism's philosophical views.

Buddhism, as analyzed in chapter 10 by Chang and Rhee, originated in a small kingdom in the foothills of the Himalayas in present-day Nepal and spread over East and South Asia. Contemplating the pain and suffering in life inevitably attendant to growth, aging, sickness, separation, and death, Buddhism finds the causes for human miseries in humanity's selfishness and consequent attachment to and craving for what is illusory and transient over what is real and durable. To be released from the chains that bind one to the ephemeral is to rediscover the real self that is buried beneath the layers of the false self. Are not reality and the true self, Chang and Rhee ask, what philosophers and psychologists in both the East and the West have searched for since ancient times, as we do today, perhaps even more so?

These three chapters illustrate that, on different levels and using different approaches, Confucianism, Daoism, and Buddhism offer different solutions for human life problems. Examining these traditional thoughts and philosophies, valued by Asian people in both the past and the present, and comparing them with the emphases of Western ethos will help us understand the different approaches advocated in the East and West and, from there, how to move into actual therapeutic work.

Presenting Unique Psychotherapeutic Approaches
from Asian Culture

If we define psychological therapy very broadly, all the therapy observed
around the world, in the past and the present, can be conceptually categorized into culture-embedded, indigenous healing practices; culture-
influenced, unique psychotherapies; and culture-related, common psychotherapies (Tseng 2001, 515–561). Using this concept, the contributors
to section 4, describe and discuss several therapeutic modes or approaches,
closely related to culture-influenced, unique psychotherapies, that originated in Asia. "Culture-influenced, unique psychotherapies" refers to certain therapeutic practices or approaches developed in certain cultures that
are heavily influenced by cultural factors. It is important to examine in
what ways cultural factors are utilized, applied, and reflected in these
unique approaches.

In chapter 11, Kitanishi, a prominent teacher and practitioner of Morita
therapy, presents his view of the philosophical background of the therapy,
an approach pioneered in the early 1920s in Japan (about the same time
that Sigmund Freud started psychoanalysis in Europe). In contrast to the
traditional understanding of Morita therapy, Kitanishi offers the updated
view that, at its core, neo-Morita therapy is a therapeutic method that resolves egocentric love and suffering caused by unwarranted attachment
and craving. He elaborates that, in the original concept of Buddhism, suffering is understood as "not being able to control things according to our
will" or "things that do not go according to our wish." We suffer because
we think that our bodies and minds and all other phenomena belong to us,
and we try to control them according to our wills. He explains that Morita
therapy emphasizes discovering a new self and moving forward with life,
rather than searching for the reasons for suffering, anxieties, or fears. The
Eastern views of nature and egolessness, or the attitude of accepting things
as they are *(arugamama)*, are used to correct pathological narcissism. In
therapy, the focus is on the development of a self that incorporates nature
(Kitanishi 1999).

In chapter 12, Kawahara, one of the key practitioners of Japanese Naikan therapy, elaborates on how Buddhist religious beliefs form the basis
of this unique, introspective method of psychotherapy. Naikan therapy
methodologically follows Zen Buddhist practices, requesting that clients
go through a "retreat" and examine their minds and lives. In principle,
this self-inspection is intended to raise a sense of appreciation and support from others, through the recollection of the experiences of love that

one has received from others (particularly immediate family members) and the recollection of one's self-centered attitudes (Kawahara 1999). This practice is considered to facilitate guilt-consciousness, by reinforcing the sense of *on* (obligation), particularly the *on* (grateful obligation) regarding one's mother. Thus, Naikan therapy very effectively uses such basic characteristics of the Japanese personality as strong potential guilt feelings, *on*-consciousness, the predominant significance of the mother, and specific moral values in the context of highly particularistic interpersonal relationships.

In chapter 13, Tseng and colleagues address an entirely different issue, namely, how to apply proverbs in the practice of psychotherapy, another unique feature of Asian psychotherapy. The proverbs used in daily life in a society often reflect the cultural views, values, and beliefs of the people in that society and are therefore useful instruments for providing suggestions and guidance in psychotherapy. They provide a highly culture-based and -colored therapeutic approach. The authors examine proverbs commonly used in the East and West, discussing the ways in which different values are stressed in coping with situations or problems, and the common issues between them. The usefulness of applying proverbs in psychotherapeutic communication is explained.

Following this, in chapter 14, Chang, based on his own personal experiences with meditation and a description of the process of Zen meditation, elaborates on the basic differences between the methodological features of psychoanalysis and Zen meditation. In psychoanalysis, the goal is enriching ego content and strengthening ego function by way of the intellect in order to replace and illuminate the darkness and chaos of the unconscious. In Zen, the ego is the obstacle to the workings of the innately healing matrix of the human psyche. Therefore, the ego must be resolved and removed. Chang explains that in Zen, as one's attention is withdrawn from the outside and directed internally, the mental stream—the flow of feelings and thinking, intertwined and conflicting—proceeds centripetally (Chang 1974) by internal and experiential logic rather than by a priori or external means. The process is inevitable under the circumstances and given the belief in the self-healing nature of the human psyche.

Reviewing Psychotherapy Experienced in Asia

Finally, section 5 of the book examines the clinical experiences of psychotherapy in Asian cultures. It focuses on the basic, traditional thoughts that guide people's ways of thinking and behavior, the potential problems or conflicts arising from such thoughts, and the therapies—based on the theoretical background of these philosophical thoughts—that are used.

In chapter 15, Kim, a leading cultural psychiatrist in Korea, describes psychiatric service and the practice of psychotherapy in Korea, elaborating on several culturally relevant therapeutic modes applied there, including indigenous, shamanistic practices, Daoist psychotherapy, and folk-related therapeutic activities. All of these therapeutic activities are based, in general, on an intuitive approach that focuses on emotional aspects. Emphasis is placed on seeing the self as a part of the group and on harmony with others and nature. Kim explains that this is different from contemporary Western psychotherapy, which is intellectual and logical, and for which a cause-and-effect relationship and logical inference are required (K. I. Kim 1999).

Echoing this, in chapter 16, Chang, using a different approach, examines the issue of culture and psychotherapy in Korea. After providing a historical and cultural background of Korea, Chang elaborates on the psychology of the Korean people within a cultural context. Specifically, he focuses on the "self" as seen in the East and West. Chang places Korean psychology and psychotherapy in a larger cultural and historical context, suggesting that the Korean situation is symbolic of the problems and potentials of the meeting of the two traditions, East and West, as well as the two realities and the two selves that have preoccupied philosophers and psychologists.

In chapter 17, Tseng, Lee, and Lü review the trend of psychotherapy in China from social and cultural perspectives. Various kinds of psychological treatments that are practiced in China, including folk healing practices, unique therapies, and contemporary psychotherapy, are traced historically. This panoramic review indicates that, in the society as a whole, multiple healing systems, whether folk or modern, exist and are utilized. Each different healing practice performs certain functions and provides certain services for the society as a whole. It is also pointed out that geographical or subcultural differences have caused many variations among Chinese living in mainland China, Hong Kong, Taiwan, and overseas. Finally, the historical situation in China illustrates clearly that the vicissitudes of psychotherapy are subject to social and cultural factors, including political ideology, social situations, war, and cultural change. Providing mental health care to meet the psychological needs of the Chinese, who are currently facing rapid, dramatic sociocultural change, is a particular challenge for clinicians.

Chapter 18 concludes by summarizing the major differences between East and West regarding views of human nature, self, personal development, the nature of suffering, and appropriate styles of resolving problems. Based on these variations in Eastern and Western thoughts, recommendations for performing culturally competent psychotherapy are made from three dimensions, namely, technical adjustments, theoretical modifications, and philosophical reorientation. The chapter aims to integrate the essential issues raised in this book and suggests practical applications for both the East and the West.

Final Comments

As far as is comprehensively possible and in various ways, the contributors to this book examine the themes and values of various Asian societies and their attendant approaches to healing. These approaches are based on the following premises: If "Asian culture" is a coherent whole, it should be possible to identify its central organizing principle, whose diverse manifestations can be seen in its various aspects, components, layers, and structures, and all the manifestations can be related to a central principle. Thus, the cultural principle and its myriad and changing expressions are like a mathematical axiom and its corollaries. We have been too preoccupied with Eastern and Western corollaries, rather than axioms. This book intends to draw attention to those neglected areas. It does not dwell on the cultural and psychological features that distinguish one Asian society from another, but on the basic principle that lies beneath the sometimes seemingly inchoate surface of society and psychology.

Throughout the book, attempts are made to integrate the aspects of psychological therapy observed in the East and the ways in which they differ from those in the West. Suggestions are made on how integration may be carried out between the two traditions, to provide a more holistic view of psychotherapy and more effective and flexible practices for people of diverse cultures in the contemporary world. After all, the East and the West are metaphors for the two divided selves that are a common predicament for modern man. They suggest that both the Eastern and Western perspectives have been one-sided. The West, in its valorization of the ego, has neglected its matrix, and the East, in its preoccupation with the matrix, has inhibited the ego. There is room for both to learn and endeavor together, to integrate views and practices, and thereby develop a more comprehensive, expanded, and balanced way of healing the mind.

I

Personality and Psychopathology

CHAPTER 2

Personality and Psychopathology: Insights from Chinese Studies

Fanny M. Cheung, Yiqun Gan, and Poman Lo

Personality has been closely associated with psychopathology in the field of clinical psychology. Clinicians can benefit from understanding "the enduring emotional, interpersonal, experiential, attitudinal, and motivational styles" of a patient in "formulating a diagnosis, establishing rapport, developing insight, anticipating the course of therapy, and selecting the optimal form of treatment for the patient" (Costa and McCrae 1992, 11, 5). Cross-cultural studies of psychopathology recognize the importance of the sociocultural contexts that affect individuals' manifestations of abnormal behavior. Studies of Chinese personality and Chinese psychopathology have highlighted culturally relevant characteristics that affect treatment. In this chapter, we review issues in cross-cultural personality assessment and introduce the culture-specific personality traits identified by an indigenously derived personality measure, the Chinese Personality Assessment Inventory. We summarize specific cultural dimensions identified in Chinese illness behavior and Chinese personality attributes. We also relate these cultural characteristics to considerations in psychotherapy with Chinese patients.

Personality and Personality Assessment
Assessment of Psychopathology Using Western Personality Tests

Personality assessment is a major activity of clinicians. Personality tests provide information pertaining to the formulation and testing of diagnostic hypotheses by identifying and differentiating specific symptomatology.

21

Early importation of Western personality tests in clinical assessment primarily involved projective techniques. With ambiguous and nonverbal test stimuli, there was no need for tedious translation. However, the use of projective techniques on the Chinese people is limited (Cheung 1996). Low reliability, lack of cross-cultural validity, and the specialized training required for interpreting projective tests accounted for its unpopularity.

The most widely used personality test in clinical assessment is the Minnesota Multiphasic Personality Inventory (MMPI; Hathaway 1943). The MMPI consists of clinical scales characterizing psychiatric categories. Its items tap the current psychological state as well as long-standing personality traits or styles that are symptomatic of psychopathology. The scales and their configurations in profiles are useful in identifying psychiatric symptoms and syndromes. The MMPI and MMPI-2 are the most widely translated and adapted clinical tests of personality in cross-cultural assessment of psychopathology (Butcher 1996). The MMPI has been translated into Chinese and has been widely used in Hong Kong and China. The Chinese MMPI was published by the Chinese University Press (Cheung 1995a), and the publication of the Chinese MMPI-2 (Cheung, Song, and Zhang 1996) is on its way. The Chinese MMPI has gone through vigorous translation and standardization in Hong Kong and mainland China and is found to be useful in clinical assessment (Cheung and Song 1989; Cheung, Zhao, and Wu 1992). The MMPI basic scales are able to differentiate between normal people and psychiatric patients, including patients with schizophrenic, bipolar, and neurotic disorders. The personality profiles obtained for the different diagnostic groups are similar to the clinical patterns observed in the United States.

Despite its clinical validity, there are cultural differences in the pattern of scores obtained by both normal respondents and patients that should be taken into account in clinical interpretation of the Chinese MMPI. In particular, normal Chinese respondents score higher on a number of clinical and validity scales, including the F, Depression (2), Psychasthenia (7), and Schizophrenia (8) scales when the U.S. norms are used (Cheung 1995a; Cheung, Song, and Zhang 1996). Compared to the normal Chinese profiles, however, the profiles for Chinese psychiatric patients are further elevated.

Does the higher elevation on these scales among normal Chinese respondents suggest that the Chinese people have more psychopathology than their North American counterparts? Further analysis on the items of these scales indicates that the different endorsement rates between Americans and Chinese respondents on the items of these scales may be due to cultural differences in the manifestation of psychopathology. Many of the items depicting "clinical features" in the MMPI were also given more desirable ratings by Hong Kong college students compared to their American counterparts (Cheung 1985b). If the MMPI is interpreted on the American norms without this awareness, there is a tendency to overidentify psychopathology. On the other hand, if the locally derived Chinese norms are adopted, the scores tend to be subdued even among psychiatric patients, so that there may be an underestimation of psychopathology. A similar pattern is found with the Chinese MMPI-2 (Cheung, Song, and Zhang 1996). In interpreting the Chinese MMPI, it has been recommended that both the U.S. and the Chinese norms be taken into account. In using the U.S. norms, the test user may find a more definite level of elevations on the clinical scales, but should allow for an adjustment of up to one additional standard deviation on scales F, 2, and 8. On the other hand, the code-types obtained by the different diagnostic groups when using the Chinese norms are better defined, although the overall scale elevations are not pronounced. (A code type is defined by the pattern of elevated clinical scales on the MMPI and their rank order in terms of elevation; please refer to Butcher and Williams 1992 for details.)

Although the Chinese MMPI and MMPI-2 have been useful in discriminating between psychiatric patients and normal adults in clinical assessment, these cross-cultural differences raise a more theoretical issue about the pattern of the relationship between personality and mental health among Chinese people. In addressing the cross-cultural differences of this pattern, we are asking two related questions: Is the pattern found in Western cultures universally applicable? Are there personality characteristics that are important to the understanding of Chinese personality and mental health that have been left out in Western studies?

Results from research and applications of the Chinese MMPI show that the answer to the first question is affirmative. The clinical profiles of different diagnostic groups in China fit those obtained in the United States (Cheung and Song 1989; Cheung, Zhao, and Wu 1992). The MMPI code-type profiles of Chinese patients correspond to the typical configurations of symptoms, behaviors, and personality characteristics associated with schizophrenic disorders and neurotic disorders.

While there has been significant research on the clinical assessment of personality (e.g., the MMPI) with Chinese patients, there has been relatively less on the relationship between normal personality domains and psychopathology. A large-scale attempt to examine the cross-cultural validity of assessing normal personality correlates of psychiatric diagnoses was made using the NEO Personality Inventory-Revised (NEO-PI-R) (Yang et al. 1999). The NEO-PI-R (Costa and McCrae 1992) provides an objective measure of the five-factor model (FFM) of personality, which asserts that there are five universal dimensions of personality: Neuroticism (N), Extraversion (E), Openness to Experience (O), Agreeableness (A), and Conscientiousness (C). The factor structure of the FFM was replicated for a large sample of two thousand psychiatric patients from ten cities in China, especially for the Neuroticism (N), Openness (O), and Conscientiousness (C) domains. Different personality profiles were identified for various diagnostic groups. Compared to normal volunteers, patients with substance-abuse disorders scored lower on Agreeableness (A) and higher on the Excitement Seeking facet of Extraversion (E). Neurotic patients and patients with major depression scored higher on N and lower on E and C. Schizophrenic patients, however, did not differ significantly from the normal volunteers on any of the five personality domains. The authors' explanation was that schizophrenia probably "reflects disturbances in cognitive and perceptual organization . . . rather than personality traits" (Costa and McCrae 1992, 364). On the other hand, it should be noted that the design of the NEO-PI-R was to assess normal personality traits, and its items did not cover manifestations of psychopathology.

McCrae and his associates (1998) concluded that the Chinese NEO-PI-R was a useful tool in understanding personality and psychopathology in China. They also asserted that the five-factor model of personality was universal and was relevant to both normal and abnormal psychology. Recent cross-cultural studies have raised a number of questions about the FFM: Is the FFM relevant and sufficient for understanding both normal and abnormal psychology of the Chinese people? This question relates to the second question raised earlier: Are there personality characteristics that are important to the understanding of Chinese psychopathology that have been left out in Western studies? Specifically, are there personality constructs that are indigenous to the Chinese culture which have been left out by imported tests?

The use of normal personality tests such as the NEO-PI-R for diagnostic purposes has also been challenged (Ben-Porath and Waller 1992). In particular, the undifferentiated composition of the Neuroticism domain of the NEO-PI-R was questioned. The facet scales of the N domain include Anxiety, Depression, and Impulsiveness. In clinical interpretation, the essential features of these forms of psychopathology are associated with different personality dimensions. The aggregation of these features into a single personality domain renders the personality domain suspect as a useful differential diagnostic tool. On the other hand, there is less dispute that these normal personality tests may be used as an adjunct to clinical measures to contribute information on stable personality characteristics that are of clinical significance.

In examining the relationship between personality and mental health among the Chinese people, the additional question is not only what type of personality test is useful, but also whether tests developed in non-Chinese societies are culturally relevant and applicable. To answer this, we must examine studies of Chinese personality.

Studies of Chinese Personality

Early studies of Chinese personality have focused on the Chinese national character (K. S. Yang 1986). In his review of the empirical studies on Chinese personality, Yang grouped the studies into three categories of personality characteristics: motivational, evaluative-attitudinal, and temperamental. Yang identified the common pattern of Chinese character included in these studies as "social harmoniousness, group-mindedness, mutual dependency, interpersonal equilibrium, relationship-centeredness, authoritarian syndrome, external-control belief, heterocentric orientation, self-suppression, social introversion, practical realism, and holistic eclecticism. These characteristics portray the Chinese as a highly social, practical, and eclectic people with a strong collectivistic orientation" (1986, 148–149). However, Yang also pointed out that many of these personality characteristics have decreased as a result of societal modernization.

Recent studies of Chinese personality adopted a more dimensional approach. Instead of focusing on the Chinese national character, intracultural and intercultural studies addressed individual differences on specific personality dimensions, including cross-cultural comparisons of universal personality traits as well as indigenous personality characteristics, particularly those associated with interpersonal contexts. Cross-cultural studies of universal aspects of personality compared Chinese respondents with their Western counterparts on personality factors that underlie specific traits. Universal personality factors were confirmed among Chinese respondents using the Eysenck Personality Questionnaire (EPQ) and the

NEO-P-I-R (Barrett et al. 1998; McCrae, Costa, and Yik 1996). The three-factor model of the EPQ consists of Extraversion, Neuroticism, and Psychoticism. Among the three factors on the EPQ, Chinese respondents scored lower on Extraversion and higher on Psychoticism than their Western counterparts (Barett et al. 1998).

Cross-cultural studies of the NEO-PI-R showed that the five-factor model was recoverable across cultures. However, cross-cultural differences have been observed in the NEO-PI-R profiles of normal Chinese and North American respondents (McCrae et al. 1998). Compared to their North American counterparts, Hong Kong students showed low E (especially Excitement Seeking), high N6 (Vulnerability), and low C1 (Competence). In addition, there was a jagged pattern among Agreeableness facets for the Hong Kong students, with high A2 (Straightforwardness) and A4 (Compliance) and low A3 (Altruism). A similar profile was obtained for Chinese-Canadians who were recent immigrants. In contrast, the profile for Canadian-born Chinese was very similar to the North American norm. Acculturation effect might explain some of the differences among the various Chinese-Canadian groups. The authors suggested that these cross-cultural differences might also be due to different cultural standards for judging these personality traits. McCrae and colleagues (1996, 203) acknowledged that, despite the universality of the FFM, "Chinese differed from Americans in their emphasis on interdependence rather than autonomy, a difference with effects on the self-concept, cognition, motivation, and emotion."

Do universal personality factors provide a complete assessment of the Chinese personality? Several indigenous approaches have been initiated to measure personality from a distinctively Chinese perspective. Yang and Bond (1990) identified five factors from a pool of Chinese personality descriptive adjectives, which they labeled the Chinese Big Five: Social Orientation versus Self-Centeredness, Competence versus Incompetence, Expressiveness versus Conservatism, Self-control versus Impulsiveness, and Optimism versus Neuroticism. Cheung, Conger, Hau, Lew, and Lau (1992) extracted five factors from the indigenously derived Multi-Trait Personality Inventory: Outgoing versus Withdrawn, Self-serving versus Principled, Conforming versus Nonconforming, Unstable versus Stable, and Strict versus Accepting. McCrae and colleagues (1996) argued that these factors could be subsumed under the terms of the FFM as they did not define unique factors beyond those of the NEO-PI-R.

Chinese Personality Assessment Inventory (CPAI) as an Indigenous Measure of Chinese Personality

The development of the Chinese Personality Assessment Inventory (CPAI; Cheung et al. 1996) is intended to address the issue of universality versus cultural specificity. As a collaborative project of psychologists in Hong Kong and mainland China, the original aim of the CPAI was to provide Chinese psychologists with an instrument that is culturally relevant to their applied needs by capturing the important dimensions of Chinese personality. The CPAI consists of twenty-two personality scales, twelve clinical scales, and three validity indices for the purpose of personality and clinical assessment.

The selection of personality constructs and the generation of items for the CPAI were based on a combined emic-etic approach in test development. In addition to including culturally universal constructs, personality characteristics that were considered to be culturally specific to the Chinese culture were identified. Scales were developed for personality constructs that are deemed to be of specific interest to the Chinese culture, such as Harmony, Ren-qing (interpersonal favor), Face, Thrift versus Extravagance, Graciousness versus Meanness, Veraciousness versus Slickness, Ah-Q Mentality (defensiveness), Family Orientation, and Somatization. Each item is a self-reporting statement describing a personal characteristic or typical behavior to which the respondent answers in a yes-no format. The items were selected on the basis of large-scale preliminary studies designed to ascertain the language fluency, content relevance, and item-scale correlations. The CPAI was first standardized on a representative sample of 2,444 adults in mainland China and Hong Kong (see Cheung et al. 1996 for a full description of the development of the CPAI).

The CPAI was re-standardized in 2001 on a representative sample of 1,911 Chinese adults. Six new scales related to openness were added to the normal personality scales, and more items were added to the clinical scales. The CPAI-2 consists of twenty-eight personality scales, twelve clinical scales, and three validity indices. Exploratory factor analyses were conducted on the responses of the standardization sample on the CPAI-2 personality and clinical scales. Four factors were extracted from the personality scales and two factors were extracted from the clinical scales. The four personality factors were Social Potency, Dependability, Accommodation, and Interpersonal Relatedness. The two clinical factors were Emotional Problems and Behavioral Problems. A list of the CPAI-2 scales grouped by the four personality factors (with a total of twenty-eight personality scales) and the two clinical factors (with twelve clinical scales) may be found in the appendix at the end of this chapter.

The Interpersonal Relatedness factor is of particular interest, because it comprises indigenous scales including Harmony, Ren-qing, Traditionalism versus Modernity, Discipline, and Thrift versus Extravagance. The characteristics associated with these personality scales reflect a strong orientation toward interdependence, instrumental relationship, avoidance of conflict, and adherence to tradition and norms.

The original CPAI factors were compared to the FFM factors in a number of studies. Four factors were found to share common domains. Three of the four CPAI factors converged in the Neuroticism, Conscientiousness, Agreeableness, and Extraversion factors of the FFM (Cheung et al. 2001). On the other hand, the Interpersonal Relatedness factor of the CPAI was not loaded by any of the facets of the Big Five. It is a dimension that is culturally specific to Chinese culture, but has not been covered in other Western personality measures. The personality characteristics associated with the Interpersonal Relatedness factor, such as Harmony and Ren-qing, would be related to conflict avoidance, self-esteem, and life satisfaction among Chinese respondents (Gabrenya and Hwang 1996; Kwan, Bond and Singelis 1997).

The CPAI scales on the Interpersonal Relatedness factor demonstrated incremental validity beyond the FFM in predicting social relationships in the Chinese culture (Cheung et al. 2001). These scales were used to predict trust of intimate persons and trust of strangers (Zhang 1997), filial piety (Zhang and Bond 1998), use of interpersonal persuasion tactics (Sun and Bond 2000), and communication styles (Leung 1999). Its usefulness in predicting mental health of the Chinese people has also been examined by relating the personality scales with the clinical scales of the CPAI in a number of studies.

Clinical Utility of the CPAI Personality and Clinical Scales

In the original standardization study (Cheung et al. 1996), the 2,444 respondents from China and Hong Kong in the normative sample were asked to indicate their level of life satisfaction in addition to filling out the CPAI scales. The Life Satisfaction Index consists of ratings in terms of satisfaction with one's job, physical health, mental health, family, and global life satisfaction. This Life Satisfaction Index had significant negative correlations with all of the CPAI clinical scales.

Would normal personality predict scores on the clinical scales? For the standardization sample, all of the individual personality scales were significantly correlated with more than one clinical scale. In particular, the Emotionality scale is a significant predictor for all the clinical scales. The Inferiority versus Self-acceptance scale also predicted all the clinical scales except for the Pathological Dependence scale. While Pessimism is a strong predictor of all the clinical scales on the Emotional Problems factor, its opposite pole, Optimism, is a strong predictor of Pathological Dependence in the Behavioral Problems factor. On the other hand, the Leadership scale is a strong predictor of all the clinical scales on the Behavioral Problems factor except Pathological Dependence.

The relationship between the indigenous personality scales and somatization is of particular interest in the study of Chinese personality and psychopathology. As will be discussed in the next section, somatization is a common form of manifestation of psychopathology among the Chinese people. The somatic presentation of psychological distress among Chinese patients has previously been misinterpreted as a denial of the affective components of distress. Kleinman (1986) later analyzed somatization from an anthropological perspective and viewed it as a contextualized response to emotional distress with implications for social relationships. The cultural significance of somatization makes it important to examine the indigenous personality traits that are correlated with this form of psychopathology.

The Somatization scale of the CPAI focuses on the pattern of complaint presentation as part of the person's illness behavior (Cheung 1995b). Items on this scale cover the expression of personal and social distress in an idiom of physical symptomatology and the tendency to seek help for these distresses from medical practitioners instead of mental health professionals (Cheung et al. 1996). The interpersonal dimension of illness behavior among Chinese patients suggests that the Interpersonal Relatedness factor of the CPAI is related to the somatization tendency.

Multiple regression analysis of the four CPAI personality factors on the Somatization scale from the 1996 standardization study shows that all four factors had significant effect, with the Dependability factor accounting for 21 percent of the total variance in the first step. In step 2, the Interpersonal Relatedness factor added another 16 percent to increase the cumulative R^2 to 37 percent. The cumulative R^2 explained by all the CPAI factors was 50 percent.

The contribution of individual CPAI personality scales to the prediction of Somatization was examined in another regression model using single scales. Stepwise regression of the individual CPAI personality scales on the Somatization scale shows that Pessimism (versus Optimism), Meanness (versus Graciousness), Inferiority versus Self-acceptance, Emotionality scales that load on the Dependability factor are among the best predictors. In addition, high scores on the Face and Harmony scales and low scores on the Flexibility and Modernization scales from the Interpersonal Relatedness factor were also strong predictors. Other personality scales that also contributed significantly to the prediction of Somatization include Self versus Social Orientation, Practical-mindedness, External versus Internal Locus of Control, and the reverse of Adventurousness. The total variance explained by the individual personality scales was 52 percent.

In her doctoral thesis, Gan (1998) used the CPAI scales to study the relationships among personality, coping behavior, and psychological adjustment in Hong Kong and Hawai'i college students. The Hawai'i student sample consisted of multiple ethnicities, including Caucasians, Chinese, Filipinos, Koreans, Japanese, mixed Asians, and Hispanics. The CPAI Somatization scale was used as one of the indicators of psychopathology. Instead of using all twenty-two CPAI personality scales, Gan administered sixteen personality scales, which were found to be related to Adaptiveness in the 1996 standardization sample. For both the Hong Kong and the Hawai'i groups, three factors were extracted from these sixteen scales: Emotional Stability, Dominance, and Relationship Concern. The Emotional Stability factor consists of a subset of scales from the original CPAI Dependability factor; the Dominance versus Submission factor consists of Leadership Introversion, Modernization, and Logical versus Affective Orientation (negative loading) scales of the CPAI. The Relationship Concern factor consists of Harmony, Flexibility (negative loading), Ren-qing, and Self versus Social Orientation, as well as double loadings on Logical versus Affective Orientation and Face. The Relationship Concern factor is comparable to the Interpersonal Relatedness factor obtained in the CPAI standardization sample.

To explore the pattern of relationships among the personality factors and the psychopathology measures, Gan ran a set of canonical correlation analyses for both the Hong Kong and the Hawai'i male and female student groups. The results showed that Somatization was correlated with high Relationship Concern and low Dominance for all four student groups. However, the pattern of associations among the psychopathology measures differed among the groups. Somatization was associated with low Antisocial

Behavior for the Hong Kong males and the Hawai'i females, with low Depression for the Hong Kong females, and high Depression for the Hawai'i males. The differential pattern of correlates between Somatization on the one hand and Antisocial Behavior or Depression on the other suggests that somatization may be interpreted as internalized aggression among Hong Kong males and Hawai'i females, a form of masked depression among Hong Kong females, and depression among Hawai'i males.

Gan also found cultural differences in the relationship between the CPAI personality factors and coping styles between the Hong Kong and the Hawai'i students. Among Hong Kong students, high scorers on the Relationship Concern factor were more likely to use problem-solving methods or to seek social support as their coping strategies. Among the Hawaiian students, on the other hand, a high degree of Relationship Concern was associated with more passive coping behaviors.

As shown from the CPAI studies, the Interpersonal Relatedness factor of the CPAI is related to manifestations of psychopathology, particularly in relation to somatization. The pattern of relationships between Interpersonal Relatedness and the manifestation of somatization for men and women in different cultures may be a complex one that deserves further investigation.

The Interpersonal Relatedness factor in the CPAI adds predictive value to models of mental health beyond those contributed by the Big Five factors of Neuroticism and Extraversion. The identification of this factor and its contributions to measures of psychopathology point to important directions in studies on Chinese personality and mental health. These studies should focus not only on universal dimensions of personality, such as neuroticism and extraversion, or of psychopathology, such as depression; additional dimensions of personality and psychopathology that are culturally relevant and important to Chinese culture should also be included. For example, somatization has been identified as an important aspect of Chinese psychopathology. Interpersonal relatedness is an important personality dimension in the interdependent Chinese culture. The CPAI personality and clinical scales have provided relevant measures of these dimensions.

As an indigenously derived personality measure, the CPAI is a useful assessment tool that taps not only universal domains of personality, but also emic constructs that have not been included in Western personality tests. This comprehensive measure provides a rich source of data on the configuration of personality patterns in relation to different forms of psycho-pathology. These patterns will help clinicians to better understand the manifestation and dynamics of psychopathology in the Chinese cultural context.

Summary of Findings: The Characteristics of Chinese Personality

Early studies on indigenous personality constructs and studies with the CPAI have highlighted the emphasis Chinese people put on interpersonal relationships. In collectivistic cultures, this interpersonal focus supple-ments individualistic personality characteristics in predicting behavioral dispositions and explaining manifestations of psychopathology. Person-ality should be examined in an interpersonal context. Gao et al. (1996) defined the Chinese self by its relations with others. In traditional Chi-nese culture, social behavior is oriented toward maintaining interper-sonal harmony and reciprocity in relationships. In studies of Chinese personality, these interpersonal characteristics contribute additional ex-planatory power beyond individualistic personality traits to predict such social behavior as filial piety, persuasion tactics, trust, and communica-tion styles. The emphases on harmony and relationship reciprocity are also related to less expression of anger, ambivalence in emotional expression, and lower likelihood of seeking professional psychological help (Cheung 2002). Studies on the relationship between normal personality and mental health in Taiwan show that extraversion is related to better mental health (Lu 1995; Lu and Shih 1997).

Other cross-cultural studies corroborate the importance of interper-sonal relationships to the mental health of the Chinese people. For ex-ample, a comparative study of the attributional style and depression in American and Chinese students found that, in a more collectivistic and interdependent culture, Chinese students accepted more responsibility for interpersonal failures than did American students (Anderson 1999). These "maladaptive" attributional styles accounted for higher scores on depression and loneliness. A review of the literature on depression among Chinese Americans by Tabora and Flaskerud (1994) showed that loss of filial piety would lead to increased somatization and depression resulting from guilt, anger, and sadness. These studies point to cross-cultural differ-ences not only in personality characteristics, but also in manifestations of psychopathology.

Chinese Psychopathology and Issues of Somatization

Cross-cultural research has shown that, although basic psychopathology is universal, cross-cultural differences are found in illness behaviors (Cheng 2001). Culture-specific features characterize patients' subjective complaints, symptom presentation, and help-seeking behaviors. In studies of psychopathology in Chinese societies, special references have been made to issues of somatization as culture-specific illness experience (Cheung 1985a, 1995b, 1998; Draguns 1996). Somatization is also associated with the use of the term "neurasthenia" *(shenjing shuairuo)* by Chinese patients to label various forms of psychological distress (Cheung 1989; Cheng 1995; S. Lee 1994, 1998). Understanding the cultural contexts that shape these illness behaviors can enhance our sensitivity to the patients' experience and facilitate treatment planning.

Indigenization of Neurasthenia as an Illness Label

Despite the lack of familiarity with psychiatric nomenclature and mental health resources, Chinese patients are more ready than American patients to admit to suffering from neurasthenia (Kleinman 1982; Lin 1989). While its imprecision has led to its decline in Western psychiatric taxonomy, "its broad range of associated symptoms as well as its ambiguous references allow for a subtlety in communication which leaves room for face-saving" (Cheung 1989, 239). Neurasthenia is used as a label to cover a variety of conditions ranging from depression and sexual dysfunction to schizophrenic disorders. Since "neurasthenia has been attributed to somatic depletion, overwork, lifestyle, and rationality, . . . it is removed from the stigma of madness" (Cheung 1989, 238). This may explain its acceptance as an illness label for psychiatric distress in Chinese folk culture. The concurrence of psychological and somatic symptoms is compatible with the holistic model of traditional Chinese medicine. The term was incorporated as a formal diagnostic category in the Chinese Classification of Mental Disorders (CCMD) and was popular with Chinese mental health professionals until the 1990s (S. Lee 1994, 1999). The core symptoms for the diagnosis include weakness and fatigue, worries and depression, excitability, nervous pain, and sleep disturbances. The disappearance of this diagnosis among Chinese academic psychiatrists in recent years reflects the transformation of the professional discourse in conformance with Western nosology. However, the concurrence of somatic and psychological symptoms and the tendency to report somatic symptoms to therapists remain prevalent features of the illness behaviors among Chinese patients.

Somatization as Illness Experience

The prevalence of somatic complaints presented by Chinese psychiatric patients has been reported since the 1970s (Kleinman 1977, 1982; Tseng 1975). The tendency to present psychological distress in the form of somatic complaints and to delay psychiatric treatment is found particularly among patients with depression. This tendency continues to prevail among individuals in non-Western cultures, including ethnic Asians living in the United States (Lee, Lei, and Sue 2001). While there is general agreement on the tendency of somatic emphasis among Chinese patients, its meaning and explanation have been a subject of debate.

Scholarly discourse on somatization among Chinese psychiatric patients illustrates the contrast between the Western biomedical model of mental disorders and the holistic model of health adopted in Chinese medicine. Cheung (1995b, 1998) critiqued the early discussions on the Chinese somatization tendency and the post hoc cultural attributions adopted to explain the tendency. The initial focus on somatization as a pathological disorder conceptualized the somatization tendency as a masking of an underlying psychological disorder whereby psychological symptoms are suppressed. The formistic and mechanistic approaches in biomedicine missed the complexity of the patterns of illness behavior through which somatization could inform the clinician about the subjective experience of the Chinese patients. In a holistic model of health, somatization could be understood in terms of the "phenomenology of discomfort and suffering, the process of communication, ways of coping and help-seeking, and the patient-doctor relationship" (Cheung 1998, 42).

Recent research has indicated that the use of body-related verbal expressions in the Chinese language to describe a wide range of personal and social concerns, including feelings, thoughts, and images, is not equivalent to somatization (Tung 1994). Studies also confirmed that presentation of somatic complaints does not preclude the presentation of affective and cognitive symptoms. Zheng, Xu, and Shen (1986) found that depressed patients described their suffering in both emotional and physical expressions. The somatic style of expressing emotions is not directly related to symptoms reported on a checklist.

Cheung (1995b) described somatization as an idiom of distress that is contextualized in a process of interpersonal communication between the patients and their social networks, as well as between the patients and their doctors. Chinese patients report different types of complaints, depending on their expectations about the nature of the consultation. The consultation experiences throughout their illness history would have shaped their interpretation and the narratives of their suffering.

The somatization tendency and the situational orientation among Chinese patients may reflect common personality characteristics shaped by cultural factors. Understanding the patients' personality dynamics can help therapists interpret the meaning of their illness behaviors and determine the appropriate course of intervention.

Implications for Psychotherapy

Scholars and clinicians have pointed out that it "is almost impossible to understand the nature of human behavior, discuss matters of abnormality or psychopathology, or elaborate on mental health care without focusing on social and cultural dimensions" (Lin, Tseng, and Yeh 1995, 3). Definitions of "normal" psychological functioning, the "healthy" mind, and the "mature" personality, which are stipulated as the desirable goals in psychotherapy, need to be examined in a cultural context. Definitions of mental health and the organization of mental health services are influenced by cultural values. The impact of cultural factors on the basic assumptions of psychotherapy varies across cultures. As such, psychotherapy with the Chinese needs to be deconstructed within the sociocultural context where it is conducted (Cheung 2000).

Leung and Lee (1996) noted the differences between the Chinese and Western value systems that shape the way in which problems are construed in psychotherapy in the respective societies. In Western theories of psychotherapy, and with most Caucasians, problems are defined as intrapsychic and individual. On the other hand, most Chinese people construe their problems as social and relational. Leung and Lee warned that without the sensitivity to these cultural differences, "Western-trained psychotherapists will treat the relationship problems of a Chinese person by advocating autonomy and independence or accommodation to the system" (1996, 447). Autonomy and independence are considered indicators of mental health in Western societies. Psychologically healthy people are assumed to be self-aware, self-determined, and self-interested, even when they are engaged in relationships with their significant others (Schneider, Karcher, and Schlapkohl 1999). However, for the relationally oriented Chinese person facing interpersonal problems, this expectation may exacerbate the original distress.

The universality assumption in theories of personality, psychopathology, and psychotherapy has repeatedly been challenged. Studies with the Chinese Personality Assessment Inventory confirm the cultural relevance of indigenously derived personality measures. The emic characteristics included in the CPAI are distinct from the personality structure found in studies using Western personality tests. These culturally related personality characteristics, such as Harmony, Ren-qing, Face, and Family Orientation, may be summarized as orientations toward interdependent relationships. In addition, the passive rationalization defense mechanisms used by Chinese people in dealing with reality problems are captured in the Ah-Q Mentality scale. The Somatization scale also highlights the dynamics of illness behavior associated with Chinese patients. These CPAI studies illustrate the need for culturally sensitive and appropriate instruments when applying Western forms of psychotherapy to the Chinese people. Without culturally sensitive assessment measures, important attributes that affect psychopathology and psychotherapy would be missed.

With the recognition of cultural differences in personality, the practice of psychotherapy in a collectivistic culture may take on different goals and styles than those in more individualistic and independent cultures. Interpersonal relationships can become a focus in these psychotherapeutic approaches. Imposing Western criteria of mental health, which emphasize autonomy and independence, may result in counterproductive therapeutic goals. Therapists who are trained to encourage patients to actively cope with psychological problems may have ignored the Chinese cultural virtues of harmony with nature and with others, and passively accepting problems as they are. They may also interpret the passive rationalization depicted in the Ah-Q Mentality defense mechanism as pathological.

Normal and abnormal, mature and immature, healthy and unhealthy are cultural constructions that need to be deconstructed. Clinically, therapists need to seek a culturally appropriate balance between active and nonactive approaches to guide patients in dealing with their problems. When Chinese patients present their somatic problems, not all of them are denying their psychological symptoms or lacking insight into their problems. The challenge for therapists is to understand the intrapsychic and interpersonal levels of the problems beyond the somatic level and to distinguish among patients who may conceptualize their problems at different levels.

In some cases, it may not be essential to forge the patients' conceptualization into an intrapsychic framework. A skillful therapist will know when and how to bypass the process of converting somatized problems into psychologized problems, and still work on the problems encountered by the patients in their lives. Insensitivity to these cultural issues would result in poorer therapeutic efficacy.

Given the holistic orientation of traditional Chinese medicine, Chinese patients are likely to accept an integrative approach to treatment that acknowledges their somatic concerns on the one hand and the personal and interpersonal problems in everyday life on the other. Therapists should first assess the readiness of patients to admit psychological problems, the stigma they attach to psychological attributions, and their psychological insight into the problems. The patients' conceptual framework should guide the therapists' adoption of an explanatory model of their illness and the form of intervention.

Culture-centered interventions have been advocated as a fourth dimension in psychology, going beyond the psychodynamic, behavioral, and humanistic perspectives (Pedersen 1999). Accurate assessment, meaningful interpretation, and appropriate intervention require a culture-centered approach. Although research with the CPAI has focused primarily on the personality of the Chinese people, its relevance to other people sharing the Confucian heritage, Chinese Americans, and other Asian Americans is suggested. Similar observations about cultural differences in psychotherapy have been made on these groups (Schneider, Karcher, and Schlapkohl 1999). Current studies on the CPAI involving different ethnic samples suggest that the indigenously derived personality dimensions may in fact be relevant to other Asian cultures and are applicable cross-culturally, rather than just to the Chinese as originally intended. Further studies in this direction will illuminate a more meaningful understanding of the roles of culture and personality in psychotherapy.

[Note: The CPAI studies reported in this chapter were partly supported by direct grants from The Chinese University of Hong Kong (# 220202030 and #2020662) and a grant from the Research Grants Council of Hong Kong (CUHK4333/00H).]

Appendix: Chinese Personality Assessment Inventory-2 (CPAI-2) Scales

---

Personality scales

Social potency factor

NOV	novelty
DIV	diversity
DIT	divergent thinking
LEA	leadership
L-A	logical vs. affective orientation
AES	aesthetics
E-I	extraversion vs. introversion
ENT	enterprise

Dependability factor

RES	responsibility
EMO	emotionality
I-S	inferiority vs. self-acceptance
PRA	practical-mindedness
O-P	optimism vs. pessimism
MET	meticulousness
FAC	face
I-E	internal vs. external locus of control
FAM	family orientation

Accommodation factor

DEF	defensiveness (Ah-Q mentality)
G-M	graciousness vs. meanness
INT	interpersonal tolerance
S-S	self vs. social orientation
V-S	veraciousness vs. slickness

Interpersonal relatedness factor

T-M	traditionalism vs. modernity
REN	ren-qing (relationship orientation)
SOC	social sensitivity
DIS	discipline
HAR	harmony
T-E	thrift vs. extravagance

Clinical scales

Emotional problem factor

I-S	inferiority vs. self-acceptance
ANX	anxiety
DEP	depression
PHY	physical symptoms
SOM	somatization
SEM	sexual maladjustment

Behavioral problem factor

PAT	pathological dependence
HYP	hypomania
ANT	antisocial behavior
NEE	need for attention
DIR	distortion of reality
PAR	paranoia

Validity scales

INF	infrequency scale
GIM	good impression scale
RCI	response consistency index

CHAPTER 3

Culture, Psychopathology, and Psychotherapy: Changes Observed in Japan

Masahisa Nishizono

Most psychotherapy is developed in a way that will allow for universal application, on the one hand, and that can be modified to fit the cultural features of certain societies or the particular eras in which the therapy is undertaken, on the other. It is believed that there are trends of acceptance in the establishment and development of particular psychotherapies according to the times (Nishizono 2000). This is true for mainstream therapies, such as psychoanalysis, which was originally developed in Europe, and culturally unique therapies, such as Morita therapy, which was invented in Japan. Both have histories of nearly a century. Both psychoanalysis and Morita therapy aimed for international or transcultural application, with the assumption that there was one true nature of human beings that would respond to a common psychopathology, beyond differences in culture and era. However, in practical application, it was found that both psychoanalysis and Morita therapy were restricted by social conditions and cultural backgrounds. There is a need to understand human nature and how, not only theoretically, but also practically, to deal with the psychopathologies that occur in a society. The nature and pattern of various psychopathologies are influenced by social background and cultural factors. The psychotherapies that are established to treat certain clusters of psychopathologies need to be modified and changed because they themselves originate from human relations and tend to be subject to changes in association with changes in society (Nishizono 1988).

Japan was the earliest Asian country to undergo extensive modernization and Westernization. The nature and process of these changes in Japanese society were different in quality and quantity during the era from the Meiji Restoration to World War II, and from World War II to the present. This chapter will describe how psychopathology has changed in relation to social changes and, associated with these changes, how psychotherapy has changed as well in order to be applicable to the society and its culture.

Changes in the Society and Culture of Japan: Three Stages of Modernization

Because of its geographical characteristics, Japan had never been threatened by foreign military forces other than the Mongol invasions between 1274 and 1281 and its defeat in World War II and subsequent occupation by the American military. Interchange with foreign countries had been prohibited by the national isolation policy of the Tokugawa shogunate government for about two hundred years, until the opening up of the country by the U.S.-Japan treaty in the middle of the nineteenth century (1854). Military affairs and diplomacy were carried out by the shogunate government, but local politics were left to a feudal lord appointed by the government. The central government's policy of leaving industry and education in people's daily lives to local administration continued for more than three hundred years and is said to have possibly been a great motivating force in the modernization of Japanese society after the Meiji Restoration of 1868. In the age of national isolation, a multilayered Japanese culture was created; based on polytheism, it included Daoism, Buddhism, and Confucianism, introduced from the Asian continent, in addition to indigenous shamanism and Shintoism.

Significant changes have occurred in Japanese society and culture from the Meiji Restoration to the present, however. These changes will be described briefly, from the perspective of modernization, by dividing them into three stages, namely, the era of the Meiji Restoration to the end of World War II, the first phase of urbanization after World War II (about three decades), and the second phase of urbanization, which continues to the present (about two decades).

The First Modernization:
Meiji Restoration to the End of World War II

Until the end of World War II, Japan was a society consisting of agriculture, and commerce and industry supporting agriculture. Agriculture requires a successor to land for continuity. The goals of the people at that time were succession to and the prosperity of the family occupation, whether it was agriculture, commerce, or industry. Because succession to and the prosperity of the family business were primary, marriage by arrangement was prevalent. Agriculture, which consisted principally of rice cultivation, required the complete agreement and cooperation of neighbors over the distribution and management of water for the rice paddies. The "logic of wa" (harmony) was valued, and served as the norm of people's behavior, both within and outside the house. Various idols of gods and Buddha were placed in the house, and family members were asked to worship in the morning and evening. Gratitude to parents, ancestors, gods and Buddha, and the public was emphasized. The public referred to here carries a peculiar meaning in Japan. It refers to people outside the house, symbolized by neighbors, whose complete agreement and cooperation are needed for one to succeed in one's family business. Individuals in the Western sense were almost nonexistent at that time. Reflecting the Japanese culture and value system, the Japanese mode of thinking emphasized consideration of others in daily communication (Nakamura 1948, 1949). The most obvious example of this is manifested in the response to the question "Don't you go?" The Japanese answer is, "*Yes,* I don't," while the Western answer is "*No,* I don't." From a semantic point of view, the Japanese answer emphasizes compliance with others, by beginning the reply with "yes," rather than indicating one's own position, and replying with "no."

Furthermore, many words representing traditional Japanese culture, concurring with the characteristics of the society, were used in daily life. Examples were *amae* (indulgence/dependent relationship between two people), *on* (obligation arising out of gratitude), *giri* (emotional/ethical duty), *iki* (emphasis on being elegant/stylish), *bokashi* (shading off/being purposely vague), *chijimi* (humility), *haragei* (psychological manipulation), and *tatemae to hone* (public conformity versus private feeling), all of which were concerned with the proper relations that were to be observed in this interpersonally oriented society.

The Meiji government introduced Western laws and systems in an attempt to centralize administrative power. With the expansion of armaments, industrialization, or modernization, was pushed ahead. However, it was modernization outside the house. The traditional ways of the family were maintained and institutionalized. These included the succession in the family of the eldest son and the submission of women to men. These ways were designed to strengthen family consciousness. As a result, amid the Westernization of society, sensitive youth suffered from conflicts between the "house" and the individual. During this period, great Japanese writers, such as Shimei Futabatei, Ogai Mori, Soseki Natsume, and Toson Shimazaki, used the conflicts between the development of the modernized self and the house as motifs in their writing. In my view, Morita therapy, a unique psychotherapy that emphasizes philosophically the acceptance of reality (including suffering) "as it is," was invented in the early twentieth century in Japan by Shōma Morita as a therapy for neuroses arising from conflicts between the self and family consciousness (see chapter 11 herein). Youth were particularly sensitive to changes in society and culture and experienced difficulty in forming their self-identities.

The First Phase of Urbanization after World War II:
The Era of Economic Reconstruction

Japan's defeat in World War II and its subsequent occupation by foreign armed forces brought about many changes in Japanese society. With the revision of the constitution and civil law, the patriarchal system that had been emphasized in the past collapsed. Women strengthened their voices by acquiring the franchise and advancing in society. They were liberated institutionally from their submissive positions, according to Confucian culture, in the house. This liberation coincided with the economic reconstruction of the nation from the ruins left by its defeat in World War II. In short, industrialization and urbanization had begun. The nuclear family emerged. The emotional motive of individuals being released from the yoke of neighbors, fellow traders, and the public in traditional society accelerated the trends of migration to the city, shunning associations with new neighbors, and holing up with their own families. The new industrial society, unlike the old agricultural society, brought about a separation of workplace and family. A husband could not help but devote himself to his work to such an extent that he was criticized severely as an "economic animal" or a "workaholic." "Being a silent male" about the things in the house was the general rule. This may be likened to the American phenomenon in the age from the end of World War II to the "women's liberation" movement in the 1960s (Balswick and Peek 1975). Responsibility for things in the house was mostly placed on the wife, leading to an atmosphere in which the wife's major role was rearing children. Having her child enter into a good school, rather than cultivating artistic sentiments or discipline, became her greatest concern. This period may be called the first phase of the urbanization of Japanese society after World War II. Young people enjoyed a certain economic happiness and social freedom, but it was not easy to break away from the traditional culture. Their parents, living in poorly populated areas after their children migrated to cities, were lonely and felt abandoned. Parents' feelings of abandonment must have weighed heavily as a debt in the minds of their children. However, it was denied and rationalized by the importance of work and child rearing.

The Second Phase of Urbanization:
From Industrial Society to Postindustrial Society

By the mid-1970s the industrialization of Japanese society had been nearly completed. The manufacturing industry increasingly shifted its manufacturing base overseas to reduce costs, including personnel expenses. With the tertiary industry developing on a worldwide scale, people started moving quickly toward a postindustrial and information-centered society. There emerged an industrial society in which one could participate beyond differences in sex, age, and race, if one could adapt oneself to the trend. With the advent of a more highly educated society, it became common for a wife to participate in society and to stand on her own. This resulted in the so-called borderless society. A communication gap between husband and wife, changes in sex ethics, and generalized "me-ism" were noticeable. A decrease in the marriage and birth rates and an increase in the divorce rate were accelerated. This period was the second phase of urbanization, in which it was very difficult for people to establish their individual identities.

Changes in Psychological Problems and Psychiatric Pathology

Among the mental diseases for which psychotherapy is administered, some are found in any society at any time, while others show differences in development and pathological patterns in relation to culture. This chapter addresses psychopathologies related to the cultural changes involved in the modernization and Westernization of Japanese society (table 1).

Psychopathology Associated with the First Modernization

As described previously, the stage of modernization of Japanese society from the Meiji Restoration to the end of World War II was different from the one that occurred thereafter. The Meiji government took measures to enable wealth and military strength to catch up with those of Western powers. With changes in the constitution and civil law, systems outside the house were patterned after those of Western countries. However, at the same time, the traditional patriarchal system was strengthened within the house. Men were encouraged to enhance their families' reputations by acquiring knowledge and technology introduced from the West to serve the purposes of the nation. In contrast, women were asked to remain in the house and support the work of the men outside.

With the systems outside the house becoming modernized (and Westernized) while the system inside the house remained traditional, youth increasingly faced cultural contradictions. Modernization in the West aims at establishing the individual self. The social systems of the West are not unrelated to this. Introducing merely the form of modernization entails difficulty. The slogan "Japanese spirit with Western learning" was created to overcome this difficulty. Still, many young people suffered from the conflict between the self and family consciousness. It is understandable that certain neuroses developed on the basis of this conflict of values.

During the development of psychiatry in Japan through the end of World War II, psychiatrists in general, other than a few Morita therapists and psychoanalysts, had not dealt with neurotic patients in the community. Instead, they focused on major psychiatric disorders in inpatient settings. It was then the attitude of society that emotional problems or neurotic disorders should be resolved within the family, by training the patient himself or through the use of folk therapies, with magical rites.

The founder of Morita therapy, Shōma Morita (1928), has classified the various kinds of neuroses observed in Japan at the time as anthrophobia (*taijinkyōfushō,* or interpersonal relations phobia), obsessive-compulsive neurosis, and common (or regular) neuroses. Hysteria was included, as well. Among scholars, *taijinkyōfushō* was once thought to be a culture-related neurosis peculiar to Japan. At present, its association with culture is being strongly debated, with the appearance of a diagnostic category called "social phobia" in the American psychiatric classification system of the Diagnostic and Statistical Manual of Mental Disorders, Third Edition (DSM-III), after 1980. It is my opinion that anthrophobia was regarded as a culture-related neurosis because it could be explained by a "psychology of shame," and Japan was characterized as a "culture of shame" (Ruth Benedict 1946). Some scholars (Kasahara 1974; Kimura 1982; Tseng 2001) have pointed out that the anthrophobia observed at that time was charac-

Table 1. Changes in Culture, Psychopathology, and the Application of Psychotherapy Observed in Japan through Three Eras

Era	Cultural characteristics	Pathology noticed	Psychotherapy
First modernization (before WWII)	Agriculture and commerce/industry society	Conflict between self and family	Invention of Morita therapy for patients with culture-related neurosis
	Patriarchal family system	Culture-related neurosis of *taijinkyōfushō*	
	Emphasis on family succession		
	Emphasis on harmony		
	Westernization of men		
	Subordination of women to men		
First phase of urbanization (three decades after WWII)	Rapid industrialization and associated urbanization	Decrease of culture-related *taijinkyōfushō*	Application of Morita therapy, psychoanalysis, and supportive therapy for newly increased anxiety, depressive disorders
	Collapse of extended family	Increase of anxiety disorders among women, school phobia among children, and social avoidant behavior among adolescents and youth	
	Rise of nuclear family		
	Separation of workplace from family		
	Weakening of community system		
	Child rearing left to women at home while men away at work		

Table 1. (*continued*)

Era	Cultural characteristics	Pathology noticed	Psychotherapy
Second phase of urbanization (mid-1970s to present)	Collapse of family and community	Increase of primitive personality disorders, depression, eating disorders, alcohol problems, and self-identity problems	Dynamic therapy for borderline disorders and eating disorders
	Borderless society		
	Decreased communication between husband and wife		Supportive therapy for peer-based self problems
	Emergence of "me-ism"		

teristically different from the social phobia recognized presently in Western society in that patients developed a fear of interpersonal contact not with strangers, but with intermediately close persons, such as friends, co-workers, and superiors whom the patients knew well. Currently, however, anthrophobia, with a cardinal picture of erythrophobia (a disorder characterized by a concern with and fear of one's face flushing in front of others), has decreased sharply, while an interpersonal phobia with persecutory elements is increasing. Further, the age of onset has become younger. In other words, the anthrophobia observed recently is becoming similar to the social phobia described for Americans in the DSM-III. This change may be attributed to the recent trend of Japanese to shun the public or traditional, regional community in their daily lives.

It may be relevant to mention the issues relating to parent-child relationship problems or conflicts observed in Japan. Heisaku Kosawa, one of the few psychoanalysts before the war, pointed out (1932) that the Japanese have guilty consciences derived from debts of gratitude to their mothers, in addition to Oedipus complexes, or guilty consciences derived from their relationships with their fathers. He named the former the Ajase complex, which refers to the negative and ambivalent emotional complex of a son toward his mother. Presumably, the self-sacrificing presence of the mother was easily understood by the people with modernized spirits in Japanese society at the time. This unique mother-son complex is elaborated in further detail by Keigo Okonogi (see chapter 4 herein).

Psychopathology Associated with the First Phase of Urbanization

Modernization after World War II was represented by the liberation of women subsequent to the abolition of the traditional patriarchal system. This change brought about the collapse or avoidance of the traditional, regional community. During this era, culture-related neuroses, such as anthrophobia (represented by the symptoms of erythrophobia) decreased and were replaced by ordinary anxiety neuroses, which increased, particularly among women, who were liberated from their traditional shackles. School phobia (a refusal to go to school among children) and avoidance or social retreat among adolescents and youth gradually increased, probably because children were raised mostly by their mothers and therefore lacked paternal support, discipline, and adequate external socialization experiences. As mentioned earlier, people at that time obtained economic happiness and social freedom, but succession to the family business disappeared, and a weakening of the familial community occurred. Husbands escaped to their work outside the home, wives became isolated, and children were driven to study for school entrance examinations. It was an era fraught with contradictions arising from the failure to meet the demands of modernization. The ambivalence between dependency and independency, as revealed in Takeo Doi's book *Anatomy of Dependence* (1973), reflected contradictions observed in the basic Japanese character. In other words, the concerns of the traditional mentality could be observed in the modernized mind. Comparing the East and the West, with relation to the self, Roland (1988) has maintained that the "familial" self is the norm of behavior in Japan and India, in contrast to the "individualized" self emphasized in America and Western Europe. I maintain that, in Japan, the familial self in daily life became less visible with the advance of social changes and the weakening of the familial community, but the intrapsychic familial self was deeply rooted and transferred to friends and peers and manifested as the "circle-based" self, or self related mainly to the peer in the immediate circle (Nishizono 1994). Psychopathology at that time reflected this psychological situation.

Contemporary Psychopathology during the Second Phase of Urbanization

Other than the universal psychopathologies found in any society, numerous mental disorders have become more prominently observed in Japan today, in association with the changes in modern Japanese society and culture. Unfortunately, political reasons led to a campaign against the government's mental health policy several decades ago in Japan. As a result, community-based psychiatric surveys have been difficult to carry out, and there is no comprehensive epidemiological data available in Japan, even now. The most recent information available came from a one-day, nationwide survey of psychiatric patients in inpatient and outpatient settings carried out in 1996 by Ito and Sederer (1999). The results showed that, among outpatients, the distribution of diagnoses was schizophrenia (26.7 percent), mood disorder (21.3 percent), neuroses (24.3 percent), dementia (4.9 percent), alcohol-related problems (4.7 percent), other substance abuse (0.3 percent), mental retardation (1.6 percent), other mental or behavior disorders (3.4 percent), and epilepsy (12.8 percent). (Epilepsy is not a psychiatric disorder, but it is customarily treated by psychiatrists in Japan.) Because of the diagnostic categories used in the survey, many nonpsychotic disorders were included in the broad category of "neuroses." Therefore, cross-cultural comparison is limited.

However, my clinical observation and my colleagues' shared opinions indicate that there has been a gradual increase in primitive personality disorders, eating disorders, alcohol abuse or dependence, and depression during this second phase of urbanization. These pathologies began emerging and increasing in the first phase of urbanization during the second modernization, but they have become more prominent. Primitive personality disorders, such as borderline personality disorder and narcissistic personality disorder, continue to increase sharply at the present time. Among the patients brought to psychiatric emergency hospitals, the proportion of borderline personality disorders is said to be increasing. The cases of eating disorders among adolescent girls and young women, depression, social retreat, various types of obsessive-compulsive disorders, and alcohol dependence or abuse are all increasing, as well. Though not much of a problem in terms of incidence, pathological bereavement cases among old widows are increasing in the aged population of Japan. The Japanese enjoy the longest life span in the world, but, without adequate family support, many aged widows suffer from loneliness and depression. Since this psychopathology is mostly accompanied by depressive symptoms and object loss, the present could aptly be called an "era of depression." These changes show that the trend of seeking pride and the need for self-realization, based on Maslow's (1968) theory of multiple layers of need, has become common. The satisfaction of those needs is based largely on the subjective view of the person concerned.

Psychotherapy at the Present Time in Japan

Psychopathologies developing with social and cultural changes show diversification in kind, while increasing in incidence. The number of psychotherapeutic organizations to meet these clinical needs is also increasing. There are currently more than a dozen scientific organizations in Japan, some directly related to the practice of psychotherapy in a strict sense, such as the Japan Psychoanalytical Association, Morita Therapy Association, Japanese Association of Behavior Therapy, and Japanese Association of Group Psychotherapy. Obviously, various kinds of psychotherapies are practiced. Interestingly, they are segregated aptly by niche. In terms of medical economy, they are mostly psychotherapies under the purview of the national health insurance system. Three kinds of psychotherapies will be discussed here, as concrete examples of segregation by niche of different psychotherapies.

Specialized Psychotherapy: Dynamic Therapy

The first segregation concerns psychoanalysis, or dynamic psychotherapy. Japan has two psychoanalytical associations, the Japan Psychoanalytic Society, a branch of the International Psychoanalytical Association, and the Japan Psychoanalytical Association, a national organization. The former is small (about a hundred members), while the latter has more than twenty-four hundred members. In contrast to other schools of psychotherapy, dynamic therapy in Japan is currently concerned primarily with two kinds of psychopathology, namely, borderline personality disorders and eating disorders, both of which have been significantly increasing recently, and the dynamic approaches that have been utilized to deal with them.

Borderline personality disorder (BPD).   A matter of primary concern among psychoanalysts who belong to the two professional organizations mentioned above is borderline personality disorder. The focus of the Japanese analysts is the same as that of their counterparts in Europe and America, namely, understanding the genetics, dynamics, and therapeutic techniques for this disorder. In short, borderline personality disorder is attributed to pre-Oedipal development and, in this respect, is not heavily influenced by cultural differences, except that it tends to occur in industrialized societies, whether in the East or the West.

Currently, borderline personality disorder has become a psychopathology so popular that it can be seen in almost all psychiatric institutions in

Japan. Fear of being neglected and abandoned and susceptibility to narcissistic injuries are characteristic of this disorder. This unstable and easy-to-split personality is said to be based on the mother-child relationship in the "rapprochement subphase" (as it was originally called by Mahler and Furer 1968), and its ego structure and function are very unstable, vulnerable, and primitive.

Eating disorders.   Recently, eating disorders have become common among young women in Japan. Eating disorders are often accompanied by borderline personality disorder. They require treatment extending over a long period, and the model treatment of choice is considered to be the psychoanalytic approach. An avoidant personality pattern or disorder, often seen among young men, is also often treated with a psychoanalytic orientation. In other words, dealing with the life histories of patients or their past experiences with their parents, which have been transferred to the therapist-patient relationship in the here and now, is necessary for pathologies that are creating major problems in the personality.

The attempt to understand the unique nature of psychopathology and to try long-term care approaches for borderline personality disorder and eating disorders was started by psychoanalysts in the West. In Japan, following this trend, analytically oriented psychotherapists, like other schools of therapists, have been paying more attention to these newly increasing clinical conditions as well and have been trying to treat them through analytic approaches. Cognitive-behavior therapists in the West have recently attempted to treat these disorders, particularly eating disorders. This is happening in Japan also. However, as psychotherapists, cognitive-behavior therapists are newcomers in Japan, and their approaches to treatment have not yet become popular.

Nonspecific Psychotherapy: In Private Practice

The second segregation by niche in psychotherapy is the private practice of general psychiatrists. Psychiatric private practice in Japan has recently been increasing at a tremendous pace. Formerly, from a public mental health point of view, it was estimated to be desirable to have one clinic per forty thousand people in cities, or more than thirty-five hundred clinics in total throughout Japan. Some of the problems of patients visiting the clinics were related to psychiatric disorders diagnosable according to formal psychiatric classification systems, but most were related to minor emotional distresses that were tied to various daily living situations or living experiences. As pointed out earlier, the familial tradition of succession to land in Japan has been lost. Instead, a tendency for youth to desire "supporting each other among peers" has become conspicuous. Associated with this is the rise of the "circle- or peer-based" self, as I call it, in contrast to the "family" self traditionally found in the East or the "individualized" self advocated in the West (Roland 1988). However, the circle- or peer-based self is primarily based on the pleasure principle, and those oriented to such a self are liable to fall into emotional distress. In psychotherapy, medications are also given to such patients as needed, but, primarily, they require minor, supportive psychotherapy. Treatment is, so to speak, an integration of an expressive-supportive psychotherapeutic approach and cognitive therapy.

Traditional and Neo-Morita Therapy

The third segregation concerns Morita therapy. Morita therapy focuses primarily on a new life experience for the patient, helping the patient learn to detach himself or herself from emotional conflict and obtain the philosophical attitude of accepting suffering in reality "as it is" (see chapter 11). The Morita Therapy Association has 500 members. I am pleased to see Morita therapy, which was initiated in Japan, attracting international interest recently. This therapy deepens the understanding of the Japanese mind and makes clear the commonalities and differences between the minds of the Japanese and non-Japanese. However, it should not be forgotten that the Japanese mind is also changing with social changes, such as Westernization and modernization.

Recently, people's interest in receiving Morita therapy seems to have increased again. This phenomenon is seen among more high-functioning, mature, and healthier people. The challenge for Morita therapists is to develop a technique that would apply the principles of the therapy to profound pathologies, for example, to people with avoidant personality tendencies. An avoidant is one who has self-pathology, and the pathology of the people for whom Morita developed his therapy is common to what was produced in the process of the modernization of Japanese culture.

Other Forms of Psychotherapy

Psychotherapies originating mainly from the West in Europe and America, particularly behavior therapy, cognitive therapy, group therapy, and family therapy, are developing in Japan as well, under excellent leaders.

The Japanese Association of Behavior Therapy has 750 members, and the Japanese Association of Group Psychotherapy, 900. However, in actual clinical practice, the use of interpersonal-focused therapy, such as group therapy or family therapy, is still limited. Japanese patients are still not used to sharing their private emotional lives with strangers (namely, their co-patients in group therapy), or even with family members in family sessions. The patients still feel that it is easier to work on their personal psychological issues through individual sessions. Therefore, group therapy and family therapy have not yet become popular in Japan.

Naikan therapy is another unique form of psychotherapy that was invented in Japan. Naikan therapy expects the patient to go through self-inspection about his or her own life, particularly in earlier stages of development, with particular focus on how he or she has been cared for by others and what he or she has done in return. It aims to help the patient grow psychologically, from a narcissistic position toward a more mature, empathic position (see chapter 12). At present, the Naikan Therapy Association is composed of about 300 members. Naikan therapy is claimed to be useful for so-called guilt-feeling-laden disorders, often related to alcohol dependence and obsessive-compulsive disorders.

Final Comments

Influenced by changes in society, familial community, and values, Japanese people have had to establish modernized selves, meaning Western, individualized selves. Consequently, many new types of psychopathology have developed. Among psychotherapies, psychoanalysis and cognitive-behavior therapies have been introduced and are developing, while Morita therapy and Naikan therapy, rooted in traditional Eastern thought, also have certain strengths. As elsewhere, conflict between modernization and tradition exists in the world of psychotherapy as well. In the book *Zen Buddhism and Psychoanalysis* (Suzuki, Fromm, and Martion 1960), the authors have emphasized insightfully the differences in psychology between the East and West. In Suzuki and colleagues' opinion, the Western spirit is analytical, discriminatory, differential, inductive, individualistic, intellectual, scientific, generalizing, conceptual, and schematic, while the Eastern spirit is synthetic, totalizing, integrative, nondiscriminatory, deductive, and nonsystematic. At the present time, when globalization has become widespread, merely stressing these differences would be of no help in developing patient-oriented psychotherapy.

Learning how to integrate these therapies without being biased is a challenge. Based on my experiences with psychotherapy aimed at the Japanese, I think that psychoanalysis is applicable to them and that the growth of personality by insight and learning, the ultimate target of modern psychoanalysis, can be obtained. At the same time, it is my opinion that, for contemporary Japanese, therapeutic intervention needs to consider culture-related factors, including the contemporary psychological needs of patients and their era-related psychopathologies, as follows:

- the necessity of offering a warm attitude and a positive stance on the part of the therapist (particularly for those patients with "circle-based" selves, who need more affection and attention from the authoritative-parental figure)
- the importance of containment and consideration of environment in the therapeutic setting
- the recognition that when his or her dependent desire is not satisfied by the therapist, the patient easily responds with defenses of the projective identification mechanism toward the therapist (particularly patients with primitive personality disorders)
- the recognition that, for most of the patients, the psychology of shame is more predominant than the sense of sin and that therefore it is therapeutically more important to focus on interpersonal relations within an actual environment rather than on the intrapsychic world
- the recognition that the patient often expects intervention at the cognitive level, with the therapist's practical advice

In summary, it can be said that most Japanese patients today are seeking a mutual relationship with the therapist in the here and now.

II

Asian Psychology: Theoretical Exploration
of Parent-Child Relations

CHAPTER 4

The Ajase Complex
and Its Implications

Keigo Okonogi

The psychoanalytic concept of the Oedipus complex that was proposed by Sigmund Freud in 1897, based on a Greek mythological story, is well known to most clinicians and scholars around the world. However, it is rare for a scholar to be aware of the Ajase complex, which was suggested by Japanese psychoanalyst Heisaku Kosawa in 1932, based on the Hindu mythological tale of the prince of Ajase. These two complexes, one derived from the West and the other from the East, both address the deep-seated emotional complex of the parent-child relationship, but they differ greatly in their analysis of the nature of the conflict and its resolution. They provide complementary concepts for a holistic understanding of the parent-child bond. Thus, it is pertinent, in this chapter, to elaborate on the background and nature of the complex, in order to provide a broader theoretical comprehension of human nature.

A pioneer Japanese psychoanalyst, Heisaku Kosawa, left Japan in 1932 to study at the Psychoanalytic Institute of Vienna. After an interview with Sigmund Freud, he underwent training analysis with Richard Sterba, under the supervision of Paul Federn. Kosawa returned to Tokyo in 1933 and took his first step as a psychoanalytic therapist by opening a private practice, as was customary in the West. He pursued this work from the 1930s until his death in 1968. During this period, Kosawa continued to assimilate Western knowledge from international psychoanalytic journals and applied his learning to the treatment of Japanese patients. Kosawa's work led him to develop his own method of psychoanalytic treatment and his own theories, of which the Ajase complex is a representative example (Kosawa 1953).

Kosawa gave close attention to the mother-child bond of early child-hood and was extremely attracted to the ideas of Melanie Klein about in-fants' sadistic oral fantasies regarding their mothers (1932). He accorded particular importance to the hate and resentment experienced by the child toward the mother, as well as to the child's oral sadism. In addition, he was strongly influenced by the methods of his former supervisor, Federn, in the psychotherapeutic treatment of schizophrenia, and noted the ma-ternal function of the therapist. Kosawa gradually found it necessary to treat not only classic neuroses, but also what are now termed borderline cases. Because of the specific nature of Kosawa's Japanese patients and his treatment of borderline cases, the question of transference and counter-transference, with regard to pre-Oedipal object relations, became an im-portant theme in his theory.

The text concerning the Ajase complex that Kosawa presented to Freud in 1932 derives from the story of the Indian prince Ajatasatru, as related in the *Nirvana Sutra* (introduced to Japan between A.D. 700 and 1000) and *The Teaching, the Practice, the Confidence, and the Realization of Shinran* (Shin-ran was a celebrated Japanese priest of the Kamakura period [1185–1333]) (Shinran 1966). Nonetheless, during the twenty years of clinical practice that followed his return to Japan, Kosawa referred principally to the Bud-dhist classic *The Sutra of the Contemplation of Infinite Life (Kan muryo ju kyo)* to elaborate his own original version of the Ajase story (1953). It is this story that forms the basis of the Ajase complex.

The Sutra of the Contemplation of Infinite Life, whose theme is the sal-vation of the mother, is rare among Buddhist texts. The central character saved by the Buddha is Ajase's mother, Idaike (characters, places, and so forth, in the legend will be referred to by their Japanese equivalents). Fol-lowing is a summary of Kosawa's version of the Ajase story.

The Ajase Story

Queen Idaike was the wife of the king of Bimbashara, ruler of Oshajo. Wor-ried that the love of her husband was fading along with her beauty, she came to ardently desire the birth of a child. The soothsayer she consulted told her that a hermit living in the forest would die in three years' time and be reincarnated in her womb. Idaike, however, was too anxious to wait three years. Obsessed by her desire for a child, she killed the hermit, who cursed her as he died: "I will be reincarnated as the son of the king, but one day this son will kill him!" Idaike became pregnant at that mo-ment with the future Ajase. The prince had, thus, already been killed once, by his mother's egoism. After becoming pregnant, however, Idaike grew to fear the resentment of the child in her womb (the hermit's curse) and decided to give birth on top of a high tower, dropping her baby to the ground below. The infant broke his little finger, but survived. Young Ajase was therefore nicknamed "the prince with the broken finger."

Ajase subsequently had a normal, happy childhood. However, when he reached adolescence, Daibadatta, the enemy of the Buddha, revealed to Ajase that his mother had attempted to kill him by giving birth to him at the top of a tower. He added that if the prince needed proof, he had only to look at his broken finger. It was in this way that Ajase discovered the story surrounding his birth. Disillusioned with the mother he idealized, Ajase was overcome with rage and attempted to kill Idaike. However, the prince's feelings of guilt led him to develop a severe illness *(ruchu)*, which covered his body with foul-smelling sores. When no one else dared to approach him, Queen Idaike devoted herself to his care. Finally realizing that these ministrations had no effect, however, and confronted with the unhappy fact that her beloved son had attempted to kill her, Idaike confided her problems to the Buddha and asked for his counsel. The instruction she received led Idaike to resolve her emotional conflicts and to devote herself to the care of her son. Ajase recovered from his illness to become an enlightened sovereign.

The Fundamental Themes of the Ajase Complex

The Ajase complex, as understood through Kosawa's interpretation of the Buddhist legend, involves several themes, which can be identified as follows.

The Mother's Desire Both to Have a Child and to Kill Her Child

Idaike wished for a child to protect her status as queen and to retain the love of her husband. Her desire pushed her to the extreme act of killing the hermit. However, believing that the hermit would return to life and occasion unhappiness, Idaike came to fear her child and considered abortion, then finally attempted to kill Ajase by giving birth to him on top of a tower. This story depicts the psychological state of a mother who, on the one hand, wishes for a child to protect her position or to satisfy her own desires and, on the other, does not want to give birth, and projects feelings of persecution and hate onto her baby to the point that she fears delivery or imagines ridding herself of her child.

Borrowing the concept of Serge Lebovici (1988), we could say that this story describes the conflicts of the mother in relation to her "imaginary baby." The mother's self-centered conflict—between an egotistical desire to exercise the right of life and death over her child and paranoid fears of the imaginary baby onto whom she has projected her own egoism— has always been part of maternal psychology. In contemporary society, as the myth of maternal love has disintegrated, mothers' conflicts have come into the open. I will later note Kosawa's experience of these issues in a Japanese clinic.

Prenatal Rancor and the Child's Desire to Kill the Mother

From the moment of Ajase's conception, he experienced a fundamental rancor toward his origins: the resentment of the hermit killed by Idaike. In other words, he was animated by the desire to kill his mother even before birth. In the Buddhist language of the sutra, resentment directed at one's origin is termed *mishoon,* or "prenatal rancor." Kosawa (1953) compared the Oedipus complex and the Ajase complex as follows: "Freud's Oedipus complex has its origins in the conflict surrounding erotic desire, where the son loves his mother and feels rivalry toward his father. By contrast, the Ajase complex involves the more fundamental issue of one's birth, or of how one came into existence." Kosawa believed that the originality of the Ajase complex lay in its themes of matricide and prenatal rancor, in contrast to the Oedipus complex, which emphasizes incestuous desire and patricide.

Freud considered the Oedipus complex a primal phantasy *(Urphantasie).* Similarly, I believe that the Ajase complex also possesses a universal character. It is a psychic state that focuses on questions linked to one's origins: the identity of one's parents and the circumstances surrounding one's birth. At the same time, I note that there are also sociohistorical factors peculiar to Japan that motivated Kosawa to present his thesis on the Ajase complex to Freud. Notably, there exists in Japan a contrast between the outward idealization of the mother and the sociohistoric reality of mothers often being forced to kill or "thin out" their children. The Japanese term *mabiki* refers to the thinning of a rice field, and indicates the killing of children as a community practice, particularly during famines. This practice was common until the Edo period (1603–1868).

Later, I will give clinical examples illustrating how children manifest prenatal rancor toward their parents and resentment and murderous desire toward their mother. This theme, incidentally, appears most often in the case of adolescents.

Two Types of Guilt

The text about the Ajase complex that Kosawa presented to Freud was titled "Two Types of Guilt." A context for this theme can be found in Kleinian (1946) comparisons of paranoid and depressive guilt, or of the movement from a punitive to a reparative type of guilt. These two types of guilt, and the defense mechanisms employed against them, are important structural elements of the Ajase complex.

Attachment between Mother and Son

One issue that needs to be addressed is the close attachment that is allowed, and even encouraged, culturally, between mother and children, which ferments the potential emotional conflict between them. Families in Asian societies, in contrast to those in the West, permit a very close emotional attachment between mother and child, particularly mother and son. Based on their comparative study in Japan and America, Rothbaum and colleagues (2000, 2002) pointed out that extremely close ties between mother and child are perceived as adaptive and acceptable and are more common in Japan than in America. In Asia, there is less need for mothers and fathers to spend time alone to rekindle romantic, intimate feelings between them. Instead, the mother devotes all of her energy and time to her children. This is particularly true when the father focuses on his work. In general, Japanese children experience less adverse effects from such relationships than do children in the West from prevailing family patterns. However, because of the close attachments with their mothers, some children, particularly sons, developed negative feelings toward their mother, particularly around adolescence. It is important to understand the mother-son complex against the background of this culture-based family relationship.

The Ajase Complex Considered from a Clinical Viewpoint

In this chapter, I examine the two fundamental themes of the Ajase complex noted above—the conflicts of the mother surrounding maternity and the prenatal rancor of the child—in light of clinical cases Kosawa treated as a psychotherapist. Concerning the former, the case of a mother with symptoms of maternal rejection will be presented; concerning the rancor of the child, the case of an adolescent.

The Conflicts of the Mother surrounding Maternity

I have noticed that more and more mothers who exhibit symptoms of maternal rejection have begun to undergo psychotherapeutic treatment in Tokyo. One of the factors contributing to this phenomenon has been the disappearance of these mothers' traditional support systems. Previously, a woman's own mother, or her mother-in-law, aided her in pregnancy and with child care. This structure of family support has been lost with the phenomenon of nuclearization of the family. The growing number of women in the workforce has, further, meant an increase in their responsibilities. In this new type of family, no system dictates who should aid the mother with the difficulties of pregnancy, delivery, and child raising. Further, in Japan, there is as yet no custom of men emotionally supporting their wives.

In these circumstances, mothers' anxieties concerning pregnancy and delivery, and accompanying symptoms of maternal rejection, have become evident. Another factor underlying this phenomenon may be the societal recognition of women's self-assertion. Both society and the family environment now permit mothers who have experienced hostility or rejection toward their children to openly express their feelings.

There have always been mothers who have experienced a rejection of maternity. In the past, however, this rejection could be rationalized as corporal punishment or discipline. Today, in contrast, respect for children's rights and the general recognition that mothers may not feel affection for their children have resulted in an increasing number of patients in Japan who complain of the maternal rejection syndrome.

Case 1.   The Ajase complex as seen in Mitsuko and her mother, who both exhibit the maternal rejection syndrome

Mitsuko is a thirty-one-year-old housewife who has been married for five years. When her son was a year old and her daughter three, she began to complain of insomnia and migraines, and harbored thoughts of killing her daughter. One day, in front of her children, she cut up her daughter's favorite doll with a pair of scissors. Mitsuko agreed to see a doctor after this event, on the advice of her husband. Thus, her individual psychotherapy with me began. Interestingly enough, Mitsuko's mother also expressed a wish for a consultation in view of the psychic changes that had occurred in her daughter, and I became her therapist as well. In this unique situation, I, as a therapist, was able to examine the intrapsychic material of both mother and daughter relating to their relationship.

Gradually, during consultations with me, Mitsuko realized that she was hypercritical of her daughter. She also felt that her daughter was starting to resemble herself at a hated time in her own childhood. In fact, her daughter incarnated all the aspects of her own personality that Mitsuko detested. On seeing her daughter, Mitsuko would be seized by the impulse to banish this "other self." She would scream, "Get out!" or "Go over there and leave me alone!" and she criticized every aspect of her daughter that she disliked. As she showered her daughter with reproaches, however, Mitsuko would be haunted by the apprehension that she was beginning to resemble her own mother, whose anxious nature she found extremely oppressive.

Until she began therapy, Mitsuko was largely unaware of the negative feelings she held toward her own mother. Rather, she considered her mother to be a fragile creature, in need of protection from a cruel father and grandmother. Mitsuko's mother had spent the thirty-five years of her marriage waiting on her husband and two mothers-in-law (her husband's biological mother, and the mother's sister, who adopted Mitsuko's father while he was in college). Mitsuko's father, furthermore, very attentive to both older women, would not take the side of his wife, who was subject to their control. He was an extremely self-centered man and showed no interest in the management of the household or his children. On arriving home, he would pick up a book; when on vacation, he would go off by himself to the mountains.

Mitsuko's first pregnancy ended in a miscarriage, for which her mother-in-law reproached her as though it stemmed from some physical deficiency on Mitsuko's part. After this, Mitsuko began to see her own mother as having sacrificed her life, in spite of her fragile health, to serve her husband and two mothers-in-law—and began to be profoundly irritated by this masochistic attitude. Mitsuko directed all her conscious feelings of anger toward her grandmothers and father; she felt sympathy toward her mother and advised her on numerous occasions to divorce.

Thus, Mitsuko began feeling in sympathy with her mother. She could not escape the idea that her mother was in danger of dying from some illness or of committing suicide, and that in order to save her mother, she must bring about her divorce. However, as her therapy progressed, Mitsuko became aware that behind these worries and anxieties on behalf of her mother lay feelings of deep resentment and animosity.

Once, Mitsuko mentioned that her mother suffered from stomach problems, and had undergone a medical examination. At the time of Mitsuko's therapy, it was determined that her mother was suffering from benign polyps, rather than an actual disease. Although her mother accepted this diagnosis, Mitsuko expressed to me the conviction that her mother was suffering from a serious illness, perhaps cancer, and became distraught at the idea of her mother's dying. She gradually recognized that behind her anxiety lay a hidden desire for her mother's death. If her mother died, her own psychic burden would be lightened, and she would experience relief.

On reflection, Mitsuko realized that she had always been treated with more coldness and severity than her younger brother. Although she had endured her mother's strict discipline—telling herself that, as the oldest daughter, she must be obedient—she lived with the fear that her mother would die or leave her family. Behind her fears of abandonment lay the idea that Mitsuko's mother had transmitted to her daughter in nonverbal form: "If it weren't for you, I'd be living happily with my little boy."

The moment at which Mitsuko began to experience unpleasant feelings toward her daughter, and to treat her cruelly, coincided with the birth of her son. Mitsuko herself had a younger brother. With the birth of this son, her position in the family had stabilized, as a daughter-in-law who had given birth to a precious heir. Mitsuko was thus in certain aspects burdened with the uncertainty experienced by her mother at the beginning of her own marriage.

As Mitsuko realized this, she began to verbalize a prenatal rancor of which she had not been conscious. "If my mother was happy, why did she force herself to have me? It would have been better for her if I'd never been born."

Mitsuko's mother had kept a secret concerning the birth of her daughter. According to what she recounted in therapy, she had married into a family of illustrious politicians. Her husband considered himself the center of the world and accorded no importance to family life or his wife. Her father and mother-in-law were extremely severe as well, and she soon bitterly regretted her marriage. At the time, however, incompatibility was not recognized as grounds for divorce.

One day, she learned by chance from a family employee that several members of her husband's family had suffered from mental illness or committed suicide. One of her husband's grandmothers, for instance, had been psychologically disturbed. On discovering this, she fled back to her own parents. She subsequently decided to divorce at once, fearing that a child conceived with her husband would be at risk of psychological abnormality. However, she was at this time already pregnant with Mitsuko.

Mitsuko's mother was torn between returning to her husband's family, and bringing her pregnancy to term, or having an abortion, and proceeding with a divorce. She hesitated, losing the opportunity for abortion, and Mitsuko was born. Mitsuko's mother feared constantly that her daughter would show signs of abnormality. Each time she fought with her husband or was bullied by her in-laws, she would feel resentment toward Mitsuko, thinking, "I wouldn't be in this house if it weren't for her."

Mitsuko was an anxious child from her earliest years, and lacked self-confidence. When her brother was born, her father's socially prominent family was delighted with the birth of a second child, a son and heir. The atmosphere of the family, and the manner in which they treated Mitsuko's mother, suddenly improved—so much so that she genuinely began to perceive the child as a blessing and to rejoice in the enviable privilege of belonging to this celebrated family. The stronger this emotion became, the more Mitsuko appeared to be a nuisance, and the mother began unconsciously to discriminate between Mitsuko and her little brother.

Mitsuko was unaware that, after she was conceived, her mother had agonized over whether or not to give birth to her. However, on becoming a mother, Mitsuko reproduced unconsciously with her own child the conflict her mother had previously experienced in relation to herself.

Ajase's mother, Idaike, like Mitsuko's mother, had desired a child to preserve her social status. After becoming pregnant, however, she had thoughts of killing her child, frightened by the hermit's curse and fearing that a misfortune would occur if the baby were born. For Mitsuko's mother, also, a child was necessary for a secure position in her husband's family; however, at the same time, she wondered if her baby would be afflicted by mental illness. The conflict experienced by Mitsuko's mother toward her daughter reveals psychological characteristics in common with Idaike's conflict regarding Ajase.

Ajase became conscious of prenatal resentment toward his mother and experienced a desire to kill her after learning as an adolescent of the events surrounding his conception and birth. Mitsuko did not have this kind of direct experience. Before beginning therapy, Mitsuko's mother had spoken to no one of the conflict she experienced while she was pregnant with Mitsuko and had repressed her feelings up until that time, considering it to be her secret alone. Over the course of her therapy, she gradually recalled, and became able to verbalize, the suffering she had experienced concerning her choice between pregnancy and divorce. In this sense, one can say that her mother's conflicts concerning the issue of whether or not to give birth had been transmitted to Mitsuko in an unconscious, nonverbal way.

Later, Mitsuko unconsciously passed on the rejection she had experienced as a child to her own daughter.

From a clinical standpoint, in psychiatric terms, Mitsuko's mother had neurotic ideas of a hypochondriacal type. One of these manifested itself in the previously mentioned symptom, a feeling of permanent heaviness in the stomach. Mitsuko's mother confided to me that this sensation had persisted for thirty years. During the course of our therapy, she underwent her eleventh exam by gastrocamera. Finally, after her treating physician diagnosed a case of stomach polyps, she had them removed by endoscopy.

After undergoing this minor surgical procedure, Mitsuko's mother confided to me that her stomach discomfort had begun with Mitsuko's birth. With this discomfort finally gone, she also felt released from an emotional sense of ill-being that had endured all that time. It gradually became clear that the stomach discomfort signified the daughter she had wanted to abort, but could not.

From then on, Mitsuko's mother was rejuvenated in a surprising manner, at times displaying the expressions and attitudes of a young girl. It was just at this time that Mitsuko believed her mother to be suffering from cancer and was seized by temporary panic. This situation, which appeared in the course of therapy, reproduced what had taken place previously, when Mitsuko was still in her mother's womb and her mother wondered whether or not she should have an abortion. For Mitsuko, her mother's stomach cancer was the child (Mitsuko herself) in her mother's womb. In addition, this fetus had the power to kill her mother. It is here that the aspects of Mitsuko's case most clearly linked to prenatal rancor became evident.

In this way, the mother's conflicts as they appear in the Ajase complex were vividly reproduced during the treatment of Mitsuko and her mother.

Changes in the State of Women in Japan and the Transmission of Conflicts from One Generation to Another

In a family with feudal values such as her husband's, Mitsuko's mother had no choice but to accept the traditional role of a daughter-in-law. Her principal duty was to serve her husband's adopted mother; however, she experienced deep frustration at being unable to experience love in the context of a happy marital relationship with her husband.

Mitsuko, who did not want to become like her mother, chose to have a "modern" marriage of love. However, after marriage and the birth of their first child, her husband devoted himself to his company rather than his family, and no longer took notice of his wife. On the surface, there had been a transition from a feudal-type family to a democratic, nuclear type. However, in light of Mitsuko's failure to find happiness in a family life centered on the couple, her mother's frustration had only repeated itself in an identical form. Further, Mitsuko projected her frustration onto her daughter and became psychologically aggressive toward her, exactly as her own mother had done.

Although at first glance mother and daughter existed in culturally different family environments, at a deeper, psychological level, the mother's conflicts had been passed on to her daughter unconsciously, through a process of intergenerational transmission. This unconscious repetition and transmission between generations, it should be emphasized, occurs in the deepest strata of the mother-child bond, transcending historical change.

The Child's Prenatal Rancor

The second aspect of the Ajase complex involves the experience of the child, and centers on the issue of prenatal rancor. Prenatal rancor is the resentment experienced by the child on learning of the mother's conflict concerning his or her birth.

In the story of Ajase, prenatal rancor is represented by the metaphor of reincarnation. As the reincarnation of the hermit murdered by Idaike, Ajase was born with the resentment of a child already killed by his mother. Psychoanalytically speaking, Idaike's conflict between the desire to have a child and the desire to kill her child was unconsciously transmitted to her son. On reaching adolescence, he attempted in turn to kill his mother.

In the logic of prenatal rancor, a child must recognize the sexual union between the parents that resulted in his or her own birth. Seen in the context of traditional psychoanalysis, which stresses the child's need to accept that the mother is a sexual object for the father, *mishoon* involves the question of the primal scene.

Prenatal rancor further involves a questioning and an investigation of one's origins: "Who were my parents?" "How was I brought into the world?" To answer the question of identity, one must know the circumstances of one's birth. It was in adolescence, when curiosity about his personal history led Ajase to discover Idaike's conflict concerning his birth, that the prince was overcome with prenatal rancor.

Moreover, while children are conceived between a mother and father, the responsibilities of pregnancy, delivery, and child rearing (or, alternately, of abortion) are often imposed on the mother alone. The story of Ajase also illustrates the mother's suffering when the father offers no support with the emotional burdens of giving birth to and raising a child. The child's empathy for the mother's suffering, and anger toward the father, are other elements involved in the theme of prenatal rancor.

In clinical practice, those who manifest most vividly the prenatal rancor aspect of the Ajase complex are adolescent boys and girls. Ajase himself attempted to kill his mother on reaching adolescence. In this connection, I would like to present the concrete example of the second clinical case.

Case 2.   Akira, who exhibits violent behavior at home and refuses to attend school, asked, "Why did you have me?"

Akira is a fourteen-year-old boy in the second year of middle school. His mother is what is known as a "kept woman" (a concubine). His father has visited Akira and his mother for nearly fifteen years. Akira came under treatment because of his refusal to attend school and his violent behavior at home. From the onset of adolescence, he suffered from his legal status as an illegitimate child and turned his anger on his father. Akira blamed his father for not having recognized Akira and his mother, and accused him of irresponsibility.

At this point, Akira's mother complained vociferously to her son that his father was a "sneak" who had deceived her and that he did not carry out his promises. They were in their current predicament for this reason. Spurred on this way, Akira began to create disturbances when his father arrived, lashing out at him and behaving violently.

During the course of events, however, Akira's anger gradually turned on his mother, as he asked himself why she had given birth to him under the circumstances. When his father was not present, he began to criticize his mother for having given birth to a child when she could not marry. Furthermore, though Akira's mother fiercely abused his father when he was absent, when his father arrived to spend the night, the two seemed to be on very good terms. The sight of this intimacy was intolerable to Akira, and only increased his anger. He would fly into a rage, feeling that his mother and father were, as man and woman, engaged in what he called "flirting." He would become violent toward his mother, screaming "Drop dead!" or "You're always complaining, but when Dad comes, you turn into a doormat and wag your tail, you're glued to him. You make me sick!" It reached the point where he threatened to strangle his mother.

As a result of these incidents, Akira stopped attending school, although he had previously been an excellent, dedicated student. He shut himself in his room, saying that he hated himself and wanted to die.

Thus, I began joint therapy with Akira, his mother, and his father. Our sessions began with Akira's expressing many doubts and frustrations concerning his parents, and proceeded with Akira's parents taking turns responding to their son and recalling the past. Finally, Akira turned to the circumstances surrounding his birth, asking why his parents had had a child when they could not marry. Akira was haunted by the belief that his mother's pregnancy had been motivated by a desire to create a bond with her lover, an idea he eventually came to express. This aspect of the case revealed a very close resemblance to the story of Ajase.

Akira's mother admitted to her son that such had been the case. She had been in love with his father, though unable to marry him, and, wanting to affirm her love and strengthen the bond between them, had decided to bring her child to term rather than undergo an abortion. In response, Akira accused his mother of irresponsibility and demanded to know why she had brought him into the world; however, his tone eventually changed. That his parents were unable to carry out an abortion (although they had certainly considered it) meant, in effect, that they had been unable to kill him. Akira gradually realized that behind his desire to know why he had been born lay a wish to discover why his parents had not aborted him. It became clear to him that they had not wanted to do so, and for that reason he now existed.

Furthermore, Akira's father explained that he had not intended to deceive Akira's mother; it was with the intention of marrying that the two had agreed to keep their child. If he had been a "sneak," he would surely have persuaded Akira's mother to accept the inevitability of an abortion. Sincerely believing at the time that he would be able to divorce and remarry, Akira's father had wanted to have the child as a pledge of their love. In present-day Japan, however, if a man falls in love with another woman, he cannot divorce without the permission of his legal wife. Akira's father is still thinking of divorce; however, according to him, his wife and children remain opposed. (He, in fact, spends approximately half the week with Akira and his mother, and the situation is to some degree acknowledged by his legal family.) As he listened to his mother and father, Akira began to realize that, in comparison to families united only by formal law, real love existed between his parents, and between his parents and himself.

Akira's violent behavior came to an end over the course of these experiences, and the family's home life returned to order. He returned to school, where, having been gifted at the outset, he was swiftly able to readjust. Two years later, he entered high school with no difficulty. Akira is leading a pleasant, emotionally healthy life.

Considered from the point of view of Akira's psychological process, when Akira entered adolescence and began individuation, the identification with his mother began to dissolve. This experience of separation led him to search for his origins and to question whether his mother had become pregnant in order to strengthen her ties with his father. Further, when she was alone with her son, Akira's mother behaved as though she lived for him alone, and abused Akira's father as a villain. When her lover arrived, however, she would do an about-face and show herself as a woman, attaching herself to his side and behaving seductively. This double aspect of his mother was extremely difficult for the adolescent Akira to tolerate.

Among the reasons Akira's anger took the conscious form of prenatal rancor were the difficulties he and his mother experienced living on their own and his anguish as an adolescent on becoming conscious of social disapproval of his family situation. However, a short period of interventional therapy sufficed to restore the unity of the family and Akira's good relations with his parents.

In adolescence, many children feel deep anxiety over the circumstances of their birth and confront the problem of their origins by searching for their true parents. These issues involve prenatal rancor. In searching to discover how they were born, how they came into existence, these children exhibit a fundamental resentment toward the roots of their identity: "Why was I born this way?" "Why did I have to come into the world under these circumstances?" Prenatal rancor is one of the fundamental themes of the Ajase complex.

Problems concerning the Feeling of Guilt in the Ajase Complex

In the context of Buddhism, Ajase was most often presented as a scoundrel who attempted to put an end to his mother. Nevertheless, he became an enlightened sovereign after being saved by the Buddha. A clear contrast can be seen with the treatment of crime and punishment in the story of Oedipus. Oedipus, feeling himself to be guilty, condemned himself to a life of blindness and exile. In other words, he lived with the burden of his crime. In contrast, Ajase was eventually saved and cared for by the mother he had attempted to kill. Through the character of the mother, the story seeks to put in evidence the vast compassion of the Buddha, a compassion that leads to the pardoning of Ajase's crime.

According to Kosawa, Ajase's feelings of guilt undergo a change over the course of the story. His guilt first appears as a fear of retaliation for wrongdoing. In my opinion, this resembles the "punitive" or "persecutory" guilt described by the school of Melanie Klein (1946). After attempting to kill his mother, however, Ajase was frightened at the possibility of punishment and fell gravely ill. His mother not only pardoned him, but also took charge of nursing him. Ajase then experienced a second type of guilt: remorse toward his mother, rather than fear of punishment. This second type of guilt is close to what Klein terms "reparative" guilt. It is no longer clear at this date to what extent Kosawa was influenced by Melanie Klein, but I would like to note again that Kosawa's argument dates from 1932.

The theme of a sinner saved by the Buddha, as it appears in the Ajase legend, is very familiar to the Japanese. This dynamism represents the other side of human relations described by Takeo Doi's (1973) concept of *amae* and is important for understanding personal relations in Japan. One party forgives, the other feels remorse, with a resulting experience of mutual pardon. This mutual pardon is clearly illustrated by the Ajase story. The centrality of sutras such as *The Sutra of the Contemplation of Infinite Life* to the popular tradition, moreover, lies in this point.

However, the psychoanalyst Ramon Ganzarain (1988) has noted several defense mechanisms with regard to the treatment of guilt in the Ajase complex. The first defense mechanism he cites is the "sharing" of guilt: by sharing guilt with another, one is discharged of responsibility. For instance, when the Buddha saves Ajase, he does so because he feels that he himself, by making Ajase's father king, initiated the string of unfortunate events that occurred between Ajase and his parents. The teaching that no one person bears guilt alone, as all people are sinners, offers a salvation that erases the problem of guilt. This process is evident in any religion. In Buddhism, however, it is specifically linked to the idea of self-renunciation, to the concept that the limiting of guilt or sin to an individual is illusion: people's crimes arrive rather from various karmic relations.

The second mechanism of defense is denial by rationalization or reasoning. The prince is told a number of secrets concerning his origins that justify his attempted murder of his mother and his anger toward her. In a psychoanalytic interpretation, it is important to understand that Ajase's inherent desire to kill his mother was rationalized and acted out when he learned the secret of his birth.

The third mechanism is confusion. The Buddhist world of salvation in the Ajase story, from the point of view of a Westerner such as Ganzarain, represents a state that should rather be termed "confusion." In this situation, no one is really guilty, and no one knows who should be blamed; everyone is saved by mutual identification. Elements such as individuality, subjectivity, and the boundaries of self are erased.

Ganzarain's identification of various psychic defense mechanisms against guilt brings into sharp focus the difference between my own Buddhist interpretation of the story and that of a Christian such as Ganzarain. Clearly, as a Buddhist, I have a tendency to affirm and idealize to some extent the idea of salvation as it appears in the story of Ajase, and to identify with it. Ganzarain's attitude, however, which considers this form of salvation to be itself a defense mechanism against guilt, is more truly psychoanalytic. Although I agree with him intellectually, I cannot disengage myself as easily emotionally. From this confrontation, I received a type of culture shock, which led me to make many new discoveries.

Mutual pardon can thus be seen as a defense mechanism against guilt, and the acting out of anger and resentment toward one's parents on learning of one's origins, a mechanism to justify inherent aggression against one's parents. This view is clearly important in the treatment of adolescents. In this light, it becomes necessary to pursue a discussion of the two types of guilt in the Ajase story from the point of view of defense mechanisms as well as in a sociocultural context.

The Difficulties of the Mother
Who Has Lost Her Husband's Support

Kosawa's version of the Ajase story focused on the conflicts between mother and child, particularly the suffering of the mother connected with the issue of infanticide. When I spoke to the well-known American family psychiatrist Theodore Lidz (1989) about the Ajase story, he suggested the following interpretation.

The tragedy of the Ajase story arises because, although the parents have together created, and should together raise, a child, the father does not assume his role and leaves the child's fate in the hands of the mother alone. In other words, Lidz suggested that the point of departure for the Ajase complex was the tragedy of the mother, as a wife or a woman, having lost the support of her husband or male partner. I believe this is a very important interpretation. Lately, I have thought of Lidz's insight as an important theme of the Ajase complex. Despite the existence of an Oedipal, triangular relationship of mother, father, and child, the mother is haunted by the idea that she must take responsibility for the child in an exclusively dyadic relationship. It is the conflict between mother and child in such a relationship, where a split appears between the idealized mother, who wields all-powerful love and control, and the frightening mother who wields the power of death, that I believe Kosawa attempted to describe with the Ajase complex.

If one approaches the problem from a cultural angle, *The Sutra of the Contemplation of Infinite Life* became central to Japanese Buddhism approximately nine hundred years ago. To give a brief historical overview, Buddhism, which originated in India, came to Japan in the sixth century by way of China and Korea. It was not, however, until the Kamakura period that there appeared a type of Buddhism that could properly be called Japanese. Its founders, who included Nichiren (1222–1282) and Shinran (1173–1262), sought to establish a popular Buddhism removed from the Chinese philosophy that had characterized it up to that time. A topic of great importance in this popularization was the enlightenment of women, in particular the salvation of mothers. Behind this topic lay the issue of infanticide, practiced in the form of "selection" or of abortion. *The Sutra of the Contemplation of Infinite Life* played an important part in assuaging the guilt of mothers who had killed or aborted their infants.

During the Edo period, the population of Japan remained stable at between thirty million and thirty-five million. This era was punctuated with many periods of famine, during which children were often killed by abortion or selection. Further, it has been the tradition that this responsibility falls solely on the mother. For this reason, the salvation of mothers who had killed or aborted their children became a central topic for Japanese Buddhism.

In Japanese shamanism, there are certain rites by which the deceased takes possession of a medium *(miko)* and returns to meet with the living. One of the most important of these rites is a memorial service for selected or aborted children (called *mizuko* or "water children" in Japanese), in which the children meet and pardon their mothers through the intercession of a medium.

Thus far I have spoken of the Ajase complex in the context of the "maternal" society of Japan, where the phrase "fatherless family" has become common and where the father continues to work outside the home while the raising of the children falls to the mother. However, it might also give insight into circumstances in the West, including the recent progress of feminism and a growing number of single mothers (particularly in the Scandinavian countries).

On the Sources of the Ajase Complex

Japanese Buddhist scholars have variously criticized Kosawa's use of Buddhist legend in his theory of the Ajase complex. They argue that, whereas the Ajase story as it appears in the *Nirvana Sutra* and Shinran's text focuses (as does the Oedipus complex) on father and son and the theme of patricide, Kosawa transformed the legend into a story of mother and child. While these criticisms are not entirely unjustified, it seems to me that one could, like Kosawa, arrive at a different interpretation of the Ajase legend by emphasizing the mother-child story of *The Sutra of the Contemplation of Infinite Life.*

In terms of constructing a psychoanalytic argument, various factors lay behind Kosawa's decision to emphasize the dyadic world of mother and child. First, he wanted to define the boundary of his theme: prenatal rancor and the question of origins, as opposed to the themes of the Oedipus complex. Second, he wanted to emphasize the essential resentment toward (and particularly the desire to kill) the mother harbored by every human being. Third, he wanted to highlight the anger and resentment of the child confronted with the knowledge that his or her mother was first of all a woman, and that his or her own origins lay in the sexual relations between his parents as man and woman. Finally, Kosawa wanted to underline the tragedy of mothers who had lost the support of their husbands. In other words, he wished to show the conflicts mothers experience in relation to their children when no help is available from their own mothers or families with pregnancy and child raising.

In addition, it is not unusual for psychoanalysts, when using a story from the classics as a metaphor for their own insights, to select and expand on those parts consistent with their own ideas, while ignoring or omitting others. In the case of the Oedipus complex, for instance, attention has recently been turned to the parts of the Oedipus legend that precede those selected by Freud—the events leading up to the birth of Oedipus to Laius and Jocasta.

As punishment for various instances of misconduct, a curse was placed on Laius: should he produce a son, the child would bring about misfortune. Laius thus determined never to have a child. However, he became drunk one evening and had sexual relations with his wife. The child born of this union was Oedipus. Because an oracle had predicted that Oedipus would kill his father, he was thrown into the river directly after birth.

Freud omitted this initial half of the legend and designated to the Oedipus complex only those conflicts experienced by the son toward his parents. If Freud had taken up the story in its entirety, several themes in common with the story of Ajase would have become evident. In Otto Rank's *Myth of the Birth of the Hero* (1914), there appear many tales and legends resembling that of Oedipus; however, all recount the story of the parents as it relates to the hero's birth.

It is this aspect of the Ajase legend, linked to the circumstances preceding the prince's birth, that Kosawa extracted from the Buddhist texts to make his principal subject. This transformation allowed him to express his own psychoanalytic insights in the form of a metaphor. Kosawa's version of the legend, which replaced a father-child story with one centering on mother and child, reflected his perception of Japanese family relations, whereas it is possible to discern in Freud's theory of the Oedipus complex the influence of a Judeo-Christian heritage.

Final Comments

It is interesting to examine the opinions recently offered by Marie Balmary (1979) and Marianne Krühl (1979) concerning how, as he was in the process of formulating his theory of the Oedipus complex, Freud moved from a theory of psychic trauma to one of interior drives. They argue that Freud's discovery of the errors of his father (with regard to Freud's own birth), and defenses against this knowledge, played a role in the above-mentioned transition.

According to these two authors, Jacob Freud (Freud's father) was already married to a woman named Rebecca before marrying Freud's mother, Amarie. While living with Rebecca, he became intimate with Amarie, at the time a young woman of twenty, who subsequently became pregnant. If Rebecca had disappeared, or committed suicide, as a result, it is easy to imagine how Freud might have associated himself with somber images in his parents' psychic world as their "imaginary baby."

If Freud had retraced the events surrounding his birth in an attempt to find his own roots, he might have read the Oedipus story as that of someone searching for his identity. However, must not there have been some repression or split in Freud's psyche concerning this theme? A reexamination of the Oedipus complex from the point of view of the Ajase theory might prove significant.

CHAPTER 5

Hindu Myth and Psychoanalytic Concepts: The Ganesha Complex

Sudhir Kakar

Ever since the advent of psychoanalysis in India in the 1920s, two questions have always hovered above its theory and practice: Is psychoanalysis at all possible in a traditional non-Western society such as India, with its different family system, religious beliefs, and cultural values? Is the mental life of an Indian patient radically different from that of his or her Western counterpart?

On 11 April 1929, Girindrasekhar Bose, the founder and first president of the Indian Psychoanalytical Society, wrote to Freud on the differences he had observed in the psychoanalytic treatment of Indian and Western patients:

> Of course I do not expect that you would accept offhand my reading of the Oedipus situation. I do not deny the importance of the castration threat in European cases; my argument is that the threat owes its efficiency to its connection with the wish to be female [Author's note: Freud in a previous letter had gently chided Bose with understating the efficiency of the castration threat]. The real struggle lies between the desire to be a male and its opposite, the desire to be a female. I have already referred to the fact that castration threat is very common in Indian society but my Indian patients do not exhibit castration symptoms to such a marked degree as my European cases. The desire to be female is more easily unearthed in Indian male patients than in European. The Oedipus mother is very often a combined parental image and this is a fact of great importance. I have reason to believe that much of the motivation of the "maternal deity" is traceable to this source.

Freud's reply was courteous and diplomatic: "I am fully impressed by the difference in the castration reaction between Indian and European patients and promise to keep my attention fixed on the opposite wish you accentuate. The latter is too important for a hasty decision" (Sinha 1966, 66).

Elsewhere, Bose (1950) elaborated on his observations and explained them through his theory of opposite wishes:

> During my analysis of Indian patients I have never come across a case of castration complex in the form in which it has been described by European observers. This fact would seem to indicate that the castration idea develops as a result of environmental conditions acting on some more primitive trend in the subject. The difference in social environment of Indians and Europeans is responsible for the difference in modes of expression in two cases. It has been usually proposed that threat of castration in early childhood days, owing to some misdemeanor, is directly responsible for the complex, but histories of Indian patients seem to disprove this. (74)

Bose then went on to say that although the castration threat was extremely common—in girls it took the form of chastisement by snakes—the differences in Indian reactions to it were due to Indian children's growing up naked until the ages of nine or ten years (girls until seven), so that the differences between the sexes would never come as a surprise. The castration idea, which appears symbolically in dreams as decapitation, a cut on a finger, or a sore in some parts of the body, has behind it the "primitive" idea of being a woman.

Indeed, reading early Indian case histories, one is struck by the fluidity of the patients' cross-sexual and generational identifications. In the Indian patient, the fantasy of taking on the sexual attributes of both the parents seemed to have relatively easier access to awareness. Bose, for instance, in one of his vignettes tells us of a middle-aged lawyer who, with reference to his parents, sometimes,

> took up an active male sexual role, treating both of them as females in his unconscious and sometimes a female attitude, especially towards the father, craving for a child from him. In the male role, sometimes he identified himself with his father and felt a sexual craving for the mother; on the other occasions his unconscious mind built up a composite of both the parents toward which male sexual needs were directed; it is in this attitude that he made his father give birth to a child like a woman in his dream. (Bose 1948, 158)

Another young Bengali, whenever he thought of a particular man, felt with a hallucinatory intensity that his penis and testes vanished altogether and were replaced by female genitalia. While defecating he felt he heard the peremptory voice of his guru asking, "Have you given me a child yet?" In many of his dreams, he was a man, whereas his father and brothers had become women. During intercourse with his wife he tied a handkerchief over his eyes as it gave him the feeling of being a veiled bride while he fantasized his own penis as that of his father and his wife's vagina as that of his mother (Bose 1949).

In my own work, fifty years after Bose's contributions, of which until recently I was only vaguely aware, I am struck by the comparable patterns in Indian mental life that we observed independently of each other, and this in spite of our different emotional predilections, analytic styles, theoretical preoccupations, geographical locations, and historical situations. Such a convergence further strengthens my belief, shared by every practicing analyst, that there is no absolute arbitrariness in our representation of the inner world. There is unquestionably something that resists, a something that can only be characterized by the attribute "psychical reality," which both the analyst and the analysand help discover and give meaning to.

It is the ubiquity and multiformity of the "primitive idea of being a woman," and the embeddedness of this fantasy in the maternal configurations of the family and the culture in India, that I would like to discuss from my observations. My main argument is that the "hegemonic narrative" of Hindu culture as far as male development is concerned is neither that of Freud's Oedipus nor that of Christianity's Adam. One of the more dominant narratives of this culture is that of Devi, the great goddess, especially in her manifold expressions as mother, in the inner world of the Hindu son. In India, at least, a primary task of psychoanalysis, the science of imagination, or even (in Wallace Stevens' words) "the science of illusion"—Mayalogy—is to grapple with Mahamaya, "The Great Illusion," as the goddess is also called. Of course, it is not my intention to deny or underestimate the importance of the powerful mother in Western psychoanalysis. All I seek to suggest is that certain forms of maternal-feminine may be more central in Indian myths and psyche than in their Western counterparts.

Exploration of Myths from India

In the Indian context, this particular theme can be explored in individual stories as well as in the cultural narratives, as we call myths, both of which are more closely interwoven in Indian culture than is the case in the modern West. In an apparent reversal of a Western pattern, traditional myths in India are less a source of intellectual and aesthetic satisfaction for the mythologist than of emotional recognition for others, more moving for the patient than for the analyst. Myths in India are not part of a bygone era. They are not *"retained* fragments from the infantile psychic life of the race," as Karl Abraham (1913, 72) called them, or *"vestiges* of the infantile fantasies of whole nations, secular dreams of youthful humanity" in Freud's words (Freud 1908, 152). Vibrantly alive, their symbolic power intact, Indian myths constitute idioms that aid the individual in the construction and integration of his or her inner world. Parallel to patterns of infant care and to the structure and values of family relationships, popular and well-known myths are isomorphic with the central psychological constellations of the culture and are constantly renewed and validated by the nature of subjective experience (Obeyesekere 1981). Given the availability of the mythological idiom, it is almost as easy to mythologize a psychoanalysis as to analyze a myth, almost as convenient to elaborate on intrapsychic conflict in a mythological mode as it is in a case-historical narrative mode (Freud 1922).

Earlier, I advanced the thesis that the myths of Devi, the great goddess, constitute a "hegemonic narrative" of Hindu culture. Of the hundreds of myths on her various manifestations, my special interest here is in the goddess as mother, and especially the mother of the sons Ganesha and Skanda.

The popularity of Ganesha and Skanda as gods, psychologically representing two childhood positions of the Indian son, is certainly undeniable. Ganesha, the remover of obstacles and the god of all beginnings, is perhaps the most adored of the reputed 330 million Hindu gods (Courtright 1986). Iconically represented as a pot-bellied toddler with an elephant head and one missing tusk, he is represented proportionately as a small child when portrayed in the family group with his mother, Parvati, and father, Shiva. His image, whether carved in stone or drawn up in a colored print, is everywhere: in temples, homes, shops, roadside shrines, calendars. Ganesha's younger brother, Skanda, or Kartikkeya, has his own following, especially in South India, where he is extremely popular and worshiped under the name of Murugan or Subramanya. In contrast to Ganesha, Skanda is a handsome child, a youth of slender body and heroic exploits who in analytic parlance may be said to occupy the phallic position.

In the dramatization of the son's dilemma in relation to the mother, brought to a head by developmental changes that push the child toward an exploration of the outer world while they also give him increasing intimations of his biological rock-bottom identity as a male, Ganesha and Skanda play the leading roles. In a version common to both South India and Sri Lanka, the myth is as follows.

Myth about Ganesha, Skanda, and Their Mother

A mango was floating down the stream and Uma (Parvati), the mother, said that whoever rode around the universe first would get the mango (in other versions, the promise is of *modakas*, the sweet wheat or rice balls that devotees offer to the god; the promise pertains to getting a wife). Skanda impulsively got on his golden peacock and went around the universe. But Ganesha, who rode the rat, had more wisdom. He thought, "What could my mother have meant by this?" He then circled his mother, worshiped her, and said, "I have gone around my universe." Uma gave Ganesha the mango. Skanda was furious when he returned, and demanded the mango. But before he could get it, Ganesha bit the mango and broke one of his tusks (Obeyesekere 1984, 471)

Here Skanda and Ganesha are personifications of the two opposing wishes of the older child on the eve of the Oedipus complex. He is torn between a powerful push for independent and autonomous functioning and an equally strong pull toward surrender and reimmersion in the enveloping maternal fusion from which he has just emerged. Giving in to the pull of individuation and independence, Skanda becomes liable to one kind of punishment—exile from the mother's bountiful presence—and one kind of reward—the promise of functioning as an adult, virile man. Going back to the mother—and I would view Ganesha's eating of the mango as a return to feeding at the breast, especially since we know that in Tamil Nadu the analogy between a mango and the breast is a matter of common awareness (Egnor 1984, 15)—has the broken tusk, the loss of potential masculinity, as a consequence. By remaining an infant, however, Ganesha will be never know the pangs of separation from the mother, never feel the despair at her absence. That Ganesha's lot is considered superior to Skanda's is perhaps an indication of the Indian man's cultural preference in the dilemma of separation-individuation. He is at one with his mother in her wish not to have the son separate from her, individuate out of their shared anima (Kakar 1987).

For the son, as we have seen, the Ganesha position is often longed for and sometimes returned to in fantasy. It does not, however, represent an enduring solution to the problem of maintaining phallic desire in the face of the overwhelming inner presence of the Great Mother. After Skanda killed the demon Taraka, who had been terrorizing the gods, the goddess became quite indulgent toward her son and told him to amuse himself as he pleased. Skanda became wayward, his lust rampant. He made love to the wives of the gods, and the gods could not stop him. When they complained to the goddess, she decided she would assume the form of whatever woman Skanda was about to seduce. Skanda summoned the wife of one god after another, but in each saw his mother and became passionless. Finally, thinking that "the universe is filled with my mother," he decided to remain celibate forever.

Elsewhere, I have traced in detail the passage of the powerful, sexual mother through Hindu myths, folk beliefs, proverbs, symptoms, and the ritual worship of the goddess in her terrible and fierce forms (Kakar 1978). Here, I shall narrate only one of the better-known myths of Devi, widely reproduced in her iconic representations in sculpture and painting, in order to convey through the myth's language of the concrete, of image and symbol, some of the quality of the child's awe and terror of this particular maternal image.

Myth of Devi and the Demon

The demon Mahisasura had conquered all the three worlds. Falling in love with the goddess Devi (Shiva's wife, known also as Parvati), he sent a message to make his desire known to her. Devi replied that she would accept as her husband only someone who defeated her in battle. Mahisasura entered the battlefield with a vast (demon) army and a huge quantity of fighting equipment. Devi came alone, mounted on her lion. The gods were surprised to see her without even armor, riding naked into combat. Dismounting, Devi started dancing and cutting off the heads of millions and millions of demons (Mahisasura's soldiers) with her sword, to the rhythm of her movement. Mahisasura, facing death, tried to run away by becoming an elephant. Devi cut off his trunk. The elephant became a buffalo, and against its thick hide Devi's sword and spear were of no avail. Angered, Devi jumped on the buffalo's back and rode it to exhaustion. When the buffalo demon's power of resistance had collapsed, Devi plunged her spear into its ear, and Mahisasura fell dead.

The myth is stark enough in its immediacy and needs no further gloss on the omnipotence and sexual energy of the goddess, expressed in the imagery of her dancing and riding naked, exhausting even the most powerful male to abject submission and ultimately death, decapitating (i.e., castrating) millions of "bad boys" with demonic desires, and so on. The only feature of the myth I would like to highlight, which is absent in the myths narrated so far, is that of the sword-and-spear-wielding Devi as the phallic mother. In the Indian context, this fantasy seems more related to Chasseguet-Smirgel's (1964) notion of the phallic mother's being a denial of the adult vagina and the feelings of inadequacy it invokes rather than allowing its traditional interpretation as a denial of castration anxiety. In addition, I would see the image of the goddess as man-woman (or, for that matter, of Shiva as *ardhanarishwars*, half man, half woman) as incorporating the boy's wish to become a man without having to separate and sexually differentiate from the mother, to take on male sexual attributes while not letting go of the female ones.

The myth continues. When Devi's frenzied dancing did not come to an end, even after the killing of the buffalo demon, the gods became alarmed and asked Shiva (Devi's husband, the most powerful god) for help. Shiva lay down on his back, and when Devi stepped on him, she hung out her tongue in shame and stopped. Shiva enters the scene supine, yet a container for the great mother's energy and power. In other words, the father may be unassuming and remote, but he is powerful. First experienced as an ally and a protector (or even as a co-victim), the father emerges as a rival only later. The rivalry, too, in popular Indian myths and most of the case histories, is not that of Oedipus, where the power of the myth derives from the son's guilt over a fantasized and eventually unconscious parricide. The Indian context stresses more the father's envy of what belongs to the son—including the mother—and thus the son's persecution anxiety as a primary motivation in the father-son relationship. This comes through clearly in another Ganesha myth.

Myth about Ganesha, Father, and Mother

In this myth, Ganesha was created solely by his mother, Parvati, from her bodily substances. (Parvati's husband, Shiva, was busy doing penance on the mountain, so Parvati, using her own power, conceived her son, Ganesha. Consequently, the father and the son never met each other.) One day, when Parvati was taking a bath, she instructed the little boy, Ganesha, to stand guard outside the door and let no one in. While the boy was standing guard, his "father," Lord Shiva, returned from his penance and asked the boy to step aside so he could visit his wife. Ganesha, following his mother's strict instructions, refused. Enraged, Lord Shiva cut off Ganesha's head. Hearing the commotion, Parvati came outside. Seeing her son lying dead, Parvati was furious and inconsolable. Shiva promised to restore the boy to life and ordered a servant to go out and bring back the first head he found, so Shiva could replace the boy's head. The servant brought the first head he found, that of an elephant. That is how Ganesha came to have a little boy's body and an elephant's head.

This particular Ganesha myth inverts the psychoanalytically postulated causality between the fantasies of parricide and filicide. It is charged with the fear of filicide and with the son's castration by the father as a solution to father-son competition rather than with the Oedipal guilt of parricide. An enduring genital inhibition—Ganesha as the perpetual boy—and a renunciation of all competitive feelings with the father seem to be the typical Indian solution of the "Ganesha complex" (Kakar and Ross 1987).

Case vignette.   The patient, Mr. Mehta, is a twenty-six-year-old counselor in a school who entered analysis not because of any pressing personal problems but because he thought it would help him professionally. Soon, though, he reported occasional problems of premature ejaculation and difficulties in maintaining erection.

Born in a middle-class family in a large village near Delhi, Mr. Mehta was the eldest of three brothers and two sisters. His memories of growing up, until well into youth, were pervaded by the maternal phalanx of four women: his mother, his grandmother, his father's brother's wife, and his father's unmarried sister, all of whom lived with them.

Like his mother, who in his earliest memories stood out as a distinct figure from the maternal-feminine continuum, Mr. Mehta too often emerged from and retreated into femininity. In the transference, the fantasies of being a woman were not especially disturbing; neither were the fantasies of being an infant suckling at a breast, which he had grown onto my exaggeratedly hairy chest. One of his earliest recollections was of a woman who used to pull at the penises of the little boys playing out in the street. Mr. Mahta never felt afraid when the woman grabbed at his own penis. In fact, he rather liked it, reassured that he had a penis at all, or at least enough of one for the woman to acknowledge its existence.

Bathed, dressed, combed, and caressed by one or the other of the women, Mr. Mehta's wishes and needs were met before they were even articulated. Food, especially the milk-based sweets, was constantly pressed on him. For a long time during the analysis, whenever a particular session was stressful, because of what he considered a lack of maternal empathy in my interpretations, Mr. Mehta felt compelled to go to a restaurant in town where he would gorge himself on sweets before he returned home. Like Ganesha's well-known appetite for *modakas*, the sweets are a lifeline to the mother's breast.

Although Mr. Mehta often returned to the Ganesha position in fantasy, he soon realized that it did not represent an enduring solution to the problem of maintaining phallic desire in face of the overwhelming inner presence of the maternal-feminine. In the psychoanalysis that followed, our major focus, then, was on his deep unconscious wish to become a man without having to separate and sexually differentiate from the mother, to take on male sexual attributes without letting go of the feminine ones.

Cultural Insight

The importance of the Oedipus complex in classical psychoanalysis lies not only in its being a dominant organizing pattern of a boy's object relations, but also in its being the fulcrum of Freud's cultural theory. Freud considered the myth of Oedipus as a hegemonic narrative of all cultures at all times, although enough evidence is now available to suggest that its dominance may be limited to some Western cultures at certain periods of their history. In other words, the Oedipus complex, in one variation or another, may well be universal, but it is not equally hegemonic across cultures. Similarly, I suggest, the Ganesha complex discussed in this chapter, together with its myth, is equally universal at a certain stage of the male child's development. It is a paradigmatic myth for relations between mother and child on the eve of the Oedipus complex, before any significant triangulation has taken place. I have tried to show that the Ganesha complex is also the hegemonic developmental narrative of the male self in Hindu India. In another of its variations as the Ajase complex (see chapter 4), it has also been postulated as the dominant narrative of the male self in Japan.

CHAPTER 6

Prohibition against Looking:
Analysis of Japanese Mythology and Folktales

Osamu Kitayama

A myth is a traditional story that existed in ancient times. It usually serves to explain some phenomenon of nature, human origins, or the customs, institutions, and religious rites of people, or to explore gods and heroes (Guralnik 1980, 942). A myth is often characterized by material of a supernatural nature, fantasy, and symbolism. Psychologically, myths provide people with the means of expressing unconscious experiences (Freud 1908). Bion (1962), a Kleinian analyst, also stressed that myths are "models" by which people can understand themselves. According to Roy Willis (1993, 10), Gambattista Vico pointed out that "myths were the imaginative attempts to solve the mysteries of life and the universe, and as such they were comparable, at an earlier stage of human development, with modern scientific theories." Folklore (or folktales) refers to popular stories of unknown authorship that are shared by folk people from the past. These stories are similar to myths, except that they are related more to human matters than to supernatural beings. However, the distinction between myth and folklore is not very clear. Myths and folktales have both been transmitted orally from generation to generation and reflect the thoughts and views shared by a people historically. Thus, they are useful cultural products for examining the issues with which people are concerned, the common problems they encounter, and the kind of coping methods that are prescribed for dealing with them.

Myths exist in many societies around the world. Roy Willis (1993, 17–34), the editor of *World Mythology,* identified the great themes of myths, which include creation (the origins of the world), the structure of the universe, and stories about humanity, supernatural beings, cosmic disaster, heroes and tricksters, animals and plants, body and soul, marriage and kinship. In Asia, China, Korea, and Japan have their own systems of myths, which may or may not share similar stories.

In Japan, the *Kojiki* (Book of myths; literally, "record of ancient things") was completed in A.D. 712. It is an account of a still earlier era, and is composed of three volumes. The first is a collection of poetic statements of early Japanese mythology. It primarily concerns the creation of Japan, including the classical story of a Japanese emperor.

I have examined some Japanese myths and folklore from a psychoanalytic viewpoint (Kitayama 1985, 1991, 1994, 1998); in this chapter, I focus on tragedies related to the "prohibition against looking." I analyze three Japanese stories: the Izanagi-Izanami myth, the myth of Princess Toyotama, and the folktale "The Crane Wife," which describes marriage between a human and a nonhuman. Understanding the tragic stories and their implications would greatly help clinicians understand their patients and the tragedies in their lives.

Besides elaborating on the child-mother relationship observed in Japan, I indicate that our clinical understanding based on these three Japanese tales would greatly contribute to the understanding of people who are so-called masochistic caretakers, a phenomena often observed in Japan. Finally, from the standpoint of practicing psychotherapy, I will explore why it is difficult for therapists to "see" patients with this problem.

Japanese Myths and Folklore
The Izanagi-Izanami Myth

According to the first book of *Kojiki,* Izanagi was a paternal deity and Izanami a maternal deity. After their union as husband and wife, they were commanded to solidify the land, and they generated the islands and deities of Japan. Finally, Izanami bore the fire-deity, who, in the process of being born, burned Izanami's genitals, causing her to die and leave this world for the land of the dead. Izanagi followed her there, asking her to return with him to the land of the living. Izanami went into another room to consult other gods, asking her husband-deity, "Pray don't look upon me." Izanagi, however, could not wait long and impatiently followed her, only to see the horrifying sight of her corpse, which was riddled with maggots and surrounded by roaring thunder-deities. He fled, feeling afraid. Ashamed and angry, Izanami dispatched ugly females after Izanagi, and finally went after him herself. In the end, Izanagi closed the pass to the land of the dead and pronounced the formula of divorce.

Many stories have a "prohibition against looking" as a turning point, including the myth of Princess Toyotama.

Myth of Princess Toyotama

The myth of Princess Toyotama is another myth from *Kojiki*. A young man, Hoori, the hero of the story, went from the land to the palace of a sea deity and married his daughter, Princess Toyotama. Several years later, Hoori went home to subdue his older brother, and became king. Princess Toyotama, who shared a bed with Hoori in the sea, visited him to tell him that she was pregnant. When she was about to deliver her baby, she told him that all people of other lands reverted to the form of their original land when they gave birth, and asked him, "Pray do not look upon me!" Hoori, however, broke his promise and watched her in secret, only to see a giant crocodile crawling and slithering around. He was astonished and frightened and ran away. When Princess Toyotama learned that he had watched her, she felt extremely ashamed and went back into the sea, leaving her baby behind.

"The Crane Wife"

Japanese people now read more folktales than myths. In many of these tales, the turning point is a prohibition against looking. A folktale called "The Crane Wife" or "The Crane's Repayment of Her Debt," well known to ordinary Japanese, is one example. The story goes as follows.

A beautiful woman visited a young man, the hero of the story, and they got married. She was good at cooking and weaving and was a devoted wife to him. Thus, they lived happily. However, she asked her husband to keep one promise: not to look at her when she was weaving. Unable to contain his curiosity, he broke the prohibition, only to find a wounded crane weaving cloth from her own feathers. Unmasked in her true figure, the crane left the hero.

"The Snake Wife"

Scholars have said that "The Snake Wife" is an older version of "The Crane Wife." In "The Snake Wife," the husband is forbidden to observe the act of child rearing. Corresponding to the part of the story in "The Crane Wife" where the wife's pain is depicted by her weaving cloth from her own feathers, in "The Snake Wife" the wife, before leaving her husband and their baby, gives the hero her own eyeballs for the baby to lick for nutrition. It is plausible that the eyes symbolize her breasts, which gave milk to her child.

"The Snow Woman"

Another folktale, which does not relate to the prohibition against looking but to being forbidden to reveal a story, is "The Snow Woman" (Yuki-onna). While many versions of this folktale exist in different places, the common opening scene describes a young man lost in a snowstorm on a mountain while collecting wood. A female snow-monster appears and almost takes his life. Falling in love at first sight with the handsome young man, the female snow-monster spares his life, as long as he promises to keep the secret of their encounter. The rest of the story, summarized here from Lafcadio Hearn's version (1904), which made it well known, highlights the breaking of a promise made by a man to a woman, resulting in their separation.

Several days later, a pretty young woman appeared in front of the young man's house, claiming that she had lost her way. He was delighted by her beauty and asked her to stay with him. She did housework and offered kind services to him. Eventually they were married and had several children. The man was envied by all the villagers for having such a beautiful and caring wife. However, one winter day, when the snow was falling, the young man told his wife of a strange recollection that he had of an encounter with a female snow-monster during a snowstorm many years before. After hearing her husband's story revealing the secret event, the wife became angry and sad that her husband had broken the promise he had made. Before he realized that the woman he had married was the female snow-monster, she disappeared into the snow, leaving him with their children and his regret at losing such a good wife by breaking his promise to her.

The Popular Legend of Urashima-tarō

"Urashima-tarō" is a story that has been passed down from generation to generation over a period of at least fifteen hundred years in Japan (Kita-yama 1985). It is the story of a fisher lad, Urashima-tarō, who rescued a tortoise that was being teased by children on a beach. Several years later, the tortoise reappeared and took Urashima-tarō to an undersea palace called Ryugujo (the palace of the dragon king). During his stay at the palace, Otohime, a beautiful princess, fell in love with him. After lavish entertainment, he married her and remained in paradise. However, he became homesick and wanted to go home. The princess presented him with a box, prohibiting him from opening it. Although he felt he had stayed in the undersea palace only for a few days, when he returned home, Urashima-tarō found only strangers. He then realized that several hundred years had passed, and he had lost his parents and his home. Feeling lost and disillusioned, he broke his wife's prohibition and opened the box. A stream of smoke came out of it, and, suddenly, Urashima-tarō became fatally old.

Analysis and Discussion

In an analysis of the stories described above, which center on the prohibition of looking (or revealing a story), several issues emerge.

Marital Union between Human and Nonhuman

The myth of Princess Toyotama, "The Crane Wife," and "The Snow Woman" all deal with marriages between human men and nonhuman women that end in separation after the men discover the true nature of the women. Similar stories occur in other folktales, such as "The Fish Wife," "The Clam Wife," and "The Snake Wife" (Kitayama 1994). The latter is known as "The Legend of the White Serpent" in China. It is very popular, and is even told in classic opera.

Associated with these are stories in which a man marries not a nonhuman being, but a fairy. A Chinese story of this nature is "Niulang and Zhinü" (The oxherd and the weaving lady), which describes the union of an oxherd and a fairy lady from the sky who are separated at the end and only allowed to meet once a year, on the seventh day of the seventh month. Modified versions of the story are shared by the Koreans and the Japanese.

Why does a man marry a nonhuman woman, and what is the hidden meaning behind these stories? Some analysts consider exogamy a defense against an incest wish. That is, marrying someone so different from one's own parents will help a person who is too close to the parents overcome the taboo of incest (Char 1977).

Prohibition against a Man Looking at a Woman

The core of the tales mentioned above is the prohibition of a man from looking at his wife in special circumstances (childbirth, death, or productive activities). The prohibition is broken by the husband, resulting in the couple's separation. What is the meaning of a woman's prohibiting a man with whom she is intimate from looking at her at certain times, and why does the man always break the prohibition, leading to an unhappy ending?

The story of Cupid and Psyche in Greek mythology also dealt with the prohibition against looking. In it, Psyche was prohibited from seeing her invisible husband, Cupid, the god of love (Hamilton 1969). Cupid was ordered by his jealous mother, Venus, the goddess of beauty, to destroy the beautiful Psyche. Instead, Cupid fell in love with Psyche on sight, and, as an invisible husband, married her, cohabiting with her only at night. Out of curiosity, Psyche broke the prohibition, putting a light on one evening to peek at her invisible husband and discovering that he was a handsome Cupid. Resentful, Cupid left her. In this Western myth, the prohibition bans a woman from seeing the man with whom she is intimate rather than vice versa, as in the Japanese tales described above.

It has been pointed out that the psychology of prohibition, that is, merely prohibiting something, induces temptation. This is well illustrated by the classic story in the Christian Bible where Adam is not able to resist the temptation of Eve, even though the action she persuaded him to do was prohibited.

In terms of male and female psychology, a woman generally feels vulnerable against a man (both physically and emotionally), and has a need for protection—the protection of keeping a secret. A woman is afraid to have her own truth exposed—not only the truth of her physical form, but of her nature and emotions. This is particularly true in most situations in Asia, where women are in less favorable social positions than men. Culturally, women are expected to show their humbleness and to avoid showing uninhibited emotions, even at home. It therefore comes as a shock to men to find that, under special circumstances, women return to their natures to express themselves.

Thus, men, still viewing their female partners as idealized mother figures, find it difficult to "see" the uninhibited side of their women, to discover that their mother figures also have "bad" sides. Thus, as if he were a small child, a man finds it difficult to have a sympathetic view of his mother figure.

Child-Mother Relations: Demanding Baby and Devoted Mother

These tragic tales usually begin with the marriage of a man and a woman and end with their separation. There are seldom stories with happy endings, such as "The Frog King" in the West, in which the frog is transformed into a human and marries the girl at the end. The heroines in the Japanese tales have both rich, productive functions and a secret that requires a prohibition against looking. To hide the secret from her husband while she produces something precious, the wife asks him to obey her prohibition. The husband, however, almost always breaks the prohibition, exposes the wife's wounded self or her corpse, and, primarily because he cannot accept the wife's secret, causes the separation of the couple.

The secret is often related to childbirth and child rearing, with the heroine described as a motherly figure. The hidden wound and death may be interpreted as the results of the devotion of a mother figure to the greedy demands of the "childish" male protagonist. It is indeed a repetition of the developmental process, in which the symbiotic mother-child relationship collapses and the fantasy about the mother leads to disillusionment. The prohibition against looking works as a signal against the confrontation and guilt feeling toward the wounded mother, the separation, and the dilemma between the "good mother" and the "bad mother" that results from confronting the wounded mother figure. The psychoanalytic theory of the difficult integration of various relations to significant objects, such as the contradictory mother figures in these stories, is fully illustrated in the object relations theory, especially in the developmental theory of Melanie Klein (1952).

Masochistic Caretaker

General speaking, the behavior of caring child is related to the emotional attachment between mother and child. The role of care taking the younger generation is socially rewarded and culturally sanctioned (universally but particularly in most Asian societies). However, excessive care for one's children, to the extent that it is harmful to the mother herself and even masochistic, could derive from another psychological factor.

The characters we share through stories usually are grounded in psychological reality. In my experience, people do exist whose lifestyles reflect those of the female characters. I call these people "masochistic caretakers" (1991); they have three main characteristics. First, they take extremely good care of people who request help, and it is hard for them to turn down such requests. Because of this characteristic, they tend to take on work beyond their capacity, have no time to rest themselves, and repeatedly find themselves in a state of exhaustion, both physical and psychological. When they fail to take good care of others, they feel ashamed; in extreme cases, they feel useless, depressed, and sometimes guilty enough to commit suicide. Second, they tend to feel guilty about having to rest and take care of themselves or have themselves taken care of by others. It is difficult for them to be easygoing and relaxed. Thus, it is hard for them to receive proper assistance from others, even when they are physically ill and psychologically hurt. The third characteristic is their self-tormenting nature. When the condition is not serious, they are just worrywarts. If the tendency progresses, however, it becomes accompanied with pleasure and satisfaction and is persistently desired, and the masochistic caretakers expend excessive effort and overwork to a point that is damaging to themselves.

It is conceivable that a narcissistic identification with a vulnerable love object and introjection of its lifestyle are the primary causes of this tendency. The primary causes develop into the secondary masochistic tendency, such as self-depreciation or self-punishment, in which anger is redirected toward the self. Moreover, as a sense of guilt deepens, a strong superego reinforces the masochistic tendency, and the self's desire to be taken care of or to be loved is projected onto people around the self. This completes an internal factor that gains self-satisfaction by taking care of people who identify themselves as wanting to be taken care of. If there is an environmental factor, such as a vulnerable mother, the masochistic caretaker tends to have a sense of guilt in expressing aggression toward it or leaving it as it is. This feeling of guilt then forcefully leads the caretaker to suppress his or her "selfishness" and take care of the other's vulnerability. Finally, when parents or the environment expect such behavior as the behavior of a "good child" and the situation becomes chronic and fixated, the role of masochistic caretaker becomes the only survival method through which the person can obtain love.

We can observe this "masochistic caretaker" lifestyle in people with personality disorders, depression, or an adaptive state of schizophrenia as well as in people with mild neuroses and in quite ordinary, "normal" people. This lifestyle may be prevalent because it may be a method by which people gain their place and successfully adapt to society. In addition, like the female characters in the stories, the positive side of this behavior is being socially loved, appreciated, and desired, and culturally beautified and idealized. At the same time, it enables one to control people around him or her by inducing a sense of guilt in others through his or her woundedness and death. In clinical practice, if "the real self," which could be assumed to exist behind this lifestyle, is carelessly exposed and robbed of its masochistic role, the exposure could lead to the tragic disappearance of "the real self" as a result of shame and anxiety, just as in the Japanese tragedies. It is quite dangerous for this kind of patient if the uncovering therapist becomes intrusive, breaking the prohibition against looking or simply advising the patient to quit this role without a deep understanding of the surrounding situation and internal object relations.

Cultural Elaboration
The Japanese Family and Child-Mother Relations

It is worthwhile to elaborate on the family system and relationships that are observed in Japan in order to have a better understanding of the child-mother relationship that has been described in the myths and folk stories recounted above.

Cultural anthropologists and cultural psychiatrists have pointed out that, in Japanese families, the mother-infant relationship is very close. While a close mother-child relationship is found in both the East and the West, including in most Asian families, the relationship may be even closer in Japanese families and have some unique features (Rothbaum et al. 2002). There are cultural reasons for the tendency toward this close relationship. The Japanese generally believe that the husband should devote his time to working outside the home, while the wife should take good care of domestic matters, including serving her husband and their children. Thus, there can be distinctive differentiations between the roles of husband and wife. The husband is often busy at work and is not available for his wife and children emotionally. Thus, the mother tends to invest her interest and energy in her children, especially her sons, with an intimacy that often involves some sexuality and interdependency. In such a close son-mother relationship, which continues even when the son has grown up and is a husband and father himself, he continues to maintain a strong emotional bond with his mother.

Amae and a Sense of Guilt

The wound hidden by the prohibition against looking is a result of the self-sacrifice and devotion of maternal women answering to the unlimited demands of the male protagonists. For example, Izanami died after producing countless deities and lands, the Crane Wife wove beyond her capacity, and the Snake Wife sacrificed her eyes to feed her baby. We can see that the prohibition against looking functions to avoid the sudden disillusionment about the beautiful maternal figures that may result from confronting their wounded figures after their self-sacrifice.

I believe these tales work as useful metaphors when we examine actual clinical cases. Therefore, as a therapist in clinical practice, I sometimes quote stories such as "The Crane Wife" to explain patients' difficulties. To put it simply, the main problem of masochistic caretakers is their masochistic thoughts or self-injuring way of living, in which they experience others' inconvenience or problems as their responsibilities. Their life histories often reveal that they have experienced feelings of surprise, confusion, and suffering when confronting the hidden aspects of an object, just like the male protagonists in the stories. They also eventually tended to experience the prohibition as their responsibility. It is conceivable that *amae* and a sense of guilt facilitate the process of identification in which a person who receives care becomes a person who gives care.

The *amae* theory was proposed by Japanese psychoanalyst Takeo Doi (1973) and, Japanese scholars believe, is a key concept to understanding Japanese psychological constructs and pathology. The meaning of this concept is ambiguous and vague, but, if I were to explain it in a few words, it is a desire or need to be loved. It is often interpreted as "dependency," but it is rather a psychology of implicit request, expecting a favor or support from others. It is interesting that dependency implies something weak and negative that could lead to pathology in Western cultures, whereas *amae* tends to have a positive connotation in Japan. I think it would be valuable for the Japanese to become aware of the possible connection between dependency and pathology by gaining a Western point of view. (Among psychoanalytic concepts used in Western countries, it is difficult to find one similar to the concept of *amae,* except in M. Balint's [1952] concept of "passive object love.")

In its studies and practices, psychoanalysis usually attempts to associate various meanings of words by utilizing the ambiguity of daily language. Doi actively used this method in his *amae* theory and connected the literal experience of tasting something sweet and the symbolic experience of dependency in a psychological sense (*amae* in Japanese literally means "to taste something sweet"). According to his assumption, the base on which *amae* develops is the mother-child relationship. In terms of early infantile experiences, in which the mouth functions as the center of experiences, there is no differentiation between the instinctive and biological desire of wanting the mother's "sweet" milk through the mouth and psychological dependency. Therefore, we can holistically grasp the entire oral experience of infants in the word *amae.*

When we reexamine Japanese folklore from the perspective of *amae,* we can see that the male protagonists' *amae* is distinctive. "Childish" male protagonists are almost passive in their encounters with and separation from the heroines. The marriage of the two is one-sided and advanced by the female when she suddenly appears to the male character. The male never actively finds and gets the heroine or actively brings her back when she leaves him. The male protagonists are also passive and powerless in the face of their wives' wounds, bleeding, or death. The heroine one-sidedly devotes herself to the male, and he strongly attaches to the beautiful, nurturing female figure, passively waiting for someone to take care of him. Therefore, we can think of the male protagonist's *amae* as one of the causes of the tragic development of the stories.

Although the male protagonist is partly responsible for the heroine's separation or death because of his demands, once he promises to obey the prohibition against looking and then breaks his promise, the sense of guilt that develops and can lead to his self-blaming remains unclear in the stories. In therapy with a patient who is like these male protagonists, one who tends to run away from this kind of situation, it is important to spend sufficient time examining the vulnerability of the other object and other causes of the situation and then to confront these causes gradually.

Simply speaking, when an environmental factor, such as a parent, is physically or psychologically vulnerable and fragile and cannot stand the child's demands but devotes herself or himself limitlessly until she or he becomes wounded, the child sometimes develops an overwhelming "forced sense of guilt" (Kitayama 1991). To resolve this sense of guilt, the child may become a masochistic caretaker, as well.

The Wounded Healer

The Ajase complex, based on a Hindu myth, describes a mother who had a complicated desire to have a child and to kill her child; the child, Ajase, when he grew up, desired to kill his mother (see chapter 4). Here, let us focus on the Ajase complex, which illustrates a typical relationship between a child and a mother, and examine the connection between the Ajase story and the tales of marriage between humans and nonhumans.

First, common among these tragedies, including the Ajase story, is the protagonist's abrupt disillusionment with the maternal heroine after he confronts her nonidealized aspect. The wounds and animality behind the devoted attitude of the female character in the stories of prohibition against looking, the betrayal that breaks the sense of fusion between the child and the mother in the Ajase story, even the shameful fact of incest in the story of Oedipus always painfully destroy the existing good relationship between the child and the mother.

Another commonality among stories with a prohibition against looking theme and the Ajase story is the caretaker's devotion and self-sacrifice. Heisaku Kosawa (1932), the pioneering analyst in Japan, first examined how this factor generates a sense of guilt. He contends that "it is not until the endless 'murder tendency' of the child is 'melted' by the 'self-sacrifice by the parents' that the child comes to have the sense of guilt (6)." If we see this as the main problem in the duplicity between the nurturing mother figure and the wounded mother figure, who sacrifices herself beyond her capacity, we can understand how it may end in one of two ways. One possible outcome is that the child accepts the self-sacrifice of the devoted mother, which leads to a feeling of penitence. The other is that the child feels the self-sacrifice as patronizing and pushing, and the mother's self-sacrifice results in an excessive sense of guilt or a forced sense of guilt in the child. As I indicated in previous papers, the forgiver in the latter case expects the forgiven to have a deep sense of guilt, and, through the caregiver's excessive efforts and devotions, the masochism of the forgiver and the identified masochism of the forgiven are repeatedly induced.

Therefore, in therapy or in child rearing, the critical issue is the vulnerability of the therapist or the mother. All therapists can be wounded and are devoted to some extent. In the discussion of the Ajase complex, I consider it necessary to focus on the devoted attitude of Kosawa himself, who originated this concept. Keiko Kida (1977) and Keigo Okonogi (1978) indicate that Kosawa possibly identified with the mother of Ajase, filled with masochistic omnipotence. Masahisa Nishizono (1986) once described Kosawa's devoted identification with the patient as follows: "The psychoanalysis of Heisaku Kosawa is referred as to the 'melting' technique. It is quite unusual in that he dives into the mind of the patient, becomes the substitute self, experiences the patient's anxiety together with the patient, and attempts to decrease the patient's anxiety (71)."

We cannot explain the power of Kosawa in identifying with the patient in a devoted manner without mentioning that he was physically one-eyed.

Here, rather than attributing everything to his personal problem, I would like to stress that being aware of the potential effect of this physical condition upon those who saw him is important. I believe that Kosawa was what Jungians such as Meier (1949) called the "Wounded Healer," which is described as the prototype of the therapist (Guggenbuhl-Craig 1971). I imagine that the figure of the one-eyed Kosawa had a great impact not only on himself, but on the patient and others, and, in fact, he seems to have been aware of this.

Thus, I would like to quote a paragraph in a letter Kosawa sent to the analyst Shigeharu Maeda (1998), who underwent psychoanalysis with Kosawa: "Confucius was a child of a mistress. This is why he became a great person. It is due to the same reason that I attained success as a therapist. It was because I was blind (200)." When Kosawa says he had success because of his blindness, just as Confucius was successful because he was a child of a mistress, he means that a person can gain power by realizing his or her weaknesses and limitations. I suppose Kosawa meant that accepting his blindness led him to a broader vision through his mind's eye.

Clinical Implications for Psychotherapy

We are all somewhat wounded, and we live by hurting others more or less. When the therapist attempts to heal someone, he or she needs to gaze at the patient's wound without being surprised or running away. In order to do so, he or she needs to see his or her own wounds, the wounds of his or her parents and their limitations, and reflect on the resulting sense of guilt and shame. The therapist who tries to avoid seeing these wounds is less able to see the wounds of the patient. Interestingly, in Japanese, *minikui* (hard to see) and *minikui* (ugly) are homonyms, as are *miru* (to diagnose or treat) and *miru* (to see). Therefore, treating the patient is "to see," and if it is hard to see, it might be because the therapist feels the "ugliness" of the patients.

In every clinical practice, psychotherapy included, the secret that the patient has hidden is often exposed. Looking at the exposed wound, the surprised therapist cannot run away or avert his or her eyes. The stories examined in this chapter can be helpful in treating the depression or psychosomatic disease of patients whom we call masochistic caretakers.

CHAPTER 7

The Oedipus Complex as Reflected in Asian Cultural Products

Wen-Shing Tseng, Kwang-Iel Kim, and Jing Hsu

There are many ways to carry out a cross-cultural study of in-depth psychology. One approach is to examine the emotional complexes that are reflected in cultural products such as folktales and children's fairy tales. Comparing the themes that appear and the ways in which problems are solved makes it easier to understand the similarities and differences of mental functioning and deep emotional complexes among people of different ethnic and cultural backgrounds (Chinen 1989; Heuscher 1963).

This chapter will explore the Oedipus complex as it is revealed in well-known fairy tales, folk stories, operas, and plays from Asia and South Asia. The Oedipus complex refers broadly here to any conflict among a father figure, a mother figure, and a child, or a parent figure and a young couple —any triangular discord that involves three figures from two generations of a family. From a dynamic point of view, one of the figures may be outside of the family or the presence of a third figure may be relatively obscure. According to the psychoanalytic theory of personality development, the parent-child triangular emotional complex becomes prominent for a child at about three to five years of age (so-called phallic stage). At that time a child will manifest a special positive affection toward his or her opposite-sex parent and a negative affection (in the form of competition and potential conflict) with the same-sex parent. However, through the process of normal development, the child will ultimately identify with the same-sex parent and gradually detach from the opposite-sex parent. If the early childhood opposite-sex attachment is not properly overcome and resolved, a neurosis can develop. Freud used the Oedipus story from

Greek myth to address this childhood-observed, parent-child complex. He believed the Oedipus complex to be a basic psychological challenge encountered in personality development and a universal phenomenon. Some scholars believe, however, that this phenomenon is subject to cultural variations.

From the perspective of depth psychology, the "primary thinking process" can be distinguished from the "secondary thinking process." The primary thinking process refers to the original thinking style that a person uses as a young child. This thought process is characterized by a disregard of logic and by influences of emotion, drive, and instinct. Various mechanisms of magic, symbolism, condensation, and displacement operate at an unconscious level. After a person grows up, the thought process gradually shifts, becoming more logical, rational, and conscience-oriented, particularly at the conscious level. This shifting of the thought process is addressed as the secondary thinking process. From a clinical perspective we analyze the mental product of fantasy, free association, and dreams, as well as the psychotic condition, because they are products of the primary thinking process and they assist clinicians in understanding the basic drives, emotions, and conflicts that a person is dealing with at an unconscious level.

In a similar way, we can analyze the cultural product of children's stories, folktales, and myths in a collective way that allows us to conduct a cross-cultural comparison of deep emotion and drive that is shared by a group of people because such cultural products deal with the mental material derived through the primary thinking process. Children's stories, folktales, and myths are a variety of projected cultural material in which the salient personality characteristics and values of a people are expressed, the covert conflicts common among its members are revealed, and ways of coping with problems provided by that culture are shown (Tseng and Hsu 1972). From a methodological point of view, we are fully aware that there is potential bias in the selection of the stories and in terms of the representation of the culture concerned, the differences in the resolution of problems, and the possibility of story diffusion crossing the boundary of culture. We are not suggesting that the stories discussed here are a presentation of the culture from which they originated; rather we analyze them to demonstrate how variations exist with respect to the parent-child complex.

By examining such stories, tales, and myths, we will explore common parent-child problems described in the East, describe how they occurred, and show how they were resolved in a cultural context. The patterns will be compared with those found in the West. This is a simple and interesting way to compare the interpersonal stresses that arise in the East and the West and the coping methods that are prescribed by each culture. It aims to explore theoretically the potential cultural variations of the parent-child complex that may exist universally throughout the East and West and to examine their implications from psychotherapeutic perspectives.

In the psychoanalytic view, the Oedipus complex is a common issue at the core of neuroses that needs to be worked out in psychotherapy. It is relevant to investigate such a well-defined and important emotional complex cross-culturally. Parent-child relationships are commonly dealt with in psychotherapy. Even if they are not directly related to clinical matters, they are often at the root of an emotional complex that indirectly contributes to the presenting problems. Understanding possible parent-child conflicts broadly and cross-culturally will provide insight for therapists and guide them in developing culturally relevant therapies. It is based on this premise that the present study is carried out.

Review of Available Literature

An interest in cross-cultural comparisons of cultural products is not new. Along with the rise of psychoanalytic theory, there was a trend among cultural anthropologists and cultural psychiatrists to collect and study folklore and fairy tales cross-culturally. Some of these studies focused on the Oedipus theme (Edmunds and Dundes 1995; Johnson and Price-Williams 1996; Murphy 1982).

In the available literature, variations of the Oedipus complex in various cultures are presented according to different family systems (Morehead 1999). After examining the matrilineal family system of the Trobriand Islanders in Melanesia, Malinowski (1927) reported that it is not a boy's father who is the key decision maker in his life, but his maternal uncle. Ilechukwu (1999) pointed out that, among the Nigerians in Africa, past custom allowed a man to have multiple wives, who could function as surrogate mothers to his son or, upon his death, as potential wives. Because a son could inherit and marry his dead father's wives, an Oedipal fantasy was eminently realizable, and the father was converted into a rival. Thus, in a polygamous family system, the Oedipal struggle is intensified, and strong taboos exist against incestuous relations (Binitie 1985; Ilechukwu 1999).

After reviewing Oedipal myths and stories from three disparate cultures —of Oedipus in Europe, Hsueh (Xue Ren-gui) in China, and Ganesha in India—Tang and Smith (1996) concluded that cross-cultural differences were found in the forms the conflict took and the precise nature of the outcomes. They also echoed the finding of others (Lidz and Lidz 1989; Weiss 1985) that the Oedipal complex must be seen as a complicated set of interpersonal dynamics embedded in a developmental line, rather than the fantasies of a single individual at a single stage of development. Therefore, parent-child relationship issues need to be examined bilaterally both before and after the phallic stage, when the Oedipus complex becomes prominent.

Rather than the fear of a father figure, some scholars have focused on the fear of a mother figure and the vagina dentata (Otero 1996), expanding the theme of the parent-child conflict. In the Hindu myth about Ajase, Okonogi (see chapter 4 herein) examined a son's hateful emotions toward a mother figure, including matricidal wishes that paralleled the patricidal wishes in the Oedipus complex. Matricidal wishes are never dealt with in Western culture.

Taking an entirely different view, M. T. Erickson (1993) suggested rethinking the Oedipus complex from an evolutionary perspective. He pointed out that secure bonding to kin may establish adaptive kin-directed behaviors, including incest avoidance. Bonding is considered the developmental foundation of a form of social attraction, called "familial attraction," which is evolutionarily distinct from sexual attraction.

Tseng and Hsu (1972) studied Chinese attitudes toward parental authority expressed in Chinese children's stories. They examined the classic *Twenty-Four Stories of Filial Piety* and others, dividing them into the stages of childhood development. Defiance of parental authority in the stories resulted in the admonition, punishment, or death of the transgressor; however, if he survived, he was given the opportunity for training and atonement. Tseng and Hsu pointed out that, in accordance with Chinese cultural values, conflicts between generations always ended in the triumph of the elders.

Hsu and Tseng (1974) also analyzed family relations revealed in classic Chinese operas. They found that, despite the importance of the father-son relationship in the patriarchal family system, the mother-son relationship was the most prominent and important in the son's emotional life. The relationship between mother and son was characterized as extremely affectionate and close, not only when the son was young, but also even when he became an adult. The father-son relationship was treated less often and rather negatively in the stories, with a great deal of mutual hostility and aggression.

Kitayama (1985) reviewed Japanese folklore concerning parent-child relations, indicating that the intensity and complexity of those relations were highlighted as more pre-Oedipal in nature (see chapter 6 herein).

K. I. Kim (1978) examined Korean Oedipal myths and found that they resolve the father-son conflict in five ways: (1) a son assumes power peacefully, after the father recognizes his worth; (2) the son's hostility toward the father is displaced to a father substitute (for example, the father exiles the son, who later becomes powerful and defeats the tyrannical ruler of another land); (3) the exiled son attacks his fatherland, not realizing that the ruler of the country is his own father, and the mother becomes a mediator who brings father and son together; (4) the tyrannical father is killed, not by his son, but by a supernatural force; (5) the son kills a dangerous animal of his father's totem. Kim commented that the deeply ingrained Korean concept of filial piety and overall social emphasis on harmony and cooperation discourages parent-child conflict and direct expression of aggression toward a parental figure. Such expression is sublimated or avoided.

Culture-rooted stories can be used in psychotherapy to facilitate culturally effective treatment. Costantino and colleagues (1986) described how to use folktales that are familiar to children as a part of psychotherapy to enhance their ethnic identity.

Oedipal Stories from Asia

Following are brief summaries of well-known fairy tales, folk stories, operas, plays, and movies from Asia (China, Japan, and Korea) and South Asia (Thailand, Indonesia, and India) selected by the authors. These stories were chosen for the sake of comparison simply because their themes highlighted the Oedipus complex in various ways. There is an assumption that stories told frequently and transmitted through generations have certain meanings and reflect issues that are stressed by a culture. Thus, they are powerful sources of insight into the values of the culture.

Stories from China

The Monkey Story from The Western Journey
This very popular Chinese children's story is based on a Chinese monk's long journey to India (thus, *The Western Journey*) to obtain a Buddhist sutra around the time of the Tang dynasty. The story is filled with imagination

and magic thoughts, and is well liked by both children and adults in China, as well as in Korea and Japan.

The story starts with a monkey king, living on a mountain, who learned magic and martial arts. He was able to fly as fast as lightning and to transform himself into seventy-two figures. He knew how to use a special weapon that he stole from the king of the dragons under the sea—an iron bar (a symbol of a penis) that could be shrunk to the size of a needle and hidden inside his ear or enlarged and used as a deadly weapon against an enemy. Even though the king was the powerful leader of a group of monkeys, he was not satisfied with himself, because he was merely a monkey, without any official title. He went to Heaven and asked the Jade Emperor for an official appointment. His request was granted, and he was given a job as a stableman. Very soon he discovered that this was an inferior position, and, feeling dissatisfied and rebellious, he stole and ate all the magic peaches that grew in the backyard of the emperor's palace and became immortal. Because he was immortal, there was no easy way to discipline or exterminate him. He misbehaved with omnipotence, causing much trouble in the world. Finally, he demanded to become the king of the world. The Buddha was called upon to help deal with the situation. The Buddha presented the monkey with a test, promising that if he could escape from the Buddha's palm, he would be granted his wish to become king of the universe. The monkey, thinking that it was an easy challenge, jumped into the sky and flew at the speed of light to the edge of the universe, where he saw five high mountains. On a hill on the central mountain, he urinated to prove his presence there. Then, with a feeling of triumph, he returned to the Buddha. The Buddha asked the monkey to smell his middle finger; it smelled of urine. The monkey then realized that he had never jumped out of the Buddha's palm. In punishment, he was subdued and was put under the Five Mountains. Thus, the first portion of the tale ended with the monkey (an omnipotent child) being punished by an almighty authority figure for his misbehavior.

In the following tale, the monkey was given the opportunity to atone for his misconduct. A monk was on a journey to the west (India) to obtain a Buddhist sutra. The monk released the monkey when he promised to follow and protect the monk on his mission. The monkey was given the Buddhist name Sun Wu-kong (monkey with enlightenment for being nothing), the name by which the story is known. The monkey (representing the ego), accompanied by a pig (representing the id) and the spirit of a fish (representing an ordinary human), made good use of his magic and martial arts skills to protect the monk (representing the superego) on the long and dangerous journey, fighting devils and other enemies along the way. After completing this task, a metal ring put on his head by the monk to control his behavior was removed, and the monkey was transformed into a human, symbolizing his maturity.

The story, filled with magic and imagination, emphasized the quality of omnipotence and described a child's rebellious behavior against parental figures. Although the child was punished, he was given the opportunity to mend his ways. While the story clearly focused on the phallic stage of development, there was no parent of the opposite sex to indicate a triangular conflict, nor was there a happy ending with a female partner, as in many Western tales. The monkey's reward at the end of the story is obtaining personal maturity.

The Story of Xue Ren-gui

There is a famous Chinese opera centered on a young hero, Xue Ren-gui, who was very smart and strong, but poor, and who later became a famous army general (Chang 1969). A series of stories titled *Hong-zong-lie-ma* (A fiery horse with red-colored mane), begins with "Cai-lou pei" (Matching at the bouquet tower), about Minister Wang's beautiful daughter, who had reached the age for marriage. Many suitable families had approached the minister about a match for his daughter, and it was difficult to turn down any of them. As was customary, Minister Wang arranged a special matching occasion. All interested candidates were asked to gather in front of the minister's house, where a tower was built. The daughter was to stand in the tower and throw a bouquet to the candidate she wanted as her husband. The evening before the event, the daughter dreamed that a big red star fell into her body. The next morning, she found a beggar sleeping in her backyard. He had a red light around his body, which was interpreted to mean that he would have a noble career in the future. She suggested that he come to the special matching event. During the event, she threw the bouquet to the beggar, rather than to any of the young men from affluent families. Her decision to marry this poor young man (Xue Ren-gui) made her father very angry, but she insisted that a promise was a promise and married him. This is one version of the first plot of the story (see figure 1.A).

In another version of the story, Minister Wang hired laborers to remodel his house. One night, his young daughter saw one of the workers, who was strong and handsome, sleeping in the yard outside the house, shivering in the cold winter air. She felt pity for him. In the dark, she found a piece of clothing from her clothes chest, which she threw to him from the window to keep him warm. The next morning, when Minister Wang found the worker wearing the piece of clothing, which he had given to his beloved daughter as a gift, he disowned the daughter in a fit of anger and chased her out of the house. The daughter had no choice but to go with the poor worker, Xue Ren-gui, and marry him, living with him in a humble hut on a mountain. Although Xue Ren-gui was poor, he was a strong young man with good shooting skills. He supported his family by hunting. Whichever version of the story is told, the first plot ends with a triangular conflict among the father, the daughter, and the young man, and the defeat of the daughter for showing an interest in a man of whom her father disapproved.

In a subsequent section (as the second plot) of the story, Xue Ren-gui left home to go to war shortly before his wife gave birth to a boy, Ding-shan. The boy, without the presence of a father, lived with his mother alone in the mountains and, when he grew up, supported her by hunting.

Eighteen years later, as the third plot of the story, known as "Ren-gui's Wild Goose Shooting," or "The Fen-River Bay" (Fen-he wan), the father, Xue Ren-qui, then a famous general, returned from the war. On his way home, at the Fen-River Bay, he met an excellent young archer who could shoot down a wild goose in flight just as easily as he himself could. He was struck with fear that the young man might become his competitor. While he was preoccupied with this thought, he noticed a white tiger that seemed about to harm the young man. To save the young man, he quickly shot at the tiger, but, by mistake, killed the young hunter instead. When he reached his wife's house, he found a man's shoes there and became angry. His wife teased him that the owner of the shoes was a young man who had her affection and had lived with her for the past eighteen years. The jealous husband then learned that not only was the man their son, but that he was the young man he had killed at Fen-River Bay. Thus, this time, the triangular conflict among father, mother, and son ended with the son's being killed by the competitive father (Hsu and Tseng 1974) (see figure 1.A).

In the next section of the opera, it was discovered that the son had not been killed after all, but had been saved by a god disguised as a white tiger, who had carried the wounded young man away. Later, this young man, Xue Ding-shan, become a famous general himself and happily met his father, Xue Ren-gui. Therefore, the story did not end tragically, as it originally seemed.

White Serpent Opera
Another folktale with a triangular theme starts with a schoolboy rescuing a small white snake from death at the hands of some other boys and setting it

Figure 1. Various Plots within a Story: *Xue Ren-gui, Nakorn Pathom,* and Oedipus

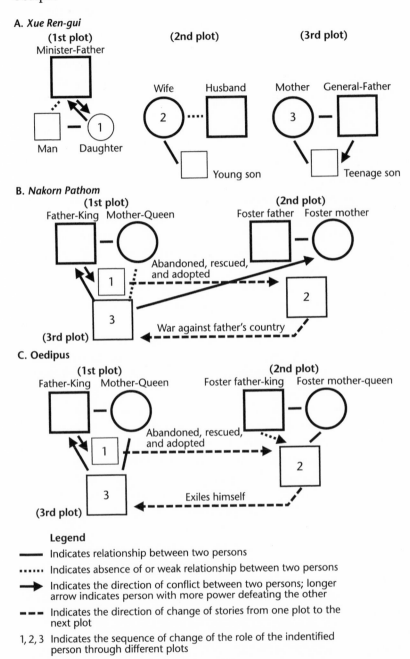

Legend

——— Indicates relationship between two persons

······ Indicates absence of or weak relationship between two persons

➤ Indicates the direction of conflict between two persons; longer arrow indicates person with more power defeating the other

− − − Indicates the direction of change of stories from one plot to the next plot

1, 2, 3 Indicates the sequence of change of the role of the indentified person through different plots

free in the beautiful West Lake. Many years later, the white serpent turned itself into a beautiful maiden called White Modest Beauty, who sought and found the young scholar, Xu Xian, who had rescued her as a boy. The young man fell in love with her the moment he met her, without knowing who she was, and they were soon married. She assisted her husband in opening an herb store and becoming successful in business. They had an infant son and lived a very happy family life.

However, one day, a powerful abbot appeared. He wondered why an epidemic of illness was prevalent in the area and suspected that someone might be making people sick. After an investigation, he warned Xu Xian that his wife was bewitched. He told Xu Xian to give her yellow wine on the fifth day of the fifth month, when all bewitched creatures in human form turn back into their true shapes after tasting the wine. Xu Xian, puzzled by the warning, did this reluctantly and saw his wife turn into a huge white serpent rising up from the bed. In terror, Xu Xian fled to the abbot's monastery on the mountain and followed his command never to return home. The white serpent was angered by this and attacked the abbot, flooding his mountain. However, the abbot overcame her and imprisoned her under a pagoda.

Xu Xian and White Modest Beauty's infant son grew up to be a great scholar, who brought honor to the house of the aunt and uncle who raised him. One day, when he had gone up to the mountain to burn incense and pray for his mother before the pagoda, the pagoda rose into the sky, and White Modest Beauty reappeared. Xu Xian was then able to join his wife in the afterlife of spirits.

In this story, the happiness of a young couple was threatened by an authority figure that claimed they had violated a rule. The authority was so powerful that the young couple could not succeed in defying it. The only solution was for their child to grow up, attain success, and, through filial piety, rescue his punished and separated parents (Tseng and Hsu 1972).

Stories from Japan

"Momo-tarō" (Peach Boy)
"Momo-tarō" is one of the most popular children's tales in Japan. The story starts with an aged couple without children. One day, in response to their wish to have a child, the couple found a large peach floating on a river. Out of it, to their surprise, came a small boy, whom they called Momo-tarō, "the peach boy." The peach boy grew up strong and, together with a mon-

key, a bird, and a dog, sailed to an island where a devil lived in a castle. The monkey climbed up and opened the door of the castle, the bird picked out the devil's eyes, the dog bit the devil's foot, and the peach boy was finally able to kill the devil. After their successful conquest, they sailed back with their boat full of the devil's treasure, and the peach boy lived happily ever after with his parents. The evil figure was exterminated and the treasure was taken, but there was no princess waiting at the end of the story for the peach boy. (This story was used by the Japanese military during the Pacific War to enhance the people's motivation to conquer the South Pacific and bring back the "treasure" for Japan.)

"Issun-bōshi" (One-inch Boy)

"Issun-bōshi" is a Japanese version of a "typical" Oedipus story. Once upon a time, there was an old couple who had no children. One day they went to a shrine and prayed for a baby. Even a tiny little thing as small as an inch would make them happy. To their delight, a little boy was finally born to them. He was a tiny little fellow, no bigger than a person's thumb. They named him Issun-bōshi, meaning one-inch boy.

When the boy became a teenager, he was still the same size. One day he asked his parents to give him a wooden bowl and a needle. He was determined to go out into the world and make a life for himself. He would use the wooden bowl as a boat and the needle as a sword. Because he was so determined, his parents granted his wish. He floated down the river, paddling with a chopstick, and finally reached Kyoto, the old capital of Japan. There he asked a lord if he could serve him. The lord found that although the boy was tiny, he was very clever. The lord became fond of Issun-bōshi and accepted him as one of his servants.

One day, when Issun-bōshi was accompanying the princess to a temple, a terrible red ogre suddenly appeared and tried to carry her away. Issun-bōshi drew his needle-sword and shouted at the top of his voice, challenging the red devil. The ogre picked up Issun-bōshi and swallowed him in one gulp. In his stomach, Issun-bōshi stabbed the ogre with all his might. This hurt the ogre so much that he rolled on the ground in pain, spit Issun-bōshi out onto the ground, and ran away. In his hurry, he left his magic mallet behind. The princess picked up the mallet and asked Issun-bōshi to make a wish. He wanted nothing but to grow bigger. The princess shook the mallet, and each time she shook it, Issun-bōshi grew bigger, until he was a strong, handsome man, taller than she. The story ends with their getting married and living happily ever after.

Ama-goshi, *a Movie*

A recent Japanese movie dealt directly with the Oedipus conflict. It was a detective story titled *Ama-goshi* (which means "crossing a place called Ama"). The story described a teenage boy who accidentally witnessed his mother making love with his father. Shocked by the scene, he ran away from home, crossing a place called Ama, and bumped into a young woman, a prostitute who had run away from her madam. They became acquainted and continued their aimless running together. On the way, needing money for food, the prostitute seduced a man, making love to him for money. The boy, witnessing this, killed the man who had made love to her, then ran away. The police originally suspected the prostitute, but no one actually knew who killed the man. Almost two decades later, through careful detective work, the police found out that it was the teenage boy who, out of jealousy, had killed the man. It is interesting that an Oedipus-themed story was used for the movie, with the Oedipus impulse acted out by a teenage boy.

Stories from Korea

The Woodcutter and the Heavenly Maiden

This is a popular legend in Korea that is told in different versions. The story starts with a handsome young woodcutter living with his mother at the foot of a mountain. He was very diligent and every day went into the forest to cut firewood for a living. However, he was still so poor that he could not afford to marry. One day, when he was working in the forest, he rescued a deer that was being chased by a hunter. In gratitude, the deer, who was actually the servant of a mountain god, promised to fulfill the woodcutter's fondest wish. He suggested that the woodcutter climb to the top of the mountain in the evening when the moon was full. The deer told him that there was a lake where maidens from heaven came to bathe. The deer also hinted that, while they were bathing, the woodcutter should hide the clothes of one of them. Without her clothes, she would not be able to return to heaven and would become his wife. Curious, the woodcutter followed the deer's suggestion. To his delight, one of the maidens became his wife, and they had children and lived happily together as a family. Then, one day, the wife began to think about her parents in heaven and wished she could see them. She asked her husband to show her the heavenly clothes he had hidden. Feeling sorry for her, and ignoring the deer's earlier warning never to show her the heavenly clothes, he did so. Overcome by her desire to return to heaven, she put the clothes on and, before the woodcutter realized what was happening, she began to float up to heaven with their children.

There are different versions of the ending of the story. In a common version, the couple was separated from then on in punishment from the heavenly father, or god. The woodcutter was given a chance to join his wife in heaven, but, because of his filial piety toward his elderly mother, he would not desert her on Earth, and he missed the opportunity (Han 1991). According to the legend, the couple now appeared as two bright stars in the night sky, separated by a river of stars, the Milky Way. They were allowed to cross a bridge to meet each other only one night a year, on the seventh day of the seventh month. This plot is common in Chinese and Japanese legends, as well.

In another version, the woodcutter and his mother were both allowed to rise to the sky to join the heavenly maiden and live together again (Souci 1999). In a movie version of the story, the heavenly maiden was punished by her angry heavenly father and changed into a wild wolf, eating human flesh for survival and eventually being killed by a hunter.

Whichever ending is used, the theme of the story is the same: a heavenly lady, not by her own choosing, marries an ordinary man, and their fates are manipulated by her heavenly father, who is dismayed by her marriage to a lowly human. There was no way for the daughter to defy her father and remain with her husband.

The Snail Lady
This is another Korean legend regarding the union of a human and a nonhuman (Han 1991). Once upon a time, there was a young bachelor who lived all alone. The young man worked very hard, even though he had no one to provide for but himself. One day he mumbled to himself, "I don't know why I'm hoeing this field to plant rice when there isn't anyone with whom to eat it." Then came a woman's voice from out of nowhere saying, "You can eat it with me." The young man was surprised. Looking around, he found nobody except an unusually large and very pretty snail at his feet. He picked up the snail and went home. A pretty woman came out of the snail shell and cooked food for him. He was delighted and married the snail lady, and they lived very happily together as husband and wife.

However, one day, the king came to their area to hunt and discovered the man's beautiful wife. The king wanted to take her for his wife and proposed a contest to the man—to see who could cut down the most trees on the mountain the fastest. The man knew that the king was going to order his soldiers to do the work for him, while the man had to do it by himself, and that there was no chance for him to win. However, the snail lady comforted her husband, and said that there was no need to worry. She revealed herself as the daughter of the Dragon King in the sea and asked for help from her father. The Dragon King sent an endless stream of tiny men with axes to help his daughter's husband.

Even though the king lost the contest, he did not keep his promise, and challenged the man to one contest after another. Each time, with help from the Dragon King, the young man won. The final contest was a boat race, in which the malicious king was swallowed by a huge wave sent by the Dragon King. The young man gave all of the king's belongings to the poor, and he and the snail lady lived happily ever after.

In this story, a man threatened with losing his wife to a malicious king, with help from another authority figure, his father-in-law, was able to resolve the conflict.

Stories from South Asia

Nakorn Pathom *from Thailand*

Nakorn Pathom is almost a Thai version of the Greek Oedipus story, except that the ending is different. According to Jumsai (1977a), the story starts with a king, Phya Kong, whose queen had just given birth to a son, known as Phya Pan. According to custom, a troupe of astrologers was consulted regarding the future of the baby, and the king heard the surprisingly bad prediction that when the prince grew up, he would kill his father. A logical solution was to eliminate the baby before the tragedy could occur, but the king could not kill his son. Instead, he ordered that the baby be put on a raft and float down the river. The boy was rescued by a woman, Home, and her husband, Chome, who had no children. They adopted the boy, and raised him. When Phya Pan grew up to be a young man, with knowledge of warfare and the tactics of fighting, he was presented in service to the king of Ratburi, another kingdom. The third part of the story notes that the king of Ratburi sent yearly tributes to King Phya Kong to avoid conflict. Phya Pan advised the king of Ratburi that there was no need to do this, and promised that he would protect the kingdom from King Phya Kong. When the yearly tributes stopped, King Phya Kong started a war against Phya

Pan's king. Phya Pan defended the king of Ratburi and, without knowing that King Pyha Kong was his biological father, killed him in battle. According to custom, the widowed queen of the defeated king was part of the victor's spoils, and Phya Pan had to show this by taking the queen as his wife (figure 1.B).

Up to this point, the story is almost identical to the Greek story of Oedipus. However, the ending is different. When Phya Pan was about to cross the threshold of the queen's chamber, two cats barred his way and gave him a premonition that a deadly wrong was about to be committed. Divine voices whispered in his ear, informing him that the queen in the chamber was his mother. He said to the gods that, if this was true, they should cause milk to come out of her nipples when he approached her. As if by magic, when he was about to embrace her by force, milk streamed out into his mouth. Then he realized that he had killed his own father. He became angry with his adoptive mother, Home, for concealing his identity, and she was put to death. Then he realized that he had committed two deadly crimes: in addition to killing his own father, he had killed the foster mother who had raised him. Not knowing how to cleanse himself of his sins, he consulted a famous Buddhist monk. The priest advised him to build a large pagoda, the tallest ever built by a man, to worship his father. He did so, and also built another one in memory of his foster mother. Thus, following Buddhist concepts, Phya Pan was given the opportunity for atonement, even though he had committed serious crimes.

The Ramayana from Indonesia

The *Ramayana* is one of the most popular stories in Indonesia (Sunardjo 1975) and, with some revisions, in other parts of South Asia, including Thailand (Jumsai 1977b). The story is told repeatedly in shadow-puppet shows, the most popular evening entertainment enjoyed by common people in Indonesia.

The story begins with King Dasarata, in the kingdom of Kosala. He had four sons, who were, in order of age, Rama (from his first wife, who died), Barata (from his second wife, Kekayi), Lesmana, and Satrugna. Rama had already married his wife, Sinta, and, as crown prince, was expected to succeed as king when the time came. The four brothers lived harmoniously, getting along well and respecting the eldest brother. However, Kekayi wanted her own son, Barata, to succeed as king. In the past, Queen Kekayi had saved the king's life on the battlefield, and the king had promised to grant her any two wishes. The queen now took advantage of this promise and requested that her own son be crowned and that Rama be banished for fourteen years to the forest. With great reluctance, the king agreed to her request.

Following the king's orders, Rama said goodbye to his beloved father, left the palace, and went into the forest with his wife, Sinta, who had begged him to take her with him. One of his younger brothers, Lesmana, volunteered to go with them. Very soon the king, saddened by what had happened, became ill and passed away. The queen was delighted and urged her son, Barata, to become king. However, to her dismay, Barata refused, insisting that the crown belonged to his eldest brother, Rama. He would only govern the country as his deputy until Rama returned, when his banishment was over.

Rama, with his wife and younger brother, managed to survive in the jungle and lived happily for thirteen years. However, one day, their presence in the forest was discovered by the evil giant king of Rawana, from the kingdom of Alengka. Being very attracted by the beauty of Rama's wife, the king of Rawana kidnaped her and hid her in his castle. Rama, in despair, promised to help another king, Sugriwa, recover his throne if King Sugriwa would help Rama fight Rawana and rescue his wife. With his powerful ally and help from a white ape, Hanuman, Rama finally succeeded in defeating his enemy and rescuing his wife. The story ends happily. Since the fourteen-year banishment had ended, Rama and Sinta returned to their home in the kingdom of Kosala, where Rama's half-brother, Barata, kept his promise and handed back the crown.

Thus, the story had two plots with triangular conflicts. In the first, the conflict was among the king, his second wife, and the crown prince. The son became the victim of the jealous stepmother and was banished into a dangerous forest. In the second plot, the crown prince's wife was abducted by an evil giant king, and the prince, with the help of an ally, defeated him. There was no direct conflict with his own father, nor any retaliation toward the stepmother who had suggested his banishment. It is interesting to note that harmonious and cooperative relations were described among the siblings, despite the conflict instigated by the stepmother.

The Ganesha Story from India

Perhaps one of the most popular and well-liked Hindu deities in India is Ganesha (also called Ganesa), son of Siva and Parvati, a deity with a human body and an elephant head. There are numerous versions of his story (see also chapter 5). The following, described by Tang and Smith (1996), is the most widely accepted. Parvati, the wife of the god Siva and a powerful goddess in her own right, wanted a son but was unable to persuade Siva to come down from his meditations on the mountain. Thus, when Parvati was bathing in the river one day, she used her powers as a goddess to form a young man, Ganesha, out of the scum of her body and breathed life into him. Parvati then charged Ganesha to keep intruders from her bathhouse. One day, Siva returned and demanded entry to Parvati's bath. Ganesha refused him entry, a battle ensued, and Ganesha was beheaded by Siva. Parvati emerged from the bathhouse, horrified and angry. She informed Siva that the young man was her son and threatened to destroy the universe unless he was restored to her. Siva, now remorseful, sent his minions to seek the head of the first animal facing north, the direction from which good things come. They returned with the head of an elephant, which was then placed on Ganesha's shoulders. In this story, the power of the mother and the mother-son bond were stressed, the father killed his son, and the mother demanded that the father make up for his behavior. This is an entirely different form of the parent-child conflict, with a different resolution.

Western Stories Compared

In comparing stories from the East and the West, we should briefly review the Western Oedipus-related stories. The story of Oedipus that Sigmund Freud used to develop his theory of the Oedipus complex originated in Greek mythology (Hamilton 1969). In the myth, there were actually three plots interconnected by the same prophecy of a father who would be killed by his son (see figure 1.C). In the first plot King Laius of Thebes abandoned his baby son, Oedipus, on a lonely mountain after hearing the prophecy from Apollo, the God of Truth. He committed this act of infanticide with the thought that his son would die there and the prophecy would not come to pass. In the second plot, Oedipus, after being rescued from the mountain and growing up, exiled himself from his "home," where he was thought to be the son of King Polybus, to avoid the fate of killing his "father," as declared by Apollo. The third plot is the one that is commonly known. In it, Oedipus kills his real father, King Laius, as a stranger on the road, marries his mother (Laius' queen) as a reward for saving the country from the monster Sphinx, has two children, and later discovers the truth of what he has done. At the end of the story, the mother kills herself in shame and Oedipus punishes himself by putting out his eyes. Thus, the best-known version was preceded by two plots that ended with the son's being abandoned by the father and exiling himself to avoid the prophesied tragedy. These were quite contrary to the last plot, in which the son killed his father incidentally.

As Weiss (1985) pointed out, the interpretation of a myth is greatly influenced by the culture at the time and by the psychological condition of the individual who interprets it. Weiss indicated that Freud used the Oedipus myth presented by Sophocles in *Oedipus Rex,* which was slightly different from Homer's version, written six hundred years earlier, and did not include a Sphinx. In Homer's version, Oedipus was neither blinded nor exiled. Freud also ignored the first plot in the myth, in which Laius, Oedipus' father, seduced and raped the illegitimate son of King Pelops, and was condemned by the angered goddess, Hera, to be murdered by his own son and replaced by him in his wife's bed. Later, Hera sent the Sphinx to terrorize Thebes.

There are popular fairy tales in the West that deal with the triangular conflict theme. Some typical examples (Cole 1982) are "Snow White" (in which the jealous stepmother queen is defeated and a handsome prince rescues the princess), from Germany; "Cinderella" (in which a stepdaughter is mistreated by a cruel stepmother and jealous stepsisters, who are ultimately defeated, and the heroine happily marries a prince), from France; "Sleeping Beauty" (in which a beautiful princess is born and a jealous fairy curses her, saying that she will prick herself with a spindle when she reaches puberty and fall into a deep sleep; after the tragedy occurs, the sleeping princess is rescued by a kiss from a handsome prince, who arrives on a white horse), from Germany. These stories all deal with conflicts between mother figures (displaced as stepmothers or disguised as evil fairies) and daughters, but end with the defeat of the parental figure and the triumph of the daughter, who is rewarded with marriage to a desirable man. A similar plot with the same ending is found in "Hansel and Gretel" (a boy and girl who are expelled by their stepmother, fight against a witch, and conquer her) and "Little Red Riding Hood" (a little girl is almost eaten by a wolf, but is rescued by a woodcutter), both from Germany. In "Jack and the Beanstalk," from England, a son, with assistance from his mother, defeats a giant and takes home the giant's treasure. All the stories thus end with the defeat of the (evil) adult figures and the triumph of the children.

Shakespeare's play *Hamlet,* one of the best-known stories in the West, is characterized by the Oedipus theme, and ends with Hamlet killing his stepfather, the king, amid agony and ambivalence.

Comparisons and Theoretical Explorations

Before we carry out a cross-cultural comparison of the emotional complexes reflected in cultural products, several issues deserve attention. First, the level of consciousness versus repression operates differently in children's stories and myths, folklore, and plays for adults. It depends on the nature of the stories and the different forms in which they are told for different audiences. Generally, in children's stories, any conflict among close family members needs to be disguised or projected onto a surrogate in order to avoid any ill feelings or reactions from the children. In contrast, in adult myths, it is less necessary to avoid direct expressions of emotional conflict, which are often already projected into the supernatural and kept at a distance because the story takes place in the past, and far away. Naturally, this is coupled with the cultural need to repress or conceal negative emotions. Thus, the issues are not suitable for direct comparison cross-culturally when the material is derived from different cultural products—myths, folklore, children's stories, or plays for adult audiences. This caution needs to be considered when cross-cultural comparisons are made.

Different Types of Parent-Child Complexes

This study makes it apparent that the Oedipus complex used by psychoanalysts to explain the parent-child conflict that occurs in the early developmental stage is merely one type of parent-child complex. There are many variations of the complex cross-culturally (see figure 2). Depending on the figures involved, the various parent-child complexes described in the East and the West can be subdivided into three major groups.

Father-Mother-Child Triangular Complex
This group involves both parents and one child, forming an apparent triangular complex among them. This complex can be subdivided further into three subgroups.

Same-sex parent and child conflict.   This subgroup includes emotional-relational complexes involving a conflict between a child and the parent of the same sex. The father-son conflict was exemplified by the Greek myth story of: Oedipus (centering on the consistent theme relating to the prophecy that a father will be killed by his own son); the British fairy tale story of Jack and the beanstalk; the Chinese opera story of Xue Ren-gui (third plot); and the Japanese movie *Ama-goshi*. The mother-daughter conflict was illustrated by the German stories of Snow White and Sleeping Beauty and the French story of Cinderella.

Opposite-sex parent and child conflict.   This subgroup includes the parent-child conflict that takes place between a child and an opposite-sex parent. The father-daughter conflict is exemplified by the Chinese opera story of Xue Ren-gui (the first plot), and mother-son conflict by the Indonesian folk story of Rama and the Indian myth story of Ajase.

Same-sex/opposite-sex parents and child conflict.   This subgroup consists of rather unusual compound complexes in which the conflict derives from both a father figure (the child's birth parents) and a mother figure (a foster parent) as illustrated by the Thai folk story *Nakorn Pathom*.

Parent-Child Bilateral Complex
This group involves conflict between a parent and a child without the presence of the other parent figure and with no sex-mate at the end of the story. Because there is no triangular relational complex, one can argue that these groups of stories represent the prephallic stage (namely anal stage) rather than phallic stage (according to psychosexual theory). This emotional complex can be subdivided further into three subgroups.

Father-son bilateral conflict.   This type of bilateral conflict is exemplified by the Chinese folk story of Monkey and the Japanese folk story of Momotarō, Peach Boy.

Mother-son bilateral intimacy.   This type of bilateral complex is characterized by the excessive closeness between a mother and a son while the father is absent. This is exemplified by the second plot of the Chinese opera story of Xue Ren-gui (while the father was away in the army) and the beginning part of the Korean folk story of the woodcutter and the heavenly maid.

Father-daughter bilateral intimacy.   Hypothetically, this is the mirror image of the mother-son bilateral complex, namely, excessive intimacy between a father and a daughter while the mother is absent. None of the stories considered here shows this complex.

Father and Grown-Up Child/Couple Triangular Complex
This group includes parent-child complexes that occur in adulthood, rather than in early childhood. The grown-up child, who has an opposite-

sex mate of his or her own, encounters conflict with an authority figure who interferes in the young couple's relationship. This "parent and young couple conflict" often occurs in cultures in which parental authority is so strong that parents continue to have an influence on their offspring, even when they are adults, with their own mates. The conflict can occur between a father (or father substitute) and a grown-up daughter, illustrated by the Chinese stories of the white serpent, and the Korean folk story of the woodcutter and the heavenly maid (third plot); or between a father figure and a son, exemplified by the Korean stories of the snail lady and the second plot of the *Ramayana*. Namely, it can be either an opposite-sex or same-sex parent-child conflict.

Thus, depending on the cultural system in which they occur, parent-child complexes have many possible variations. They can be triangular or bilateral, occur in early childhood or in young adulthood, and involve either homosexual or heterosexual parent-child relations. The traditional Oedipus complex is merely one type of parent-child conflict.

Displacement of Parental Figures

If the direct conflict between a parent and child is considered too threatening from a cultural perspective, a parent substitute is used instead. Since it is emotionally uncomfortable to directly ascribe the parental figure with an evil nature, it is common to disguise or project it onto a surrogate figure. Using a stepfather or stepmother is the most common way to split the parental figure and displace the negative feelings toward the stepparent. If any open conflict occurs, the person often does not know that his own parents are involved when the negative action is undertaken (such as in the second plot of Oedipus or *Nakorn Pathom*). Beyond this, the parental figure is often disguised as a witch (as in "Snow White"), an evil giant (as in "Momo-tarō"), or a powerful authority in the form of a monk, Buddha, or the emperor of heaven (as in many Eastern stories, such as those of the white serpent and the monkey Sun Wu-kong). Thus, there are many ways to project the parental figure, depending on the material offered by the culture and how far the father figure needs to be disguised from the actual father.

The Nature and Intensity of the Conflict

The conflict between parent and child can be described intensely, vividly, and directly, or subtly and symbolically. For instance, in the Japanese story *Ama-goshi* and the British *Hamlet*, which were written for adult audiences, the wish to kill the rival is explicitly described; however, in many other stories, particularly of stories for children, the negative conflict is left almost untouched, such as in "Momo-tarō" and *The Western Journey.*

After reviewing the theme of family complexes revealed in folk literature, Johnson and Price-Williams (1996) summarized that, although it is observed around the world, the degree of father-son hostility varies from one society to the next, reaching its peak in competitive, patriarchal, class-structured societies. They commented that the Oedipus complex is a culture-specific and essentially pathological outcome of a male-dominated, class-structured society. They also pointed out that the Oedipus tale needs to be understood in historical context. For instance, the story has two endings. An earlier one, reported by Homer, had Oedipus living on as king long after his crimes of incest and patricide were revealed and dying heroically in battle. Later, in *Oedipus Rex,* Sophocles added Oedipus' self-punishment by blinding. This change suggests that the attitudes toward such crimes had hardened. The shift in society toward patriarchy and stratification was the variable behind the change in attitudes.

In the same vein, whether or not the theme is sexualized varies in the East and West. In many Western children's stories, such as "Snow White," "Sleeping Beauty," and "Cinderella," the conflict is not only related to jealousy, but the story always ends with the girl getting a prince (even in the story of the princess and the frog). However, happy endings with sexual partners usually do not occur in stories from the East (such as the story of Sun Wu-kong). There are some exceptions, such as in the story of Issunbōshi, the one-inch boy, who is permitted to marry a princess after defeating the terrible ogre who tried to kidnap her.

Different Solutions Provided

The impact of cultural factors is more explicit in the solutions to parent-child conflicts, namely, who wins. In the West, particularly in children's stories and folktales, the young child almost always defeats the parental figures. From an analytic point of view, it can be said that the children are allowed to compete with and conquer the parental figure. The triumph of the youngsters is permitted and encouraged on a fantasy level. This kind of ending is found in the Japanese stories of Momo-tarō, who conquers evil, and Issun-bōshi, who defeats an ogre. However, this is not always the case. Where cultural value systems respect authority figures, the youngsters are expected to be defeated by the authorities. This is illustrated in the Chinese stories *The Western Journey* and the first and third plots of *Xue Ren-gui* as well as the Indian story of Ganesha (relating to father-son conflict), and in the Chinese story of the white serpent and the Korean story of the woodcutter and the heavenly maiden (relating to father-daughter conflict).

But even though the children are defeated by the authorities in Eastern stories, they are often given the opportunity to amend their defiant behavior and grow up. This is well illustrated in the story of the monkey, who was allowed to amend his misconduct and be accepted as a human being after protecting the monk. In *Nakorn Pathom,* the guilty child was given the opportunity for atonement by building a pagoda to worship the killed parents. Thus, the younger generation is not eliminated as a result of the conflict, but is encouraged to become more mature.

Theoretical Formulation

Through the material analyzed in this chapter, we reveal that the parent-child complex is subject to cultural influences and various types of the complex (figure 2). Based on this study we can summarize certain hypothetical issues concerning the parent-child complex as follows:

- The parent-child emotional complex appears as a part of the psychological task during personality development and is observed universally. However, the type and the nature of the complex varies greatly among different cultures so that the "typical" Oedipus complex as described in psychoanalytic theory is merely one kind of complex among many types of parent-child complexes that can be observed cross-culturally.
- The parent-child complex becomes a triangular one in cultures that tend to sexualize interpersonal relations; the parent-child complex exists as a bilateral one in cultures that desexualize interpersonal relations.
- The story line wherein a young child is allowed to defeat his parents reflects a culture that values individuality and youth; the story line wherein the parents defeat children reflects a culture that values authority and age over its younger generation.
- In cultures that stress parental authority, parent(s) will have a continuous influence on younger generations even when a child matures and becomes part of an adult couple.
- In cultures that value continuity over generations, the child is given the opportunity to atone for his or her mistake and grow up.

Implications for Psychotherapy—East and West
"Universality" of the Oedipus Complex

The universal existence of the Oedipus complex described by the school of psychoanalysis has been questioned and the validity of the complex as the core of neuroses doubted by some clinicians and behavior scientists (Schrut 1994). However, from this presentation, it is clear that the potential conflict between parents and children is observed in many cultures in both the East and the West as long as it is broadly defined. Therefore, there is no argument that parent-child complexes exist in different cultures. However, the forms in which the conflicts occur and the resolutions prescribed by the culture vary significantly.

It would be a mistake to consider the East entirely different from the West or, conversely, to deny that there are any differences between them. It would be more useful to find out what they have in common and what differences exist. It is clear that examining in depth the cultural products that reflect their emotions, impulses, and conflicts will theoretically help us to broaden our examination of the scope and nature of human conflict. It will also assist us to realize the many ways in which conflict can be resolved and which methodological or technical models can be incorporated into psychotherapy.

Clinical Implications

The results of the present study clearly suggest that when a therapist provides psychotherapy to the patient, cultural considerations are necessary to help the patient deal with problems in parent-child relations. The younger generation of patients with Eastern backgrounds, in general, needs to be encouraged to confront authoritative figures of their parents' generation when necessary, rather than following the traditional passive approach. Further, the parent-child triangular conflict needs to be desexualized to minimize the anxiety associated with an awareness of it. For confrontations involving an authority figure, psychotherapy must be carefully carried out by adjusting to the culture to preclude negative repercussions by the parental figure who, by tradition, values and stresses parental authority.

As usually prescribed in mainstream (Western) psychotherapy, the younger generation of Western patients is generally encouraged to be independent, assertive in facing sexualized conflicts, and aggressive in over-

Figure 2. Various Types of Parent-Child Complex: Observed from East and West

A. Father-Mother-Child Triangular Complex

(1) Same-sex parent and child conflict
(a) Father-son conflict

Son defeated father

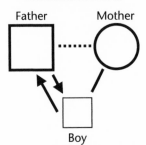

Oedipus (3rd plot) [Greek]
Jack and the Beanstalk [England]
Ama-goshi [Japan]

Father defeated son

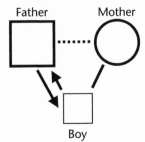

Oedipus (1st plot) [Greek]
Xue Ren-gui (3rd plot) [China]

(b) Mother-daughter conflict

Daughter defeated mother

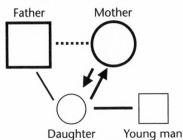

Snow White [Germany]
Sleeping Beauty [Germany]
Cinderella [France]

(2) Opposite-sex parent-child conflict
(a) Father-daughter conflict
Father defeated daughter

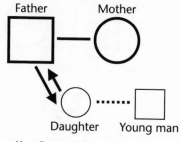

Xue Ren-gui (1st plot) [China]

(b) Mother-son conflict
Mother defeated son

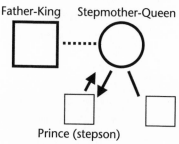

Ramayana (1st plot) [Indonesia]

Mother-son mutual hostility

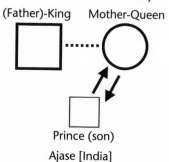

Ajase [India]

(3) Same-sex/opposite-sex parent-child conflict
Son defeated both father and mother

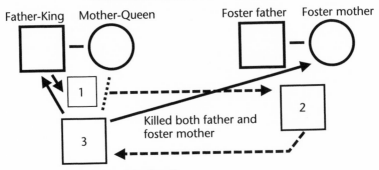

Father-King   Mother-Queen   Foster father   Foster mother

1

2

3

Killed both father and
foster mother

Nakorn Pathom [Thailand]

B. Parent-Child Bilateral Complex

(a) Father-son conflict

Father defeated son

Father-King   (Mother)

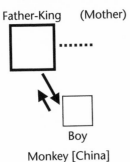

Boy

Monkey [China]

Son defeated father

Devil (father figure)   (Mother)

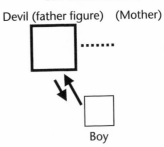

Boy

Momo-tarō [Japan]

(b) Mother-son bilateral closeness

Father   Mother

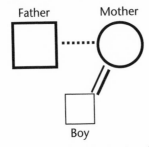

Boy

Xue Ren-gui (2nd plot) [China]
The Woodcutter (1st plot) [Korea]

(c) Father-daughter bilateral closeness

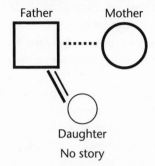

Daughter

No story

C. Father and Grown-Up Child/Couple Triangular Complex
(a) Father-daughter conflict

Father defeated daughter   *Daughter defeated father*

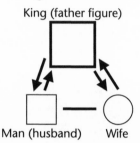

White Serpent [China]   The Snail Lady [Korea]
The Woodcutter (3rd plot) [Korea]

(b) Father-son conflict
Son defeated father

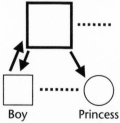

Issun-bōshi [Japan]
Ramayana (2nd plot) [Indonesia]

coming conflicts with authoritative, parent-generation figures. However, it may be beneficial for them to know that compliance, negotiation, and compromise are among the options that can be considered for problem solving between generations. From a cultural perspective, one of the functions of psychotherapy is to help the patient to learn how to use culturally "alternative" ways to solve problems.

The task of dealing with the conflicts involved in parent-child relations is a universal one. However, the insights obtained from a comparative analysis of the parent-child conflicts reflected in cultural products of the East and the West show vast differences in the ways in which people deal with these developmental challenges. This statement may overgeneralize and polarize the situation, but it does highlight the potentially different approaches needed to deal with parent-child relational complexes among patients of different cultural backgrounds.

III

Traditional Thought, Philosophy, and Psychotherapy

CHAPTER 8

Confucian Thought:
Implications for Psychotherapy

Yan Heqin

Confucian thought is considered to be at the core of the traditional thought shared for centuries not only by the Chinese, but also by many other people in Asia, particularly the Koreans and the Japanese. In China, it was regarded as the mainstream of thought that was officially taught through many dynasties, even though a number of people were influenced simultaneously by other systems of thought, such as Daoism (Taoism) and Buddhism.

One way to examine the characteristics of people's minds from a cultural perspective is to review their traditional systems of thought. Confucius' thought has been examined from various perspectives by scholars in the past, with countless articles published, predominantly in Chinese, some in Japanese and Korean. The essays have focused mainly on aspects of literature, thought, and history; a few related to mental health or psychotherapy (Y. X. Xu 1997). There are some writings in English that approach the topic from various angles, such as the concept of personality (Tseng 1973a), interpersonal relations (Lin 1939; Huh 1995), sociological aspects (King and Bond 1985), and philosophical views (Tong 1969)

From a mental health point of view, examining traditional thought will help us gain a basic understanding of the nature of human beings, a unique view of mental health, and philosophical thoughts that can be used in psychotherapy, the art of healing a person's emotional problems and obtaining a healthy mind.

First, several issues need to be clarified. Confucian thought, originally taught by Confucius and his disciples, deals with various issues, including a general philosophy of life, ethics, education, and political philosophy. It is not a religion, as some Western scholars think (such as Smith 1958), even though Confucius has been respected (and even worshiped) by people as a great teacher. The Chinese consider Confucian thought useful for improving human qualities, stabilizing harmonious interpersonal relationships, and cultivating a scholarly manner, particularly when life is going well. However, when a person's life is not successful, the philosophy of Daoism can be helpful, and when a person is suffering, Buddhism can be beneficial. Thus, the Chinese mind is characterized by multiple synthesized systems of thought, rather than a single way of thinking. Also, political and social changes have created changes in what is considered "Confucian thought."

A Brief History of Confucian Thought

To further pursue Confucian thought, it is necessary to briefly review the historical background of Confucius as a person and Confucian thought as a movement. According to historians, Confucius was born in 551 B.C. and died in 479 B.C. He was an important philosopher, scholar, politician, and, most significant, educator. In his early life, he worked as an officer of rites. He soon became interested in teaching knowledge, a way of life, and human ethics. As a scholar, he had many disciples. Tseng-Zi and, particularly, Mencius were among his famous disciples. His followers taught, transmitted, and expanded his thought, which was known as the school of Ru. Confucius' teachings were written by his followers into four books: *Da-xue* (Great learning), *Zhong-yong* (Doctrine of the mean), *Lun-yu* (Analects), and *Men-zi* (Mencius). The books were written mostly in the style of dialogues between the master and his disciples.

Confucius was born in a time known historically as the era of Chun-Qiu (which literally means "spring and autumn"; 770–476 B.C.). It was at the end of the Zhou dynasty, and was characterized by the existence of many states that were frequently in conflict. It was an era full of unexpected change politically and, thus, was named the Spring and Autumn period by historians. It was also a time when many philosophers and scholars promoted different schools of thought that rose and fell. After the era of Zhan-Guo (the Warring States period; 475–221 B.C.), China was united by Emperor Qin Shi-huang (who built the Great Wall) in the Qin dynasty (221–206 B.C.), which later became the Han dynasty (206 B.C.–A.D. 220) It was then that Confucian thought became officially regarded by Emperor Han Wu-di as the only respected school of thought; other schools were abolished. In the later interpretation of historians, Confucian thought (which emphasizes the importance of proper hierarchical relationships among people) was used politically as a means to enhance the autocratic feudal system.

In the following eras of the Wei, Jin, and Sui (Three Dynasties) and the Tang dynasty (roughly 220–907), Buddhist thought was transmitted from India to China. By the time of the Song dynasty (960–1279), scholars incorporated Buddhist as well as Daoist views into Confucian thought, making it more of an integrated philosophical system and ethical guide for the regulation of society.

Thus, Confucianism had a significant impact on the Chinese mind for many centuries, until the end of the Qing dynasty (1911). It was at the beginning of the Republic, during the famous May Fourth movement (Wu-si yun-dong) in 1919, led by scholars and college students, that antitraditional and anti-Confucian thought emerged as part of an effort to modernize China. It was charged that, through history, many people had come to regard Confucian thought as the only way of thinking. It was learned through recitation and interpretation, with Confucius' words often quoted as if they were the words of a saint, until they became almost like shackles confining people's thoughts. Since Confucian teaching was merely concerned with humanity, it did not consider any other systems of knowledge, such as natural science. Thus, intellectuals considered it an obstacle to promoting modernization through technological science.

During the Cultural Revolution (1966–1976), Confucian thought again came under severe criticism. Contemporary intellectuals still considered Confucian thought a part of the Chinese cultural heritage, but it was criticized in its application to modern life.

Mental Health Concepts Reflected in Confucian Thought

As already pointed out, Confucian thought is basically concerned with the philosophy of life, education for knowledge, cultivation for personal maturity, and humanistic ideology for political application. Its major emphasis is on how to systematically and consequentially cultivate oneself, manage one's family, regulate one's country, and give order to the world (*Great Learning,* 1). Many mental health concepts that deserve mention were included among these philosophical teachings.

For example, concerning the basic nature of human beings, Confucius' disciple Mencius stressed that "human nature is basically benevolent," thereby contradicting Xuan-zi's teaching that "human nature is fundamentally evil." However, both shared the common view that human nature can be educated and cultivated to achieve a better quality. This view was stressed in the saying, "By nature, near together; by practice, far apart" (*Analects,* XVII, 2), which implies that people are inherently alike, and that external influences and their own efforts cause them to become different. This saying clearly expressed the importance of developing one's potential and ability to cope with life's problems. It was also stated that "the demands that a gentleman makes are upon self; those that a small man makes are upon others" (*Analects,* XV, 20), thereby emphasizing that it is healthier and more mature to depend on the self than on other people in seeking to attain goals in life. Mencius also pointed out that "affluent children are mostly lazy; children of famine are mostly violent; different temperaments are not inherited, but depend on how the mind was raised" (*Mencius,* VI-A, 7). This passage stresses the effect of environment on the human mind.

Confucius stated that "at fifteen I set my heart upon learning. At thirty, I had planted my feet firm upon the ground. At forty, I no longer suffered from perplexities. At fifty, I knew the biddings of Heaven. At sixty, I heard them with a docile ear. At seventy, I could follow the dictates of my own heart; for what I desired no longer overstepped the boundary of right" (*Analects,* II, 4). He described his personal experience of the psychological stages of growth from youth through late adult life. He explained how a person could, by self-cultivation of the mind, attain moral perfection and personal maturity in life. He also mentioned that "in his youth, before his blood and vital humors have settled down, he is on his guard against lust. Having reached his prime, when the blood and vital humors have finally hardened, he is on his guard against strife. Having reached old age, when the blood and vital humors are already decaying, he is on his guard against avarice" (*Analects,* XVI, 7). This passage cautions that different mental health issues deserve attention in the different stages of the life cycle. Basically, it emphasizes that a person needs to be liberated from his or her personal desires in order to become an ideal person.

Similarly, Mencius pointed out that "there is nothing better than to have less desire for cultivation of mind; for a person to have less desire, some may not survive, but it is rare. For a person to have many desires, some may survive, but it is rare" (*Mencius,* VII-B, 36). Mencius also indicated that "those who are hungry will eat without proper choice of food; those who are thirsty will drink without careful choice of water. It is hunger and thirst that make them not eat or drink properly, suffering from the harm of hunger and thirst. In the same way, desire could bring harm to a person's mind" (*Mencius,* VII-A, 27). Therefore, it was advocated that "when a gentleman eats, he does not seek over full; lives in residence, does not demand over comfort. Be sensitive to things and cautious to saying things, then life will follow the correct way, merely as the result of learning" (*Analects,* I, 14). Mencius does not propose that people simply deny or suppress their basic desires, but properly guide and control them for the sake of maturity. This is the basic concept of mental health in life.

Confucius described his own personal experiences as "striving [so] resolutely [for studying] that he omit[ted] eating, and enjoying [learning] so much that he overlook[ed] worry, without noticing the approach of aging" and noted that "he who seeks only coarse food to eat, water to drink, and a bent arm for a pillow, will without looking for it find happiness to boot. Any thought of accepting wealth and rank by means that I know to be wrong is as remote from me as the clouds that float above" (*Analects,* VII, 15). In these passages he indicated how much he valued the obtaining of knowledge, the training of the personality, and the cultivation of morality in seeking the road to mental maturity. This view has significant implications for modern people, who seek only practical benefits and material success, ignoring the mental satisfaction and integration of the mind, the essence of good mental health.

Confucian Thought and Psychotherapy

In my opinion, there are several ways that Confucian thought can be applied in the practice of psychotherapy.

Establishment of Benevolent Love toward Others

Ren-ai is the core concept of Confucian thought. *Ren* in Chinese means benevolence or kindheartedness in human relationships. *Ai* literally means love. Thus, *ren-ai* emphasizes the humanity in interpersonal relationships. When one of his disciples, Fan-chi, asked Confucius about the meaning of *ren,* Confucius replied, "To love people" (*Analects,* XII, 22). In the *Great Learning,* it was said, "To know the bright virtue, to be close to the people, to the extent of goodness." In this saying, the words "bright virtue" and "goodness" imply the inherited benevolence that needs to be brought into full play. Another disciple, Zi-gong, inquired of Confucius, "If a ruler not only conferred wide benefits upon the common people, but also compassed the salvation of the whole state, what would you say of him?" He was asking if offering kindness and compassion was *ren*. Confucius replied, "It would no longer be a matter of good, but, without doubt, he would be a Divine Sage, even Yao and Shun [legendary emperor and saint] could hardly criticize such a ruler" (*Analects,* VI, 28). Thus, when Confucius emphasized the proper hierarchy among people in a society, he not only stressed the importance of obedience toward authority, but, reciprocally, the importance of the authority to be benevolent and care for his subordinates.

If this concept is applied to the therapist-patient relationship, we can say that it is necessary for the patient to cooperate with the therapist, but, at the same time, it is essential for the therapist to be able to demonstrate benevolent love and care toward the patient. Certainly this reciprocity will improve the quality and effect of psychotherapy.

Mencius said, "To love [someone] without being close affectionately is not *ren*" (*Mencius,* IV-A, 4). This means that even if you have a good attitude toward others, but they are not close to you, you need to examine your affection toward them; perhaps you have not shown real *ren* (benevolent affection) toward them. This view is very useful when a therapist is relating to a patient in psychotherapy.

The same concept can be used in therapy to encourage patients to develop genuine love toward others. This is particularly true not only with immediate family members and close friends, but also with working colleagues, especially in relationships between superiors and subordinates. Developing the capacity for genuine love—learning to be close to people to the extent of one's goodness, to forgive others for their mistakes and to accept them unconditionally, without harsh criticism—enables one to maintain desirable interpersonal relationships with family and colleagues. These relationships are the basis for happy lives for one's self and others.

"Harmony" as the Principle for Interpersonal Relations

Tension related to interpersonal relations is often a major cause of psychological distress, which contributes to the occurrence of psychopathology. Helping a patient deal with interpersonal conflicts and adjust to her or his social environment are among the major tasks in psychotherapy.

Confucian thought stresses the virtue of etiquette *(li)* and harmony *(he)* as the basic principle for interpersonal relationships. This principle is reflected in the words "application of rite for the valuables of harmony" and "not knowing rite, will be unable to behave as a person" (*Analects*, XX, 3). Confucius considered that, through a system of etiquette or rites, humans can regulate their desires and behave properly.

The closely associated concept of *he* in interpersonal relations is also important in Confucian thought. It is said, "Difference, but harmony." That is, even though there are often differences among people, those differences do not necessarily prevent people from being able to coexist and strive together toward goals. On the contrary, their differences will allow them to be complementary to each other for their mutual benefit. There is no need to force every person to become the same. It was said, "Harmony avoids isolation." If you know how to relate to others harmoniously, you will not become an isolated person. Confucius emphasized, "Heaven time is less valuable than earth benefit; earth benefit is less important than human harmony" (*Mencius*, II-B, 1). Competing with and attacking others for self-benefit will only end in harming one's self. This view is still valuable in guiding people, including patients, in how to relate to others.

The Golden Mean as the Principle for Dealing with Problems

The concept of the golden mean stressed in Confucian thought is against having too much or too little; everything should be right in moderation. In the *Doctrine of the Mean* it was said, "The [emotions of] delight, anger, sorrow, and joy, when they are not expressed, are in the middle [without extreme]; when they are expressed, manifested in the middle with regulation, they are harmonious [and blended]. Maintaining in the middle is the basic rule of the universe, and being harmonious is the fundamental way of functioning. If the mean and harmony can be sustained, then heaven and earth can be stabilized properly and everything in the universe can thrive."

This view is also true from a psychological perspective. If a person can regulate his or her emotions in the right way, without being too extreme, it will be beneficial for the person's health. Expressing emotions of delight, anger, sorrow, and joy in the extreme, without proper control, will cause a disturbance in the person's mental condition. One of the goals of psychotherapy is to help a patient manage emotions properly. It is not merely a matter of regulating emotions, but also dealing with conflicts and problems. The Confucian concept of the golden mean is one of the most useful principles for coping with problems.

Performing One's Proper Role as the Base of Stable Social Order

It is the Confucian goal to establish a stable and happy social order by first establishing proper relationships among people in all aspects of life. Confucius said, "Let the prince be a prince indeed, the minister a minister indeed; let the father be a father indeed, the son be a son indeed" (*Analects,* XII, 11). It is the Confucian idea to define proper relationships in the five basic interpersonal relationships evident in society (*Doctrine of the Mean,* 20). Although Confucius did not define in detail the proper way for a person to behave in each basic interpersonal relationship, he emphasized that, if a person behaved "properly," according to the socially defined interpersonal relationships, society could be maintained in order and stability. Mencius later elaborated this concept into five basic ethical relationships among human beings, namely, "Affection between parents and children; righteousness between sovereign and subordinate; differences between husband and wife; order between the older and the younger; trustworthiness among friends" (*Mencius,* III-A, 4). This concept can be applied to the behavior of patients within family and societal settings.

Contemporary family therapists have pointed out that one of the major problems encountered in dysfunctional families is the absence of properly defined and performed roles within the family, preventing appropriate relations to occur between husband and wife, parents and children, and siblings of different ages. The goal of family therapy, therefore, is to ensure that each family member performs his or her proper role (Tseng and Hsu 1991, 83, 119). This therapeutic concept is in line with the Confucian emphasis on proper roles and relations among people, starting with the family and extending outside it to include work and social situations, so that a proper, harmoniously functioning society can be achieved.

Emphasizing Empathy toward Others

It is not only important to have genuine love for others, but, as Confucius emphasized, it is essential to be able to empathize with others. Confucius repeatedly indicated this point: "Never do to others what you would not like them to do to you" (*Analects,* XV, 23); "You yourself desire rank and standing, then help others to get rank and standing; you want to turn your own merits to account, then help others to turn theirs to account" (*Analects,* VI, 28); or "Take care of your own elderly and others' elderly; raise your own youngsters and others' youngsters" (*Mencius,* I-A, 7). From these statements, it is clear that Confucius considered important qualities of mind to be the ability to understand others, to think from the perspective of others, and to do things for the sake of others. These are among the qualities that contemporary psychologists consider to be elements of maturity, allowing a person to move up from a narcissist perspective to a level at which the person is able to show empathy toward others.

Many mental health patients are suffering from narcissistic tendencies. They are concerned only with themselves, are disappointed that they cannot fulfill their own needs, and ignore others' feelings and needs; they therefore find it difficult to relate to others. It is useful to help those kinds of patients learn to leave their self-centered, immature positions and move up to a more mature level, at which they are able to think, feel, and do things for the sake of others, showing the capacity for empathy toward them.

Self-Cultivation as a Means for Achieving a Mature Personality

In addition to the points above, there are numerous other concepts described in Confucian thought that can be used in guiding patients in therapy. Confucius encouraged people to have active attitudes in life, blaming neither heaven nor others. He encouraged people to concentrate on cultivating themselves, coping with reality, and learning to accept any consequences with calm and ease. Most important, he believed that every person has the potential to live and grow with satisfaction in life, as long as the person knows how to pay attention to the psychological life beyond the material life and how to keep balance and harmony deep in his or her mind.

The suggestion that obtaining internal satisfaction is the essential way to achieve happiness is one of the most valuable contributions of Confucian thought. People who diligently make use of their potential to obtain knowledge, develop their talents, cultivate their own personality, be good to others, be good to themselves, and "know" how to be satisfied with the condition of striving itself, disregarding the outcome, are gaining real happiness in life. One who fails in spite of every effort to make use of his or her potential to improve his or her life is advised to accept the result as fate, without resentment toward others or him- or herself. Confucius proposed the optimistic view that a person contains all that is necessary for self-governance, that the individual is self-sufficient and has the potential to obtain mental maturity and happiness, even though that person must be ready to accept any outcome with equanimity. This view of mental health and personal maturity is attainable, and will be useful in advising patients who are either too anxious to obtain achievement in their lives or are so frustrated with life that they withdraw from reality (Tseng 1973a). As Liu (1993) pointed out, the psychotherapeutic function of Confucian discipline is based on working with *hsin* (or *xin*, meaning "mind-heart").

From Self, to Family, to State, to the World

Finally, from the standpoint of practice, Confucius drew a guide on how to successfully obtain one's goals in life. He emphasized starting with the cultivation of the self, then establishing and maintaining a harmoniously functioning family, working toward a desirable state, and, finally, learning how to rule the world (*Great Learning*, 1). Thus, he visualized a certain course in working on one's life, step by step, systematically, starting with the self, moving outward to the family, the state, and the world. This is an ambitious and logical mission for a scholar.

Among these steps, besides starting with self-cultivation, Confucius placed a strong emphasis on establishing proper order within the family, with relevant role-playing and genuine affection among family members. As King and Bond (1985, 32) pointed out, in the Confucian model, the individual is conceptualized as a relational being. Confucius described five cardinal relations *(wu lun):* those between sovereign and subject, father and son, elder and younger brother, husband and wife, and friend and friend. Of these five basic dyads, three belong to the family and the other two are based on the family model, with sovereign and subject as father and son, and friend and friend as brothers. In Confucian social theory, the family occupies a central position; it is not only the primary social group, but the prototype of all social organization (Mei 1967, 331).

For those people, whether Chinese or not, who live in contemporary society and face the threat of the disintegration of the family system, it is particularly pertinent to stress the importance of family in our lives. The primary task of every person, beyond the cultivation of the self, is still to learn how to establish and maintain a functional family. Confucius' emphasis on family remains valuable for those who tend to ignore this important aspect of life.

Experiences of Practical Application

It must be clarified that Confucianism is one of the main streams of thought and is highly regarded in China and other parts of Asia as a guide to cultivating one's knowledge, thought, and behavior. However, it is not a school of psychotherapy for healing mental health problems. No special psychotherapy model has been developed in China (or any other part of Asia) that is primarily derived from and geared toward Confucian thought in the way that Naikan therapy is closely related to Buddhist thought, particularly the thought of Pure Land Buddhism (see chapter 12). Morita therapy is strongly influenced by Zen Buddhism (see chapter 11), and a Daoistic cognitive psychotherapy recently emerged in China (see chapter 9). However, Confucian thought has prevailed for so long in the minds of the Chinese people that no form of psychotherapy undertaken in the past or present in China can escape the impact of its philosophical attitudes. Clinical experiences in China indicate several points that need to be mentioned from the perspective of clinical practice.

First, Confucian thought is developed mainly for scholars and promotes intellectual cultivation. It is characterized by ideal situations that cannot be obtained. It is a goal for which to aim, an ethic to be desired; however, it is far from the real lives of common people in a practical sense. Psychotherapists have to realize that ordinary people, suffering from mental problems or emotional difficulties, are in need of practical guidance that is beyond ideal situations and meeting ethical goals. In this regard, many teachings from ordinary life experiences are more useful, such as the knowledge and advice reflected in proverbs and sayings (see chapter 13). The Chinese realize from experience that life is full of harshness and difficulties, mixed with hate and love, greed and generosity, deception and honesty. The ideal ethical situation advocated by Confucian thought is great, but it is not sufficient to deal with practical daily life. Much of the accumulated wisdom derived from actual life by ordinary people is reflected in commonly used proverbs. Many strategic approaches for dealing with potential enemies or competitive rivals are derived from military books and may be used in commercial or political situations. Thus, Chinese people have learned how to adapt to the complexities of life. It would be naïve for a therapist to believe that all Chinese are simply followers of Confucian thought. Confucian thought merely described the ideal goal for which a person should aim; it did not necessarily reflect the actual life situation of every Chinese. Even the Chinese family, which is supposed to be harmonious, with proper role-playing within the hierarchy and an emphasis on filial piety, in reality may be colored with tendencies toward disharmony, disobedience, chaos, and even conflict, and may require family therapy. It is important for a therapist to recognize and be aware of this. In the practice of psychotherapy, the therapist can reasonably expect that the Chinese patient will usually show respect toward him or her, as an authority figure, and that the family is the basic unit on which to work (Huang and Charter 1996). However, a skillful therapist needs to know how to go beyond these basic assumptions and how to distinguish the ideal from the real. Otherwise, the ideal prescribed by Confucian thought may overshadow the real. An experienced cultural psychiatrist needs to know that culture can be addressed at different levels: the ideal, the actual, the stereotypical, or the deviant (Tseng 2001, 34–35).

It has been pointed out frequently that, when a person is young and successful, Confucian thought is useful, as it provides hope for human nature and the maturity that is obtainable. It promises social order and civilization. Given the official civilian examination system that was observed in the past, studying Confucian thought was one of the best ways to achieve social success. However, when a person becomes old, and realizes that life is full of vicissitudes and suffering, unfairness and lack of hope, Daoistic philosophy is beneficial because it operates according to the rules of nature, coming from nothing and returning to nothing (see chapter 9 of this book).

In other words, Confucian thought, as a system of knowledge and ethics, has both merits and limitations. Its basic views about human nature, desired interpersonal relationships, and social order are useful for certain patients, depending on their stage of life and the nature of their problems.

Obviously, the practice of psychotherapy is influenced by cultural factors. To carry out therapy of the mind, Chinese analysts cannot ignore Confucian thought. An important professional task is to learn how to select and use the relevant concepts rooted in ancient Confucian teachings to conduct appropriate and effective therapy for contemporary Chinese—many of whom face the problem of how to promote material achievement and catch up with the technology emphasized by modernization.

It is also a challenge to determine to what extent and in what ways basic Confucian thought can be applied in therapy for people in the West, who tend to ignore the importance of maintaining the integration of their own minds, establishing and maintaining a functional marriage and family, creating harmony among people, and seeking the golden mean in resolving problems in life. Psychotherapy practiced in the West, particularly individually and analytically oriented dynamic therapy, tends to focus primarily on the activation of the self. Learning how to integrate the interpersonal and social-system aspects of Confucian thought into individually focused therapy, to expand the scope of family therapy and produce socially rooted, mature individuals, is a challenge awaiting Western psychotherapists.

CHAPTER 9

Daoist Philosophy:
Application in Psychotherapy

Dersen Young, Wen-Shing Tseng, and Liang Zhou

Daoism is an ancient school of Chinese philosophical thought. It is believed to have been founded by Lao-zi (also known as Lao-tse, in the Wade-Giles spelling), a legendary person who was born about 2,570 years ago. It was later further elaborated by a follower, Zhuang-zi (also known as Chuang-tse), who was born about 2,300 years ago. The primary emphasis of Daoist thought is the importance of following the Dao (Tao), meaning the Way of the universe (*dao* = road), and it is therefore known as Daoism. (Throughout this chapter, the term "Dao" will be used to reflect the actual Chinese pronunciation of the word.) About 2,000 years ago, Daoism was gradually incorporated into a loosely existing folk religion to form the Daoist sect, which identified gods, practiced mysterious acts, and searched for immortal life. Thus, it is necessary to distinguish between Daoist thought (a school of philosophy) and Daoist religion (Wei 1979; Xiao, Young, and Zhang 1998). In this chapter, we are referring only to Daoist philosophy, which has nothing to do with the Daoist religious sect.

Daoism as a philosophy has been summarized by the well-known Chinese writer Lin Yutang (1948, 14) as a philosophy of the essential unity of the universe (monism), of reversion, polarization (yin and yang), eternal cycles, the leveling of all differences, the relativity of all standards, and the return of all to the Primeval One, the divine intelligence, the source of all things.

There are significant differences between Confucian and Daoist thought. Confucianism is a philosophy of social order, primarily focused on interpersonal relations in social life. Confucians worship culture and reason; Daoists reject them in favor of nature and intuition. Confucius was a positivist; Lao-zi was a mystic (Lin 1948, 4).

Most Chinese historians and scholars regard Confucian, Daoist, and Buddhist thought as the three basic foundations of Chinese philosophy. Among them, Confucian thought has historically been the officially supported ethical thought, while Daoism has been viewed as a mysterious philosophy that deviates from the mainstream. However, many intellectuals have enjoyed reading Daoist books for their philosophical views and the Daoist enlightenment on the nature of life. It has also often been said by laypeople that, if you are successful in your life, you adhere to Confucian thought; if you are not successful, you are more appreciative of Daoist thought.

We know very little about Lao-zi as a person, except that he was born in 571 B.C.; that he was a contemporary of Confucius, probably twenty years older; that he came from an old, cultured family and was a keeper of the imperial archives at the capital; that he retired and disappeared in midlife and probably lived to a great old age (Lin 1948, 8). He was born during the Spring and Autumn period, as was Confucius, an era characterized by frequent wars among the feudal lords, during which people suffered greatly. It may be said that Lao-zi's thought strongly reflected his reaction to and disapproval of the wars, conflict, and competition that resulted from the search for power and material gain.

The book later referred to by scholars as the *Daode-jing* (Oracle of morals) is believed to have been written by Lao-zi before he retreated to a mountain. Over time, through the process of hand copying, some of the characters and words were changed, resulting in variations in the writing. Scholars have pointed out that several hundred versions of the book have been published in China over the years, offering different interpretations and explanations of the original text. In addition, the meanings of some of the words may have changed over time. Further, there was no punctuation between words or characters at that time, and the words and sentences could be read in different ways. Readers of the text would have been influenced by the interpretations of outstanding commentators. There are many English translations of the text. Needless to say, the translations are greatly subject to the translators' ability to comprehend the original meaning. Therefore, careful reading and explanation are necessary (Barrett 1993; Guo 1999). Two versions of the *Daode-jing* written in the second century B.C. were discovered in 1973, during the excavation of a ruin. This discovery has brought modern scholars closer to understanding the original reading of the text, during the first phase of its existence.

To understand Lao-zi's *Daode-jing*, it is important to understand the social and historical context of his time, to comprehend his unique style of writing, his special ways of expression, and the unorthodox logic he used to explain his philosophical thought.

In reaction to his time, with its frequent wars among states causing the suffering of the people, Lao-zi was firmly against a life full of desire and achievement; instead, he valued peace and the rule of nature. He emphasized the importance of the Way, referring to the universal truth and rules, and the way they regulate the world, including human life. He valued nature and stressed the importance of not-doing, or no-action *(wu-wei)*, rather than trying to overrule, overachieve, and become successful. Clearly, he was against wars. He stressed the importance of a simple, plain life, and treasured natural institutions rather than acquired knowledge and cognition.

In his writing, Lao-zi frequently used terms of opposition to illustrate dualism and states of opposition (such as yin and yang, soft and hard, full and void, bright and dark). He purposely used unorthodox logic to communicate his ideas to others (for instance, being soft is being strong; knowing is not knowing). He often used certain analogies symbolically to explain things (such as the stream is the origin of the ocean, or the valley is the origin of the stream, implying the origin of things). Thus, a certain skill is needed to read his essays.

In discussing Lao-zi's style of writing, it is necessary to refer to the *Yi-jing* (Oracle of change). The *Yi-jing* is one of the most ancient Chinese texts, emerging more than three thousand years ago in China (Yang 2001). It is a resource of thought that had a significant influence on Lao-zi's later thought, as well as on Confucius (Yang 2001), and deserves some elaboration here.

The *Yi-jing*, originally called *Zhou-yi* (Oracle of change of the Zhou dynasty), was a text historically used for divination. It was utilized to divine and explain the universal rules that regulate the cosmic world, as well as the world of humans. Associated with the *Yi-jing* is the supplementary text, the *Yi-zhuang* (Interpretation of change), which offers interpretations of the *Yi-jing*. The *Yi-jing* not only provides explanations about the divine rules, it also offers descriptions of historical life patterns and thoughts shared by ancient Chinese in the early stages of the Shang and Yin dynasties, when the *Zhou-yi* was written. The fundamental concept of the *Yi-jing* is the existence of opposite forces that maintain a balance in the world.

The Wisdom of Lao-zi

We are now ready to discuss Lao-zi's thoughts as reflected in the *Daode-jing*. The *Daode-jing* is a relatively short document composed of eighty-one brief essays or statements (even though each statement is referred to as a "chapter" by later scholars). The book was written with a total of no more than five thousand characters. The issues that are addressed in the chapters include the nature of the universe, politics, society, war, and the nature of human behavior. Only the basic concepts and issues that are relevant to human psychology and the principles of psychotherapy will be considered here. Basically, the English translation by Lin Yutang (1948) is used, with some modification, following Guo's (1999) linguistic insight and logical analysis. Reference has also been made to an English book on this subject by Jonanson (1991).

The Truth about Dao

The fundamental concept of Lao-zi's thought is that an eternal rule, truth, or principle has existed from the beginning of the universe, regulating the world, as well as the lives of humans. This way or truth is often invisible and unrecognized. Therefore, in the beginning of his text, Lao-zi defined the absolute being of Dao: "The Dao that can be told of, is not the absolute Dao; the Names that can be given, are not Absolute Names. The Nameless is the origin of Heaven and Earth; the Named is the Mother of All Things" (chapter 1). He further clarified that the Dao is "looked at, but cannot be seen—that is called the Invisible; listened to, but cannot be heard—that is called the Inaudible; grasped at, but cannot be touched—that is called the Intangible" (chapter 14).

Lao-zi was fully aware of how people would react to his definition of Dao and recognized different qualities of the Daoist. He stated, "When the highest type of men hear the Dao, they try hard to live in accordance with it; when the mediocre type hear the Dao, they seem to be aware and yet unaware of it; when the lowest type hear the Dao, they break into loud laughter—if it were not laughed at, it would not be Dao" (chapter 41). He recognized the clear order that exists among humans, the Dao, and nature. He explained that "man models himself after the Earth; the Earth models itself after Heaven; Heaven models itself after Dao; Dao models itself after Nature" (chapter 25).

The Concept of Opposites (or the Existence of Two Poles)

Like the cognitive style of the ancient *Yi-jing*, which is characterized by dualism, Lao-zi's writing often followed the rule of opposites to explain the dynamic phenomena observed in the world. For instance, he stated that "reversion is the action of Dao; gentleness, the function of Dao. The things of this world come from Being; and Being [comes] from Non-being" (chapter 40). Further, he mentioned that "out of Dao, One is born; out of One, Two; out of Two, Three; out of Three, the created universe. The created universe carries the Yin at its back and the Yang in front; through the union of the pervading principles it reaches harmony. To be 'orphaned,' 'lonely' and unworthy is what men hate most. Yet the princes and dukes call themselves by such names. For sometimes things are benefited by being taken away from, and suffer by being added to. Others have taught this maxim, which I shall teach also: 'The violent man shall die a violent death.' This I shall regard as my spiritual teacher" (chapter 42).

Lao-zi not only suggested we pay attention to the existing being, which can be observed, but also stressed the utility of not-being. As he said, "Thirty spokes unite around the nave; from their not-being [the hollow space in the center] arises the utility of the wheel. Mold clay into a vessel; from its not-being [in the vessel's hallow] arises the utility of the vessel. Cut out doors and windows in the house [wall], from their not-being [empty space] arises the utility of the house. Therefore, by the existence of things we profit; and by the non-existence of things we are served" (chapter 11). This passage illustrates that his concern went far beyond the reality that could be observed and grasped; it leads us to pay attention to matters of existence and to function at a higher level.

Rule of Nature: The Virtue of Doing Nothing

In a paradoxical way, Lao-zi helped us view the nature of our lives from entirely different perspectives. He elaborated the virtue of not-contending. He stated, "The brave soldier is not violent; the good fighter does not lose his temper; the great conqueror does not fight with others; the good user of men places himself below others. This is the virtue of not-contending, is called the capacity to use men, is reaching to the height of being mated to Heaven, to what was of old" (chapter 68).

In a similar way, he said, "Who is brave in daring [you], gets killed, who is brave in not daring [you], let live. In these two, there is some advantage and some disadvantage [even if] Heaven dislikes certain people, who would know why? Therefore, even the Sage regards it as a difficult question. Heaven's Way [Dao] is good at conquest without strife, rewarding without words, making its appearance without call, achieving results without obvious word. [Using] big meshes, yet letting nothing slip through" (chapter 73).

As an extension of this thinking, he proposed the virtue of the void. He stated, "The student of knowledge [aims at] learning day by day; the student of Dao [aims at] losing day by day. By continual losing, one reaches doing nothing; by doing nothing, everything is done. He who conquers the world often does so by doing nothing. When one is compelled to do something, the world is already beyond his conquering" (chapter 48).

This concept is difficult for the beginner to comprehend and accept. It is even regarded as a nihilistic attitude of life. However, if we listen carefully, we may understand the point he was stressing. Using the analogy of water, he tried to elaborate what he meant by doing nothing. He said, "The best of men are like water: water benefits all things, and does not compete with them. It dwells in [the lowly] places that all disdain, wherein it comes near to the Dao" (chapter 8).

Way of Life: Sparing Desire

Lao-zi also emphasized dealing with our desires and emotions. He warned of the danger of overweening success. He stated, "Stretch (a bow) to the very full, and you will wish you had stopped in time. Temper a (sword edge) to its very sharpest, and the edge will not last long. When gold and jade fill your hall, you will not be able to keep them safe. To be proud with wealth and honor is to sow the seeds of one's own downfall. Retire when your work is done, such is Heaven's way" (chapter 8). In a concrete way, he further elaborated this issue by referring to our senses. As he said, "The five colors blind the eyes of man; the five musical notes deafen the ears of man; the five flavors dull the taste of man; horse-racing, hunting, and gambling madden the mind of man; rare, valuable goods induce the misbehavior of man. Therefore, the sage provides for the belly (for inner satisfaction) and not for the eye (for external gratification). Hence, he rejects the latter and accepts the former" (chapter 8).

He summarized how we should handle our satisfaction, stating that "when the world lives in accord with Dao, racing horses are turned back to haul refuse carts; when the world lives not in accord with Dao, cavalry abound in the countryside. There is no greater curse than the lack of contentment. No greater sin than the desire for possession. Therefore, he who is contented with contentment shall be always content" (chapter 8).

Rules of Adaptation: Dealing with Hardness by Softness

Again, in a paradoxical way, but with great insight, Lao-zi suggested ways to deal with situations in life. He said that "when man in born, he is tender and weak; at death, he is hard and stiff. When things and plants are alive, they are soft and supple; when they are dead, they are brittle and dry. Therefore, hardness and stiffness are the companions of death, and softness and gentleness are the companions of life. Therefore, when an army is headstrong, it will lose in battle; when a tree is hard, it will be cut down. The big and strong belong underneath; the gentle and weak belong at the top" (chapter 8). Again, he continuously pointed out that "to yield is to be preserved whole, to be bent is to become straight, to be hollow is to be filled, to be tattered is to be renewed, to be less is to gain, to have plenty is to be confused" (chapter 22). He restated, "He who stands on tiptoe does not stand [firm]; he who strains his stride does not walk [well]; he who reveals himself is not luminous; he who justifies himself is not far-famed; he who boasts of himself is not given credit; he who prides himself is not chief among men. These in the eyes of Dao are called 'the dregs and tumors of Virtue,' which are things of disgust, therefore, the man of Dao spurns them" (chapter 22).

Further, he pointed out that the rhythm of life is as follows: "He who is to be made to dwindle (in power) must first be caused to expand; he who is to be weakened must first be made strong; he who is to be laid low must first be exalted to power; he who is to be taken away from must first be given— this is the Subtle Light. Gentleness overcomes strength. Fish should be left in the deep pool, and sharp weapons of the state should be left where none can see them" (chapter 36).

Lao-zi strongly advocated the importance of following nature and returning to the origin with innocence. He clarified his point as follows: "He who is aware of the (forceful) Male, but keeps to the (gentle) Female, becomes the stream of the world. Being the stream of the world (as the origin of the ocean), he has the eternal virtue, returning to the original character of (innocence) of an infant. He who is conscious of (apparent) honor, but keeps to (hidden) obscurity, becomes the valley of the world. Being the valley of the world (as the origin of the river), he has the eternal virtue, returning to uncarved, original wood. He who is familiar with white (bright place), but keeps to the black (dark place), has the eternal model, maintaining eternal virtue, returning to the final condition of the void" (chapter 36).

Knowing about the Self

Finally, Lao-zi valued the importance of having insight into the self. As he said, "Who knows that he does not know is the best; who does not know what he knows has a (worse) problem. Who recognizes problems as problems is not a problem. The Sage has no problems, as he recognizes problems as problems, therefore, he has no problems" (chapter 36). He restated that "he who knows others is learned; he who knows himself is wise. He who conquers others has the power of muscles; he who conquers himself is strong. He who is contented is rich; he who is determined has strength of will. He who does not lose his center endures; he who dies yet (his wisdom) remains has long life" (chapter 33).

Application in Psychotherapy

As a school of philosophy, Daoist thought is characterized by an emphasis on nature. It downplays a person's desire for success and achievement, stressing the importance of following the nature of the universe, pointing out the phenomenon of opposites or the rule of dualism, revealing the cyclical swing between extreme poles, and valuing the unorthodox way of coping by using softness against hardness. Historically, scholars have regarded Daoism as "nihilistic," with a "mystic" attitude toward life; administrators have seen it as rebellious against the establishment. However, the value of Daoism lies in its unique insight into the nature of life and its alternative ways of dealing with life—even though much emphasis is placed on its extremes. It has been pointed out that the core concept of naturalness stressed by Lao-zi in ancient times is characterized by the ideas of spontaneity, primordiality, and continuity. With some modifications, this basic concept can still be applied to modern technological society, promoting the natural development of human affairs and society (Liu 1999).

It has been pointed out that, from a cultural perspective, psychotherapy has several implications, namely, to enforce culturally sanctioned coping patterns, to provide temporary cultural time-outs, to seek culturally alternative cultural resolutions, and to exchange and expand the cultural system for a more flexible and adaptive life (Tseng and Hsu 1979). Lao-zi's contribution to psychotherapy is to provide an alternative perception of life and the suggestion that we approach problems in an entirely different (and even unorthodox) way.

Provision of an Alternative Perspective on the Way of Life

A person caught in a narrow view of life and rigidly obsessed with certain goals tends to feel trapped and to suffer agonizingly from problems. The goal of psychotherapy is to provide such a person with an opportunity to review the situation and examine his or her attitudes and orientation toward life, thereby rescuing the patient from the dead end that he or she has reached. In this regard, Daoist thought provides an entirely different view of the world and of the life of a human being. It can certainly be utilized in cognitive therapy, providing a person with an alternative perspective on life as a whole.

Management of the Desire for Achievement

Many people are preoccupied with endless desires and the pursuit of never-ending goals. As a result, they suffer from despair and dissatisfaction. Such people need therapy to adjust and reduce their desire for achievement and success and to learn to enjoy life in a different way—being content with what they have. Knowing their limitations and being satisfied with what they are is very useful for those who are blinded by excessive desires and expectations.

Application of Different Coping Patterns

Instead of aggressively fighting back when challenged, vigorously dealing with problems, confronting situations face-to-face and violently, Daoism suggests entirely opposite ways of approaching challenging situations, such as dealing with hardness with softness and doing nothing except following nature. At a glance, it is difficult to comprehend the beauty of these patterns of coping, which may sound unrealistic. However, after careful thought, you will see the usefulness of these ways of dealing with problems. Perhaps the best example of the application of softness against hardness is a situation of conflict between a man and a woman. Instead of arguing forcefully according to reason or relying on threats or violence, using a tender voice and affection will resolve the problem with much greater ease. Friendliness and kindness, rather than suspicion and guardedness, are the best weapons with which to relate to your neighbors. In terms of government, too many rules and too many ambitious plans requiring high taxes do not allow people to enjoy their lives but instead lead them to suffer from excessive burdens and rules. In the same way, in a family, too much discipline and competition and too many expectations will ruin the joy and happiness of the family members. Living naturally and affectionately, without necessarily doing too much of anything, tends to bring more contentment and joy. That is the spirit of doing by doing nothing.

Obtaining Philosophical Enlightenment

One of the final goals of psychotherapy is to help people obtain a different view of and philosophical attitude toward life. By viewing life at a higher level and obtaining enlightenment regarding the nature of life, a person can accept and deal with life with more meaning. We tend to see what we can see and ignore the things that we are not able to see. Recognizing hollowness—that is, recognizing the important function of the central hole of a wheel, realizing the usefulness of the space in which to load things into a car, appreciating the usefulness of the space in a house for living—is among the inspirations of Daoist thought. Listening to others for what they do not say, rather than paying attention to what they express; recognizing the invisible contribution of others to you, rather than busily complaining about them; acknowledging the hidden desire inside you that influences your behavior, rather than paying attention to what you think rationally in your head are all practical examples of noticing and appreciating "hollowness," as hinted at in Lao-zi's view. Revising and expanding one's philosophical cognition and attitude are ultimate goals of psychotherapy, with which mainstream contemporary psychotherapy is seldom fully concerned.

Comments from the West

From a philosophical perspective, numerous insightful comments indicating the basically different ways psychotherapy is performed in the East and West have been made by Western scholars and clinicians (Ehrlich 1986; Knoblauch 1985; Williamson 1992). For instance, Pedersen (1977) pointed out that Western personality theory assumes a separation and opposition of the individual and the environment and builds systems that assume the ego to be an actively independent observer and controller of the environment. In contrast, Daoist philosophy stresses experiential evidence, intuitive logic, and the interrelation of all things. These factors are not used to resolve conflict, but to transcend it through acceptance of the conflict. Ehrlich (1986) contrasted Eastern notions of transcendent liberation to the traditional psychoanalytic model of personal transformation.

However, there are some psychotherapies unique in the West that have principles similar to those advocated in Daoism. For example, Williamson (1992) explained that the essential notion of self-psychological therapy is that empathic attunement itself facilitates the natural growth of the personality. It is not the interpretation (as valued in classic psychoanalysis) that is primarily curative, but empathic understanding. Since the spirit of Daoism is the natural, spontaneous, and gentle following of transformations, without interfering, Williamson indicated that, in a broader sense, "empathic understanding" (advocated by self-psychology) and "natural unfolding" (stressed by Daoist thought) seem to be linked together at a conceptual level.

The clinician Knoblauch (1985) pointed out that Daoist thought values intuitive logic, rather than the Western concept of rationally defined evidence, and acceptance, rather than the Western concept of control. He advocated the application of Daoist thought to actual counseling in the West. He proposed five counseling constructs relating to Daoist thought that can be used in the practice of psychotherapy: nowness, not trying, de-emphasis on the ego, guilt desensitization, and observational acceptance. He commented that clients seek counseling when their efforts to find answers or solutions are unsuccessful. They may have thought that the only way to improve their lives was to struggle persistently in the application of "good" intentions. Unfortunately, they often become trapped in a mire of well-meaning stubbornness. Therefore, counselors must help clients get off the track on which they have been circling. When clients (following Daoist thought) begin to trust in all things and stop trying so hard, the circle will be broken.

Daoist Cognitive Psychotherapy Practiced in China

Although numerous scholars and clinicians in the East (H. A. Kim 1995; Rhee 1990; Young 1997; Zhai 1995) have stressed the usefulness of Daoist thought in psychotherapy for Asian patients, it was only recently that a special form of cognitive therapy emerged in China that specifically utilized Daoism in the treatment of neurotic patients. In contrast to psychoanalytic-oriented psychotherapy, which focuses primarily on the analysis of unconscious emotional conflict and obtaining insight to resolve the intrapsychic complex, cognitive psychotherapy chooses to work with patients at a conscious, cognitive level, to correct the patients' own thoughts, beliefs, and attitudes that are causing dysfunction. Since the early 1990s, a team, mainly from the Mental Health Institute of Hunan Medical University, led by Dersen Young has been carrying out Chinese Daoist cognitive psychotherapy (Young et al., n.d.). Because the main thrust of the therapy is to help the patient obtain cognitive insight and become "detached" (or relieved) from excessive desires or expectations, the therapy is called *chaotuo xinlizhiliao* in Chinese (literally, "detachment psychotherapy," meaning transcendental psychotherapy in English).

Core of the Therapeutic Program

After studying Daoist thought carefully, the team identified eight phrases (or slogans) in four categories that form the basis for their cognitive therapy: *li er bu hai* (doing things that are beneficial for the self, others, or society and are not harmful to the self, others, or society) and *wei er bu zheng* (doing things as best as one can, according to one's ability, but not competing with others); *shao si gua yu* (being less selfish and less occupied with desire) and *zhi zu zhi zhi* (knowing how to feel contented and how to stop desires properly); *zhi he chu xia* (knowing how to relate to others harmoniously and to place one's self in the subordinate position) and *yi rou sheng gang* (knowing how to defeat hardness with softness); *huan pu gui zhen* (returning to the simple state of self and belonging to the innocent truth of life) and *shun qi zi ran* (complying with naturalness).

Cognitive therapy is provided for patients suffering from minor psychiatric disorders by utilizing these basic phrases, which are familiar to and easily understood by lay people. In addition to cognitive counseling, a treatment program is combined with the practice of relaxation exercises and meditation, as well as group discussions. The main thrust is to change the patient's basic attitudes toward the self, to regulate negative affects, and to revise the patient's lifestyle in accordance with Daoist philosophy, as represented by the eight basic concepts.

Case Vignettes

Case A.   Mrs. Wang, a forty-five-year-old junior-high-school-educated accountant suddenly developed an acute anxiety state, with restless, disturbed sleep, which continued for three months. Her condition started after she was investigated by the police for a financial crime committed by a superior in her company. She became nervous, worrying that she herself might be prosecuted for wrongdoing in her accounting work. She became irritated and tended to lose her temper. She criticized her son for not studying enough and for not getting better grades. She argued with her husband over any trivial matter that occurred in the household. The major focus of her cognitive therapy was to help her establish the attitude of *shun qi zi ran* rather than worrying about everything. As the Chinese proverb says, "If you have done nothing wrong in your mind, there is no need to worry that anything will happen, including that a ghost will knock at your door at midnight." She was encouraged to accept a new attitude, expressed in the phrase, *wei er bu zheng,* and to learn not to be too harsh with her son and expect unreasonably high achievement. After ten therapy sessions, her anxiety diminished and her family noticed that she was no longer as temperamental and anxious as she had been for the previous three months.

Case B.   Mrs. Liang, a fifty-seven-year-old college-educated retired woman visited a clinic with a chief complaint of irritability, sleep disturbance, and episodic occurrences of anxiety, with palpitations and the fear that she might be suffering from a heart attack. After a physical checkup that revealed no heart problem, brief cognitive psychotherapy was offered for what was diagnosed as general anxiety disorder. In addition to helping her learn how to practice relaxation exercises and meditation daily, counseling focused on the factors that contributed to her anxiety. It was revealed that, after her recent retirement, she focused her attention too much on family matters, including the behavior of her husband and their children. For instance, she would become irritated if her husband messed up the newspaper that she had carefully folded, or she would become annoyed when her young adult children would not listen to her advice on how to be successful in life and instead argued with her. The core of the cognitive therapy focused on how to tolerate others' different behavior or styles of living (as they were, "naturally") rather than trying to change them (according to her own desires), and not to expect too much of her

children (by not being competitive). By emphasizing acceptance and tolerance, she was able to relate harmoniously with her family members. After
she learned how to adjust to (and enjoy) her postretirement life, her clinical symptoms eventually subsided.

Studies of the Effectiveness of the Cognitive Approach

Preliminary studies have indicated that such a cognitive therapeutic approach is beneficial for patients suffering from generalized anxiety disorder
(Zhang et al. 2002), as well as so-called type A personality disorder (people
who tend to be overly serious in dealing with things and competitive in
their relations with others) (Xiao, Young, and Zhang 1998). The concept
is simple and the procedure easy to carry out, even for junior therapists.
In addition, the ideas utilized for therapy are not very complicated, and
are easily understood by laymen. They are culturally familiar concepts and
attitudes, filled with "ancient wisdom" by the therapist. Clinically, it was
found that people who have already reached or are beyond middle age, a
time of diminished ego struggles and greater compliance with nature, can
more easily make use of the Daoist attitude of accepting naturalness and
limiting desires.

From an academic point of view, there is a need to investigate whether
there are any specific effects of this unique, cognitive therapy on Asian
people, who are familiar with these traditional thoughts, and people in the
West, for whom these philosophical ideas are foreign.

CHAPTER 10

Buddhist Teaching:
Relation to Healing

Suk Choo Chang and Rhee Dong-Shick

Buddhism is an experience-based teaching of life, a means of release from suffering, and a way of healing. Since its beginning more than two thousand years ago in the foothills of the Himalayas, it has spread widely in Asia and beyond, taking up colorful local and temporal features in the process. Beneath the surface, however, its essential message remains common to all schools of Buddhism. It suggests that human truth and reality exist in a realm beyond words, because "words" are inherently conditioning and limiting. Buddhism is not a religion: it does not believe in dogma, but in silence; and it does not ask to believe, but to experience. Therefore, it does not conflict with "religion," but can embrace it. For the teaching to be more understandable and practically helpful, however, it needs the tools of language and analytical work.

The following is a brief sketch of the birth and development of Buddhism and some psychological inquiries into a few of its basic tenets—karma and nirvana—a view of healing mechanisms, and comments on a few common questions.

History and Development

Buddhism arose more than two thousand years ago, with an "awakening" of the historical Buddha, the son of a prince of a small kingdom in the foothills of the Himalayas, in present-day Nepal, in 563 B.C. (Fischer-Schreiber et al. 1994). The circumstances of his birth were blessed, as the prince (or the son of a raja) was surrounded by luxury and comfort, and, at a young age, married well to a majestic, constant, cheerful, and dignified woman, who produced a lovely son. However, the luxury and comfort and his father's efforts to shield him from all the miseries of the world outside his estate could not keep Buddha from seeing the sorrows of separation, sickness, aging, and death, the universal human predicaments. Deeply troubled, one day he departed, renouncing his fortune and privilege, in search of the meaning of life and a way of healing. After six years of pilgrimage, he found the answer, "awakened," and began to teach those who gathered around him. Thus, Buddhism was born (Humphrey 1972; Ross 1966; Smith 1958).

Since then, Buddhism has spread throughout Asia. It continues to spread into the West, especially since the beginning of the twentieth century. In the process, two major schools, the Southern and Northern, or Theravada and Mahayana, developed. But despite different appearances or the forms of local and temporal manifestations, certain basic ideas are common not only among different schools of Buddhism, but also in Hinduism, in the context of which Buddhism arose, not unlike the birth of Protestantism in reaction to the then-corrupt practice of Catholicism in the West.

In the course of its development, the Mahayana school, in interaction with Daoism (Taoism), produced Zen (Chan in Chinese, Son in Korean) Buddhism. Zen has become the principal school of Buddhism in Korea and Japan (Bodde 1953; Wright 1959; Fairbank, Reischauer, and Craig 1973). Together, Buddhism, Confucianism, and Daoism came to be known as the Three Teachings, the main intellectual framework of East Asian culture and consciousness on an educated level. Each of the three streams of thought has been able to maintain a separate identity while liberally interacting with and learning from the others because none insists on its exclusive possession of the truth, all believing that the truth lies beyond words, in silence and experience, and that each school is a different expression of the same truth. The rationale for experiential learning is the belief that, since every human being is an integral part of the cosmos and an expression of its principle, one can learn the truth by being true to one's self. This can be achieved by removing one's culturally, personally, and idiosyncratically conditioned self, the "ego," the "small self," so that what Buddhists call the "greater self" may emerge.

The Basic Teachings:
The Four Noble Truths and The Eightfold Path

Buddhist teaching begins with the premise that life is fraught with conflicts and sufferings. (This means that it has little meaning to those who are surrounded by luxury and comfort and who do not see or experience the pains and anguish of life.) To be freed from sufferings, one needs to conduct one's life and relations to others morally, first, by cultivating (or rather cleansing) one's consciousness. These instructions are contained in the Four Noble Truths and the Eightfold Path (Humphrey 1951, 1972; Ross 1966; Smith 1958; Wood 1959).

Suffering comes from undue attachment to and craving for the transient and illusory because "desire means those inclinations which tend to continue or increase separateness [of one from all others] . . . all forms of selfishness, which necessarily separate one from others (Humphrey, 1951, 91). Selfishness alienates one not only from others but, equally importantly, from one's own true self. We may recall that seeing a person's "self" in two layers—true and false—is consonant with all the major modern psychological views, including those of Freud, Fromm, Horney, and Jung.

In Buddhism, the two selves consist of the "small self" and the "greater self," and ideal psychological development means experiencing the greater self by removing the small self, by clearing out the idiosyncratic personality layer so that the underlying personal potential can be realized. On the level of the smaller self, one is separate from all others and alone, but on that of the greater self, one is related to all others. In Humphrey's (1951, 91) words, "Man's duty to his brothers is to understand them as extensions, other aspects of himself, as being fellow facets of the same Reality." In the words of Smith (1958, 115), one can be released from the bondage of attachment, if one can free oneself from "the casket of self-interest into the vast expanse of universal life." In Wood's (1959, 23) poetic metaphor, an overcoming of the smaller self is like a dewdrop merging with the ocean.

The Truth includes the Eightfold Path (or eight steps) to be taken toward liberation, and it begins with right association. This refers to the necessity of associating with those who are like-minded, moral in orientation, intent on self-improvement and self-discovery, motivated for and valuing peace of mind. It involves a search for community with those oriented toward health and suggests that health is as contagious as sickness.

It may be noted that, in Buddhism, one's personal and social lives are seen as integral processes. This is a reflection of a general "Asian" thought pattern, for better and for worse, which sees things "holistically" and intuitively, rather than individually and analytically. Right association is followed by right knowledge and right aspiration.

The second and third paths refer to right speech. They concern the way one uses daily language. As the most characteristic human attribute, language contributes to the best in life and society, but also to the worst in human behavior and history. This is because language can obscure and mislead as much as it can illuminate and guide. A glance at world history amply illustrates this point.

This is a why the third path urges us to be mindful of the way we use language in social relations and to be charitable to others. The admonition, like all others, is easy to say, but hard to practice. For instance, how honest are we in our daily lives? Often we do not even know that we are being untrue or dishonest. Also, one's culture can be so ethnocentric that a person sees others as he or she wishes or fears them to be, rather than as they are. Trying to be totally honest may be "too advanced" for most of us, but one can begin to be truthful. Therefore, each time we say something that is less than true, it is necessary that we reflect upon our motivation in doing so. (This is reminiscent of Confucius, who reflected upon his behavior three times daily.) The essential reason for the untruth is likely to be selfishness, the belief that one's interests are in basic conflict with those of others.

The fourth path is right behavior, which may remind us of the Ten Commandments. Then there is the fifth path, right livelihood. If the nature of one's work is such that it pulls him or her away from the truths and the paths, it will be difficult for that person to attain peace of mind. The sixth path is right motivation, without which hardly any work, especially self-improvement, can be done. Self-improvement (or recovery of health and release from suffering) requires a basic change in personality, and a meaningful change in personality for the better is, indeed, a difficult thing, as modern studies of personality disorders indicate. In other words, Buddhist teaching is directed toward a basic change in personality, for which a strong motivation is essential. A common source of the motivation can be a need to free oneself from suffering, whereas a major obstacle to such change in modern venal society is the prevalent illusion that one can attain health and peace easily. The seventh and eighth paths, respectively, are right mindfulness and right absorption, or concentration and meditation.

Concentration and meditation can be considered problems of "consciousness." Consciousness is like a space. Space can be understood in terms of all the objects, visible and invisible, in it, and their energy. Consciousness can also be understood in terms of its content (feelings, sensations, thoughts) and energy (in the form of attention and concentration).

Concentration (on an object or a task) is possible if one is motivated and undistracted from outside as well as from inside. What is most difficult to control, even when one is motivated and in a quiet place, is the endless stream of thoughts, feelings, and sensations in our minds. Concentrated attention is most possible, therefore, when inner stirrings are calmed down.

The mind is normally filled with thoughts, feelings, and sensations, though their configurations are conditioned by one's idiosyncratic background. Examples of concentration abound in our daily lives. A child is absorbed in his or her play, a master craftsman or performer in his or her craft; a scene or story may move a person to go "beyond himself." D. T. Suzuki (1956, 279–294) cites master swordsmen in a tournament as an illustration. In the match, both (A and B) are totally concentrating on each other. In this concentration, they are also aware of their surroundings, but they do not become emotionally invested in the surroundings. Instead, their mental energy is focused on each other (or they identify with each other). It is said that the one who wins is the one whose quality of identification is better, meaning for A to know B as B knows himself. Such identification requires that the observer suspend his or her own prejudice and presumptions, or what Buddhists call "abolishing or killing one's ego." In other words, concentration is possible only if one's consciousness is cleared of its contents.

It is to this end that meditation is conducted. In meditation hall, one may often find an admonition in two Chinese characters, *ting xue,* which mean "listening to snow fall." To listen to the normally inaudible snowfall, one must silence the environment. The snowfall is still inaudible, however, so one proceeds to silence the mind within. In short, the admonition tells of the purpose of meditation. In the words of Patanjali, the author of *Yoga Sutra,* circa 300 B.C., meditation is an "unbroken flow of thoughts toward the objects of consciousness . . . [to reach a] shining of the true nature of the objects . . . not distorted by the mind of the perceiver." This, in Wood's paraphrase, is a "continuation of ideation . . . [to reach] complete thinking . . . but with the shining of the mere object, as though with a voidness of one's own nature" (Wood 1959, 235; see also Humphrey 1972). Please refer to chapter 14 in this book for a view into the nature of meditation.

How Meditation Heals

The concepts of karma and nirvana (see Wood 1959; Humphrey 1972; and Fischer-Schreiber et al. 1994) help our understanding of the spirit and rationale of meditation.

Karma is a belief that all phenomena, including human psychological phenomena, are interrelated and interdependent. It is a belief that one's present psychological state is the consequence of one's past actions, as well as nonaction, and that one's present deeds are the causes of one's future state. Past negative conduct results in present suffering (neurosis), and present negative deeds cause future suffering. To liberate one's self from the chain of suffering, one needs to accumulate good deeds, for which one begins recollecting the past. This process is called cleansing, clearing, and stilling of the mind—or meditation. An apt metaphor can be found in the chained ghost in Charles Dickens' *Christmas Carol.* A motivationally positive life frees a person, whereas a motivationally negative one chains him or her. Is this not an essential message of psychoanalysis? A view of the mechanisms of loosening and resolving negative psychological chains is presented in this book (chapter 14) and has been presented elsewhere (Chang 1974). Also see Thondup (2001) for healing through positive motivation.

Nirvana has been commonly translated as "egolessness" (or selflessness) and has often been misunderstood. It is the state that cannot be expressed in words because each word conditions and limits its meaning. " 'The Tao (or Dao) that can be expressed is not the eternal Tao, and all that is said about it is necessarily untrue. . . . All positive description is adding predicates to the All . . . a limitation of the All. . . . Nirvana is!' It cannot be conceived; it can only be experienced" (Humphrey 1951).

Nirvana begins in overcoming the idea that all individuals are separate, with the self-interest of each conflicting with that of all others. The state of nirvana is an ultimate affirmation of life (Suzuki 1956), but, to Freud (1930), it was an expression of thanatos. These views illustrate contrasting perspectives and premises of the two traditions. Individualism is based on a belief that all beings are innately irrational and predatory. From this perspective, a separation of all individuals becomes a categorical imperative, human relations have to be necessarily contractual (Tocqueville 1835, 104–108), and a "strong ego" becomes the psychological ideal. We thus see an interesting lineup of psychological theories in the way the individual and the ego are defined by Freud, Jung (1954), and Buddhists. See also Dumont (1966) for the meaning of the "individual" in the Hindu tradition.

For the purposes of this chapter, the Kantian view of the nature of the "self" (or the ego and, by implication, the individual), as interpreted by William James (1890), if I understand them both correctly, is strikingly close to, if not identical with, the concept of nirvana.

Kant (as interpreted by James) divides the self into four components —material, social, spiritual, and pure ego. The first three selves are what we would today call, respectively, the biological, social, and psychological selves, and do not require reiteration. What is most interesting is his "pure Ego." For him, it is the basis or vehicle of all thinking. Introducing Kant's transcendentalist theory, James suggests that if there is an object or an idea that cannot be perceived, it cannot become a part of that person's experience. "All things, then, so far as they are intelligible at all, are so through combination with *pure consciousness* [my emphasis] of Self, and apart from this, at least potential, combination nothing is knowable to us at all." He continues, "At the basis of our knowledge of our selves there lies only 'the simple and utterly empty idea *I;* which thinks, nothing more is represented than the bare transcendental Subject of the knowledge . . . which is only recognized by the thoughts which are the predicates, and of which, taken by itself, we cannot form the least conception' " (James 1890, as quoted in Chang 1988, 361–362).

I am not aware of a better description of the state of nirvana or pure consciousness in English than Kant-James' "pure Ego." This insight suggests that the cultural patterning of thought can be understood and transcended toward a higher ground and an integration of disparate cultures of the world.

Commonly Asked Questions about Buddhism

We learn as much by unlearning as by acquiring new data, especially about one's self and one's culture. One can know others to the extent one knows one's self. With this in mind, a few commonly asked questions about Buddhism follow.

Buddhism: A Religion?

It is interesting to note that the two eminent dictionaries of religion and philosophy (MacGregor 1989; Fischer-Schreiber et al. 1994) and one standard dictionary of psychiatry (Campbell 1996) do not list "religion" as an entry. Does this mean that the term is too well known to reiterate or too controversial? A popular dictionary (*Webster's New World Dictionary*, 3rd College Edition of American English [New York: Simon & Schuster, 1988]) suggests that the etymological meaning of "religion" is "to bind back" *(re-ligare).* In other words, the fundamental meaning of religion is to relate and unite. Unfortunately, conventional perspectives and practices have often been antireligious, contentious, and divisive.

The question is important for more than semantic reasons, because "religious" upbringing colors and conditions, parochially, one's view of life and the world. This is so because "religious" practices and beliefs, even though they are local and temporal adaptations and expressions of universal religious needs, pattern and structure our feelings, sensibilities, and thinking. Since the practices and beliefs inculcate particularistic views of universal issues, from infancy on, one grows up believing in one's own view of the world and life. Such an upbringing can be a source of personal conflict and of cultural misunderstanding, and a rationale for war.

Is Buddhism a religion? has often been asked. Intellectually, Buddhism is nontheistic, nondogmatic, nonconceptual, and nonexclusive. It is inclusive, experiential, and psychological, despite any contrary surface expressions on a folk level. It does not insist on what the truth is, but suggests what it is not. It is a teaching of life: how to relate to others, how to conduct one's self, and how to be. This is why, despite kaleidoscopically varying surface meanings—local and temporal—Buddhism, on a philosophical level, can and does embrace various religions as an expression of the same truth. Consequently, in Asian households, one commonly finds the peaceful coexistence of family members who follow various religious affiliations, such as Christianity, Buddhism, and Confucianism. Related to this is an interesting experience Asians have in Western societies: In Asia, "religion" can be a most interesting topic at social gatherings, but the topic is essentially taboo at Western social gatherings. The average Asian is not normally conscious of what religion he belongs to and does not feel that the classification of religions is useful, except in terms of its local and temporal manifestations.

On the Teachers of the Teachings

The quality of the teachers of Buddhism, as in any other fields, covers a wide range. How can one recognize a good teacher? This is as difficult as recognizing who would make a good future psychotherapist. One basic attribute may be being least needy—in a material, physical, emotional, and intellectual sense. Those who have experienced much suffering, but have overcome it, learn much about themselves in the process, not in their separateness from others, but in their relatedness. They can see themselves as a part of the whole. Their perception is not of the undifferentiated world of a child, but the de-differentiated world of an adult, one who has experienced alienation, to borrow Erich Fromm's metaphor in another context.

Meditation, a representative Buddhist approach to self-improvement and healing, is an essentially solitary and lonely undertaking. A good teacher is like a companion on a long journey, or like a mountain guide, who can lead the climber to a safer and more effective pathway. A good teacher may be like a good book, which leaves little detailed memory, but brings about significant change for the better in the reader's personality. The best teacher is then a person who neither asks nor demands, yet changes students for the better simply by his or her way of being. One needs to make one's own judgment about the teacher. Ultimately, choosing a teacher may be a matter of one's karma.

A Problem with the Clinical Application of Buddhism

A number of questions have been raised regarding the clinical application of therapeutic methods derived from Buddhism in Asian, as well as in non-Asian, contexts. To what extent, for instance, can technicalities be separated from Buddhism's underlying premises? This is a reversal of an analogous question that has been asked in applying the psychoanalytical approach in Asian societies. Observing the practice of psychoanalysis in Japan, Okonogi (1967) suggested that the practice begins, sooner or later, to look like Morita therapy, including the characteristically Japanese mode of human relations (or patient-therapist relationships). There is little reason to suggest that the situation would be otherwise elsewhere in Asia.

This is a part of a larger question that Asians have been asking for the past two centuries in adopting and adjusting to incoming Western culture. One answer has been to adopt Western techniques, but maintain Eastern spirit. This common and well-known answer is insufficient, however, because the technicalities themselves are the product of a long Western tradition. This is to say that, on the surface, Western sciences may seem, from a Western perspective, discontinuous from Western traditions, including the theological, but, in depth (or from an Eastern perspective), they are continuous. These are theoretical questions requiring much more clarification.

From a practical standpoint, however, the healing approaches known in association with Buddhism, such as meditation, are applicable in Western contexts, because healing does not depend, ultimately, on technicalities, but follows universal principles. This means that in Western contexts meditation reawakens the West's own dormant healing potentials, which have been eclipsed by its characteristic patterns of thinking. On these and related issues, readers are referred to Kim and Berry (1993) and Lee and Zane (1998) for a broad range of perspectives.

Buddhism and Hinduism are highly analytical on an intellectual level, as Smith (1958) observes. Wider use, including clinical application, however, requires further analytical effort, which has been restrained for two cultural reasons, among others. The ethos and themes of Buddhism are peace, harmony, and unity. However, a compelling source for analytical drive is found in conflicts. One "analyzes" not in love, but in conflict. The other restraint has to do with the larger cultural and historical context of the meeting of Eastern and Western traditions. The circumstances in which the two met induced the East to overidentify with the West, so that Eastern phenomena were seen through Western conceptual schema. This is like viewing non-Euclidean space according to the corollaries of Euclidean geometry: it gives an illusion of understanding. Creativity is born in an authentic ground. To reach that ground, however, the technicalities developed in the West can be highly useful. Instructive in this regard is a series of recent works on the relationship between Buddhism and psychoanalysis, including Fromm, Suzuki, and DeMartino (1960); Molino (1998); Roland (1988); Rubin (1998); Watts (1961); and, for East/West comparative philosophy, Northrop (1960).

In summary, Buddhism is a teaching of life, of how to conduct one's life to be freed from suffering and attain peace and clarity of mind. It is not a religion, but an experience-based teaching that embraces, rather than conflicts with, religion. If the "individual" is a logical outcome and culmination of Western values, the individual as a part of the "whole" is a consequence of Eastern values, including those of Buddhism. Neither is sufficient by itself. For a more wholesome and effective approach to life, each needs to understand the other better.

IV

Unique Psychotherapeutic Approach from Asian Culture

CHAPTER 11

The Philosophical Background of Morita Therapy: Its Application to Therapy

Kenji Kitanishi

Morita therapy is a unique psychotherapeutic approach that was established in Japan by Shōma Mori, a professor of psychiatry at Jikei University in Tokyo in the early 1920s (Kondo 1976). As a procedure, it was originally characterized as a treatment that took place in a residential setting, with an initial stage of absolute bed rest and isolation (for about one week), followed by a stage of gradual restoration and experience of normal life, with instructions given through a diary to produce changes in philosophical attitude (with an emphasis on accepting things as they are).

In contrast to this traditional view of Morita therapy, I would like to indicate that, at its core, it is a therapeutic method that resolves egocentric love and suffering caused by desires. Many people may be surprised by this statement, because Morita therapy is often associated with stereotypical images that are distant to modern conditions. Images are most frequently associated with inpatient therapy, bed-rest therapy, the technique of emphasizing "leaving things unquestioned" (*fumon*, i.e., no question) as well as images of the therapy as being stoic, religious (similarities with Zen are often pointed out), authoritarian, paternalistic, and with limited applicability to certain pathologies.

This chapter begins by departing from the traditional notion of Morita therapy, namely, as an inpatient therapy primarily for Morita *shinkeishitsu* (neurotic temperament). When we free ourselves from the confines of this notion, we are able to discover the tremendous potential of Morita therapy for modern daily problems in outpatient settings, beyond the treatment of neurotic temperament problems in residential settings. This is the new trend of Morita therapy, called neo-Morita therapy. It is first necessary to clarify the basic understanding of Morita therapy, the implications of this understanding, and the ensuing ideas that are associated with the treatment of "suffering." This new view is based on clinical experiences of Morita therapy with Japanese outpatients suffering from modern daily problems. Morita therapy seeks to resolve suffering by focusing on the love and desire that cause it.

Originally, Buddhism viewed the love and desire at the root of suffering as "egocentric love" and sought ways to resolve it. Buddhism's original word for "egocentric love" in Japanese was literally "thirst for love." This signifies the way humans attach themselves to various desires, as if they are desperately seeking water to quench their thirst. This love and desire are egocentric, and based on attachments to the self and others (Nakamura 1970).

The Chinese philosophies of Lao-zi and Zhuang-zi also questioned the nature of human desire (Mori 1994). In East Asia, problems emanating from love and desire were not understood in the context of interpersonal relationships such as parent-child relationships, but in relation to "living." Love and desire were referred to as pathological narcissism, and viewed as the roots of our suffering. Morita therapy draws from the understanding and methods of resolution of pathological narcissism, which are found in East Asian philosophy, religion, and psychology.

Morita Therapy and Living

Neo-Morita therapy views the cause of human suffering as excessive self-centered love and desire. It centers on each person's "living," and is based on the core East Asian understanding of humanity. The therapy incorporates the ideas of egolessness (not having a mind of self) and mind-body unity (not separating mind and body and their relations with nature), which are based on East Asian naturalism (which views nature as having the power to guide humans in the way they are supposed to live). The totality of these ideas points to a natural and unique way of living, and, for the sake of discussion, the author addresses this East Asian philosophy. Empathy and understanding toward this natural way of living enable us to understand the problems of those who suffer because of self-centered love and desire. In other words, East Asian philosophy enables us to understand the unnatural and unbalanced way in which those who suffer live their lives. People who are obsessed with anxiety are living against nature or forcing themselves to live unnaturally. People who suffer because of excessive love or desire live excessively and are limited in their existence as natural and unique beings.

Morita therapy helps people explore their unnatural and unbalanced way of living. With the assistance of a therapist, they try to modify their way of living and seek a more natural way of being. This task in and of itself is a transformation from the attachment to egocentrism and narcissism to living with love or living naturally according to one's individuality (real self).

The effectiveness of Morita therapy depends on whether or not patients can share the human understanding of East Asian philosophy. In the past, Morita therapy was not easily accepted in the West because East Asian philosophy, on which it was founded, was not easily comprehended. On the other hand, Morita therapy has proliferated in China after its recent introduction there because East Asian philosophy originally developed in China, and Morita therapy's understanding of human nature and problem-solving methods are familiar to the Chinese. One of the most important treatment techniques in Morita therapy is the establishment of a common understanding of this background knowledge with the patient. In other words, it involves psycho-education of this particular way of understanding human nature and communication of this understanding.

In Taiwan, it was reported that the Chinese method of cognitive therapy applied to patients with panic disorder. In the therapy, Confucian sayings were utilized to modify patients' attitudes toward life. The sayings included statements that described a more natural way of living, such as "follow nature," "be calm with whatever you encounter," and "be forgiving." These statements indicate that those who suffered from self-centered love and desire were able to find a natural way of living with nature (Chien 1999). On mainland China, the Dao's concept of and attitude toward life were utilized in cognitive therapy (Young 1997). Chinese psychiatrists and patients understand Morita therapy and its notion of suffering and ways to solve this suffering. This cultural understanding probably accounts for the recent popularity of Morita therapy in China. Morita's concept of *arugamama* (acceptance as it is) is translated in Chinese as "to follow nature." In East Asia, the treatment of neurosis signifies that the patient has discarded self-centered love and desire and is adapting to nature. There seems to be a common process through which a person goes and a state that a person reaches when becoming free of suffering. Morita therapy seems to present a common framework for the understanding and resolution of this suffering in East Asia. In fact, it may not only be limited to East Asia, but may be universal. In the future, the understanding of the problems and problem-solving methods that are elucidated by Morita therapy will probably be emphasized in the West, as well.

Historical Perspective of Morita Therapy

The Japanese psychiatrist Shōma Morita, at the age of forty-five in 1919, developed a psychotherapy method that he originally called "personal-experience therapy," which his followers later named after him. Morita was born in Meiji 7 (1874) and spent his young adulthood as a physician during the Meiji and Taisho eras (1868–1912). These were periods of dramatic change in Japan. The country reversed its exclusionary policies. In addition to Western government systems, modern science and medicine were introduced, as well as various Western ideologies, all of which had a significant influence on Japanese intellectuals.

Morita studied and examined Western psychotherapeutic techniques that were introduced during that period in Japan. He sharply criticized them and attempted to establish his own form of psychotherapy. He criticized Freud's psychoanalysis and Dubois's "persuasion method." By examining his criticisms, we find the originality of his understanding of psychopathology and of theories of treatment and the philosophical background of Morita therapy.

Morita (1922, 633) stated the following in his criticism of Freud's psychoanalysis: "As I see it, it is the way people separate their body and mind, the way they think they are the only ones that can understand their mind, and the way they think they can control and achieve their goals that causes contradictory thinking in the world. People can only control an extremely small portion of their bodies and mind according to will. Forgetfulness and sudden remembrances cannot be controlled at free will for it is a phenomenon of nature."

Morita was extremely critical of analysts' attempts to control anxiety by examining and recognizing the causes of anxiety. He asserted that repression is a natural phenomenon and that many people experience psychological trauma. For Morita, trauma could not be the cause of neurosis.

Morita's (1922) criticisms were also directed at Dubois's "persuasion method." He criticized Dubois's argument that neurosis was caused by false thought processes and that it could be cured through rational persuasion and correct educational methods. Morita asserted that experience is what is important.

Morita viewed human suffering and anxiety from the perspective of "circular theory" rather than linear causality. He placed "nature" at the foundation of his psychotherapy. This is an Eastern criticism of Western psychotherapy that centers on the logos. Morita also proposed a psychotherapy modality that is based on Eastern ideology.

In the following, I will attempt to explain Morita's understandings of mental phenomena by discussing circular theory and the conflict between the "real" and the "ideal" in human conflicts (namely, contradiction between ideas and reality). Following this, I will present the ideologies of Eastern naturalism, mind-body monism, and egolessness as a way to understand Morita's treatment theory (Kitanishi 1999).

Various Theories of Morita Therapy
The Circular Theory

Circular understanding is a basic epistemology in Morita therapy. It recognizes the Buddhist concept of *in-nen* (in Japanese, *in* means cause, and *en*, relation or connection). Buddhism teaches that there cannot be a sole cause to a phenomenon even though there may be a major cause behind an event. For the major event to actualize, other supportive causes must exist; these are called *en*. In other words, a phenomenon is caused by *in-nen*: cause and relational connection. Events that occur in the body and the mind are understood in relation to other things. This is the basic epistemology behind Morita's understanding of mental phenomena. In Morita therapy, the first goal of treatment is to break away from the negative circularity, that is, a simple, lineal causality.

Psychotherapeutic Significance of the Circular Theory

The circular theory holds the following therapeutic significance for Morita therapy.

- It is natural for people to want to know the reasons for their suffering, anxieties, and fears. However, they must change this attitude if seeking the causes will destroy or damage their power to live. For example, in the course of therapy, patients may discover how they were wounded from their relationships with their parents. However, it is extremely important for them to recognize that this awareness is on a different dimension from healing the suffering, discovering a new self, and moving forward with their lives.

A clinical example may serve to explain this point. A female patient sought treatment from me because of anxiety and depression. She had been in psychotherapy for over a year with another therapist and had come to realize that her difficulties, anxiety, and depression stemmed from her past relationship with her mother. There were no changes, however, in her pain and suffering. She did not know how to go on living. She wanted to change. Whenever she asked her therapist what to do, he told her that she had to endure the suffering. The patient bitterly complained that she sought therapy precisely because of this suffering.

For this patient, as Schulte (1964) pointed out, there was a difference between understanding the painful events of the past and finding a way to live. It is too simplistic to think that a patient's suffering can be helped by searching for and finding its cause. Suffering is not caused by one thing. Suffering is constantly activated and strengthened in relationships.

The resolution for suffering is not to find its cause. Searching for the cause often reinforces one's suffering. Patients must free themselves from this process and instead examine their interaction with the surrounding world in the here and now and try to break away from the negative cycle. They must also work toward reclaiming their sense of living.

This recognition is important for the therapist as well. If the therapist is obsessed with the past and with anxiety and does not pay attention to the patient's suffering, the patient will also end up focusing on the past. This will destroy or damage the patient's power to live in the present.

- The Morita therapist is a specialist who identifies and eliminates the negative cycle. It is important to recognize the negative cycle in which the patient is trapped and to work with the patient to enable him or her to break away from this pattern. The therapist believes that destroying the negative cycle will activate the patient's hidden abilities and natural healing power. In fact, with patients who are not severely obsessed, breaking the negative cycle is often all that is necessary in therapy.
- Suffering is not equal to being obsessed with anxiety. Those who are obsessed with their internal pain often sever their relationships with significant family members and their other social relationships. They suffer in isolation or in a closed world with their family, thereby increasing and deepening their suffering. The therapist assists patients to establish new familial and social relationships and helps the patient break away from a negative cycle with these relationships at the core.

The notion of "leaving things unquestioned" in Morita therapy signifies a passive approach in which the therapist does not question the past, the symptoms, or the therapeutic relationship. Instead, Morita therapy actively explores the patient's relationship with the world and assists the patient in establishing new relationships.

Conflict between the "Ideal" and "Reality"

What is human suffering and conflict? In the original concept from Buddhism, suffering is understood as "not being able to control things according to our will" or "things that do not go according to our wish." We suffer because we think that our body and mind and all other phenomena belong to us, and we try to control them according to our will.

Morita (1926) also tried to explain neurosis and general human suffering by using the concepts of desire and fear. Morita, in line with the Buddhist understanding of suffering, thinks that desire causes fear. In other words, the desire to live produces the fear of death—that is, suffering. The desire to live contains the fear of death, and Morita thought that the harmony of desire and fear (suffering) was important. Thus, for Morita, desire and fear were natural phenomena that were "real." Morita viewed the basic organization of human conflict as an opposing structure to nature, that is, the "real" and the "ideal."

The natural or "real" as espoused by Morita (1922, 1926) comprises physicality, senses, and emotions; desire and fear (emotions in general); and general activities of the mind. The "ideal" is the narcissism of the ego or an attachment to the self that opposes the existence of the natural (real) and tries to gain control through thought (which is a medium of language). This "ideal" is characterized by thinking of the self and the world as "one's own," logic that is formulated on this thinking, an enlarged sense of ego, and the superiority of logic and the inferiority of the body (or emotions) that are supported by language. In Morita therapy, this type of ego or sense of ego must be destroyed or eliminated. Morita therapy is a psychotherapy that treats the pathology of narcissism by bringing it to the fore according to a unique way of thinking.

Unlike the denial of desire in Buddhism, Morita therapy employs paradoxical treatment strategies. The ego (narcissistic ego) that clings to possessing the self and tries to manipulate it according to one's will must be broken down. In addition, desire must be experienced as desire, and fear must be experienced as fear. This is the harmony between desire and fear that is considered the natural way of human beings.

Desire and Fear

Desire itself is a paradox in nature. As with narcissism, we cannot exist without it, but, at the same time, it creates suffering when it becomes pathological. The desire to live later became one of the key concepts of Morita therapy. This concept, like desire, has two contrasting characteristics. On the one hand, it promotes the act of living itself, but, on the other, it brings about suffering. Desire makes us attempt to rebel or fight against suffering, which in turn brings about *toraware* (obsessive preoccupation). This understanding of desire and fear is what makes Morita therapy effective in resolving modern-day suffering as well as the suffering of the future. Morita (1926) is unique not only because he developed his treatment method in a home environment, but also because he discovered the meaning of desire in an Eastern context and placed it at the core of his treatment. The focus of Morita therapy is on living and on the discovery of desire.

Morita (1921) identified the hypochondriac temperament (tendency to become anxious) as the basis of Morita *shinkeishitsu* and psychic interaction as the mechanism that strengthens and fixates anxiety, which is a natural human reaction. A hypochondriac temperament is a psychic reaction toward incidents that is regulated by temperament. We can speculate that in naming this term Morita had thought of the fear of death and the fear of illness as the bases of suffering. Making the fear of death the basis of human fear came to hold two meanings. One was to see the fear of death from the perspective of living. Fear comes about because we try to live. We cannot eradicate this fear. To eliminate this fear is to deny "living." In other words, humans live with this basic paradox. The pathology of narcissism is not being able to accept this paradox and to pursue a perfect, secure, and self-centered life. Pathological narcissism is a state of mind in which one tries to control things that do not exist in reality, things that are temporary or that one cannot control. A person with a hypochondriac temperament experiences the suffering of living more than others. In other words, such a person has a stronger experience of the suffering of being born, of illness, of aging, and of death. He or she is clumsy at living, is intense, easily experiences difficulties, and sometimes finds it difficult to accept and love him- or herself.

However, pathological narcissism itself is a paradox. Pathological narcissism, on the one hand, causes obsessive preoccupation with fear. On the other hand, it promotes a natural and unique way of living that leads to creativity. Desire exists behind the fear, and the uniqueness of a person lies in the way he or she looks at this desire and actualizes it. This phenomenon can be found among people with social phobias who have succeeded at occupations such as acting. Despite their social phobias, they are in a profession that requires expressing themselves in front of others.

In other words, we all live with problems. Is there a person who is perfectly healthy with no problems? To suffer over living and to overcome this suffering is the beginning of living. At the point where we think we have overcome suffering, we face suffering again. We then overcome it again. It is in this process that our mental capacity to contain this suffering becomes larger. This is what it means to live and to grow. Through failures and disappointments, we are able to modify our excessive unrealistic narcissism, which lacks flexibility and needs omnipotent control. This modification, in turn, enriches our process of living.

Pathological Narcissism: Self-centered Excessive Love and Desire

To be fixated on the self signifies a life that is full of suffering; this suffering comes from trying to control the self, others, and the surroundings because of the inability to love one's self adequately. Alternatively, it is the story of love that is filled with suffering because the self has to continuously seek love and validation from others. This desire and love create suffering such as anxiety, fear, and depression, and become the sources of obsession. Neo-Morita therapy uses Eastern philosophy to resolve this suffering of desire and love. Pathological narcissism includes pathology with which Eastern psychology, religion, and philosophy have dealt. It is the extreme desire that tries to control the ever-changing nature of things or relationships according to one's desires. When searching behind this suffering, we find the minimization of this natural and unique way of living and the inability to love one's self. This is an extreme form of perfectionism, and behind it we find a strong desire for control. Other issues are closely related to this pathological narcissism. In the United States, the problem of narcissism and how to love one's self has received much attention since the 1970s (Kohut 1971). At the focus is the suffering of the person who excessively seeks the love of and validation by others. This desperation for attention, notice, and love leads to feelings of inferiority and depression and to interpersonal anxieties. Moreover, one cannot acknowledge this self. This inability leads to the pathology of excessive self-consciousness and narcissism. Even here, it is found that self-centered and excessive love and desire create fear.

Eastern Naturalism and Egolessness

For Morita (1922), body, emotions, and desires are a natural part of being human. Human contradictions and conflicts are caused by the attempt to control emotions and desires, which Morita considered the ego, with thought and knowledge. Furthermore, self-actualization comes from becoming aware that nature exists within one's self and by acting according to the laws of nature. This type of thinking about nature is not unique to Japan.

For example, the Chinese philosopher Lao-zi points out that the moment humans discard intentionality, nature starts to exert its function (Mori 1994). In other words, for people to survive and develop, they must adapt to nature, and learn from it. In nature there is an order that cannot be comprehended by human intellect; rather, that order becomes apparent in the conditions of selflessness or egolessness. This is what Morita therapy considers following nature or accepting reality as it is.

The notion of placing nature and the theory of egolessness at the base of psychotherapy has been easily understood and shared by Chinese psychiatrists. Many Chinese Morita therapists point out the commonality of the view of nature in Japan and China. Furthermore, Zhuang-zi, the follower of Lao-zi, stated that truth cannot be transmitted to others through writing or words and that one cannot transmit truth through teaching. He stated that truth can be understood only through direct experiential intuition. Morita's thinking about the importance of experience and the limitations and distrust toward language and the logic that is behind words can be seen in the Eastern view of nature and egolessness; the ideology of egolessness is woven into the philosophical background of Morita therapy. Furthermore, the ideology of the Eastern view of nature and egolessness, in addition to the awareness of nature in the East and the perception of relationship between humans and nature, illustrate the way of the self. This basic philosophy of Morita therapy rests on the same foundation as the ideologies of Lao-zi and Zhuang-zi, the original Buddhism of India, and the ideologies of Mahayana Buddhism (Kitanishi 1999).

Egolessness and *Arugamama*

Thus far, we have discussed the unbalanced way of an unnatural life, especially on the attachment to ego. Discussion has been based on the assumption that Eastern philosophy has an established perspective that stands in contrast and offers a solution to this state. There is probably no disagreement that psychotherapy based on Eastern philosophy is concerned with the understanding and treatment of this "ego" or narcissism. According to Murase (1976, 1977), Naikan therapy (another unique Japanese psychotherapy, which is carried out through self-inspection) and Morita therapy shared the same view—that individual unhappiness and maladjustment were caused by a self-centered way of life—and that both therapies aimed at changing this condition. To state this in Japanese terms, the treatment goals are "to get rid of the ego and to become *sunao*" (plainly mind). This means that the treatment goals of both Naikan and Morita therapy are to treat this pathological narcissism and to get rid of the ego, which means reaching a state of egolessness. Morita referred to this state as "pure mind." Morita (1934, 361) also states, "This is first experienced when a person becomes free from the belief that things should be a certain way, or free from concern about those around us." He notes that this is a state that is learned in the process of treatment.

There is no doubt that the state of mind is in contrast to what Morita calls the paradox of thought. The following diary entry was written as an understanding of Morita's notion of a "pure mind"(Morita 1934, 361):

> The pure mind is a mind of *arugamama* where what I don't like, I don't like; what I like, I like. If I don't want to work, and work reluctantly, then I can improve this situation. People try so hard so that they will not feel this feeling of dislike. That is why they become less human, and are full of mistakes. An honest mind follows reality. It is necessary to accept things as they are. When we can accept reality, then we become more obedient. In reality, there is no such thing as making great strides. To think that one suddenly becomes enlightened and becomes a better person is not based on object reality. It is an assessment based on moods. One becomes great by taking one step at a time. One should not take it for granted that one has become great.

People can experience two states of mind when they overcome this pathological narcissism. In one, they can actualize their feelings and instincts; in the other, they can do things reluctantly while making an effort to master their feelings of reluctance. In other words, in the latter state of mind, they contain what they don't like, while continuing to move forward and tackle issues. When we are internally able to take care of the pathological narcissism that is at the root of obsession, then we can experience a pure mind, a sincere mind, which, in turn, enables us to be in harmony with our surroundings. There is no doubt that it is this state of mind for which Morita therapy and Naikan therapy aim. How does one reach this state of mind? Kora (1965) called it *arugamama* (being as it is) and explicated it as follows: The first point of *arugamama* is to genuinely recognize one's symptoms and accompanying suffering and anxiety, and to accept them. This "notion of acceptance" is the key to preparing one's mind to accept one's emotions. The second point is to accept the symptoms as they are while behaving constructively according to one's original desire to live. In other words, eliminating pathological narcissism (accepting symptoms as they are) and exerting narcissism (actualizing the desire to live) must progress simultaneously. This psychological process has several aspects.

Narcissism, Which Must be Destroyed or Discarded
Here the ego signifies the way of being, which, according to Kora, resists, denies, cheats, avoids, and is unable to recognize one's symptoms. In order to discard narcissism, one needs to know one's self and to know one's limitations.

Knowing oneself.   We suffer when we encounter difficulties in life and become stuck. This is an opportune time for us to search for ourselves, to modify the way we are, and to grow. However, for many, their pathological narcissism, in other words, their perfectionism and excessive self-consciousness, comes to the fore. Thus, the first step in overcoming the self is to know one's self. It is important to recognize that people become more perfectionist or excessively self-conscious when trying to overcome their problems. We understand this to mean that people do not become stuck because something is lacking, but rather, they suffer because of excessiveness.

Knowing one's limitations (actualizing one's self).   It is difficult for those who are suffering to know their own limitations. They may object, stating, "I am suffering because I have been confronted so much by my own limitations." However, when people become stuck, they easily become extreme perfectionists. In other words, they fall into a limbo between the self that is a total failure and the self that dreams of becoming a superman. Knowing the limitations of a perfectionist or excessive self-consciousness enables one to modify the self. Modifying the excessive self and excessive way of living is what it means to live according to one's individuality and in a natural way. On the one hand, one discards pathological narcissism, while, on the other, one activates one's strength.

Sense of Helplessness

A sense of helplessness is the most important experience in giving up pathological narcissism. It is the most important element in the task of living, as well. Quite often, patients experience a sense of helplessness with elation, in which they state, "I had been trying to control everything" or "I was a self-centered person" at a turning point in therapy. There is a sense of giving up, which also connotes a sense that "it is only me, but it is me." To give up not only means giving things up; it also means gaining more clarity about a situation. What is given up is a way of living that is attached to the ego. Also included in this task are the giving up of pathological narcissism and the process of clarifying a way of living that is natural and according to one's individuality. This transformation has to be accompanied by a transformation toward a new way of living. This process is what Kora (1965) calls the actualization of the desire to live. The "sense of helplessness" and the "giving up" that occur during treatment serve as the key impetus for the experience of egolessness.

Toward a New Self: Living According to One's Individuality

Treatment does not end when one is able to discard one's ego. A person must also discover a natural way of living according to his or her individuality. What is this discovery like? There are other aspects besides actualizing the desire to live. They include the following.

Strengths of recognizing one's weakness.   The image of the new self is one in which one lives actively according to one's desires. This means that one recognizes one's emotions, pain, and state of mind and body and is able to express them. This is understood as real strength and the natural way of living according to one's individuality. A person with attachment toward self seeks strengths and perfection in her- or himself and cannot accept personal weakness, fearing that others will discover this weakness. This attachment is what creates suffering. *Arugamama* means to recognize and accept one's weakness. It also means to reawaken from narcissistic, perfectionist illusions about one's self and to find one's natural self.

Strengthening one's foundation.   This weakness indicates a person's imperfections and ambiguities. For people to acknowledge this weakness,

they must have a foundation in real life. It is important for people to experience a sense that they are actively involved with their families and
society. The Morita therapist always encourages the patient to face the
reality of the here and now because a patient's sense of being grounded
is strengthened through active involvement with reality, failures, and the
correction of failure. The experience of *arugamama* cannot exist without
the task of grounding one's self in a life that is based on reality.

Arugamama *and Disillusion*

Arugamama means accepting one's anxieties internally and recognizing
and exerting one's natural desires. However, this is not all there is. It is also
important to get out of one's pathological narcissism toward one's self and
the surrounding world and to change it to a more realistic understanding.
A person must see things as they are and accept them. Then one can behave
according to one's inner natural desire. By awakening from such pathological narcissism, one is able to accept anxiety as one's own, become aware
of his or her desires, and actualize them. Such awakening and acceptance
are not unique to neurotic patients. When we face psychological crises, we
are influenced by pathological narcissism. In other words, in the process
of living, we all fall into this sort of pathological narcissism, and then go
through the process of awakening from it. To awaken from this pathological narcissism, one needs to interact with therapists and significant others
to examine the illusions in real-life situations. This interaction requires a
therapist's assistance. Naturally, there are areas in which people will fail.
However, it is important to incorporate this failure and disappointment for
a person to be able to modify pathological narcissism. Perfectionists and
people who are excessively self-conscious become stuck because they have
failed to fail appropriately. In addition, these people view little failures as
signs of total failure on their part and do not learn to modify their illusions
from these failures. To be *arugamama* means that people live according
to their individuality, become free from "pathological narcissism," which
dictates how a person should be. It means achieving the developmental
tasks of adolescence and young adulthood of becoming autonomous from
one's parents and becoming involved with society. In middle adulthood,
it means psychological separation from one's parents and living one's life
according to one's individuality. In late adulthood, it means accepting the
aged self and actualizing one's potential.

Body-Mind-Nature Monism

As stated previously, Morita (1922) returns all bodily and emotional phenomena to nature. There is absolute affirmation of nature and a latent optimistic affirmation of humans. This view of nature opposes Western dualism, and tries to see mind and body as one. These are traditional Eastern ways of understanding and, at the same time, an antithesis to the logos-centered ideology that was introduced from the West. In concrete terms, Morita recognizes that physical activities must be included if changes are to be brought about in the mind. In addition, according to traditional Japanese thinking, mastering physical forms is very important in the process of acquiring or learning a skill or achieving enlightenment. For example, when craftsmen learn their trade, they learn the form of their work before learning the content. The form of sitting is emphasized when sitting in meditation *(zazen)*. This is the logical foundation for the sequence of bed rest in the treatment system of Morita therapy. In addition, this type of understanding of the mind and body naturally leads to the importance of physical activity and a concept of self that includes the body.

Morita therapy emphasizes consciousness. A narcissistic ego that eliminates nature must be broken up. The goal of treatment is the development of a self that incorporates nature. This is the state of *arugamama*. Wisdom in this case is knowledge that is based on nature, that is, facts, and is always in harmony with nature. People in this condition can experience and express nature, and express the way of the open self.

Studies of Treatment Effectiveness

Morita (1921–1974) originally divided neuroses into the *shinkeishitsu* type and the hysteria type, of which the former (later identified as *Morita shinkeishitsu*) was regarded as the subject of Morita therapy. *Morita shinkeishitsu* corresponds to anxiety disorders that also embody mood disorders and personality disorders (especially cluster C as defined in the American classification system of DSM-IV as avoidant, obsessive-compulsive, and dependent personality disorders) (Kitanishi et al. 2002).

Three types of neuroses were included (Kitanishi et al. 2002): (1) obsession (obsessed with ideas, mainly corresponding to obsessive-compulsive disorder, social phobia); (2) ordinary *shinkeishitsu* (obsessed with somatic symptoms, no corresponding diagnostic category in DSM-IV); and (3) paroxysmal neurosis (obsessed with anxiety attacks and anxiety, mainly corresponding to panic disorder with or without agoraphobia, generalized anxiety disorder). Morita found that these three types of neuroses shared the same mechanism of symptom formation, which he called *toraware*.

When reviewing treatment outcomes of different Morita therapy institutions, we find that Morita therapy has been effective for *Morita shinkeishitsu* from the 1920s when it was first developed to the present day. Although there are some variations in the judgment criteria, we find a high rate of effectiveness when selecting the population for treatment. The improvement rate from the Morita therapy for *Morita shinkeishitsu* has been reported, in chronological order, as 93.3 percent for the period 1919–1929 (Morita 1974); 92.9 percent for 1929–1937 (Kora 1938); 92.7 percent for 1963–1974 (Suzuki and Suzuki 1979); and 77.6 percent for 1972–1991 (Kitanishi et al. 2002). The rate for the last period is lower because it represents findings from a study conducted at Jikei University, where the treatment of atypical cases other than *Morita shinkeishitsu* was conducted.

According to clinical experiences (Kitanishi, Fujimoto, and Toyohara 1992; Kitanishi and Nakamura 1989), the treatment effectiveness is found to be best among male patients who are in their twenties and thirties, who have typical *shinkeishitsu* symptoms, who have adequate time for treatment, and who have voluntarily sought Morita therapy. Treatment is not found to be as effective among patients who have social phobia, who are delusional, or who have an obsessive-compulsive disorder that includes compulsive behaviors, irrespective of age at the time of admission for treatment.

Although Morita therapy has been focused toward the treatment of patients with *Morita shinkeishitsu* since its development by Morita, this approach has been applied to patients with a variety of disorders. When Morita therapy is applied to patients with mood disorder, it has been found that such treatment approach is effective for chronic unipolar depression (including Bipolar II) and dysthymic disorder (Kitanishi and Nakamura 1989).

In summary, traditional Morita therapy has evolved into contemporary neo-Morita therapy, which focuses on the basic concept and theories of human nature, with broad application to the client who suffers from contemporary daily problems. The core of neo-Morita therapy is helping clients resolve basic philosophical attitudes toward living.

The therapy is based on the circular theory, according to which things are influenced by cause and relation with endless, multiple, interactional factors, rather than by lineal cause. As a therapeutic approach, it emphasizes discovering a new self and moving forward in life, rather than searching for the reasons for suffering, anxieties, or fears.

The circular theory takes the view that people who suffer tend to be preoccupied with self-centered excessive love and desire. The Eastern view of nature and egolessness, or the attitude of accepting things as they are, is used to correct pathological narcissism. The therapy focuses on the development of a self that incorporates nature. Thus, Morita therapy is not as concerned with technique or procedure as it is with the enhancement of a philosophical view that is strongly rooted in Asian culture and the Buddhist and Daoist views of life and their relationship with nature.

CHAPTER 12

Japanese Buddhist Thought and Naikan Therapy

Ryuzo Kawahara

Naikan therapy is a unique style of psychotherapy invented in Japan in 1941 by Ishin Yoshimoto. *Naikan* in Japanese literally means "internal inspection or self-examination" *(mishirabe)*. In Naikan therapy, a client goes through a process of psychological self-inspection, with basic instruction and minimal supervision from the therapist. The therapy is based on the philosophical thought of Buddhism, as well as Japanese cultural concepts relating to interpersonal relations and psychological structure. It would be interesting to examine the way in which culture influences the theory and practice of psychotherapy. Because Naikan therapy has its roots in Buddhist thought, particularly that of the Japanese sect of Pure Land Buddhism, it is appropriate to briefly describe that thought before discussing Naikan therapy itself.

The Thought of Pure Land Buddhism

Buddhism was initiated about 2,500 years ago, in the fifth or sixth centuries B.C., at the midpoint of the Ganges River near Nepal in the northern part of India. It is known that the prince Siddhartha Gautama, dissatisfied with his spiritually barren life, left his home and family to find enlightenment. After searching for many years, he finally reached enlightenment (nirvana). Thereafter, he became known as the Buddha (the Enlightened One), and his teachings (that life is full of suffering that can be overcome by following the path to enlightenment) and the example of his life formed the basis of Buddhism (Morgan 1993).

In time, Buddhism was subdivided into two major schools: Theravada Buddhism and Mahayana Buddhism. Theravada (the Way of the Theras) Buddhism is more conservative in its approach, reflecting the earliest and most authentic Buddhist beliefs and practices. Because the Theravada scriptures are written in the ancient Indian language of Pali, Theravada is sometimes called Pali or Southern Buddhism. Mahayana (Great Vehicle, or Great Way) Buddhism emphasizes the variety of paths for reaching the final state of enlightenment. Its scriptures are written in Sanskrit; therefore, it is also called Sanskrit or Northern Buddhism. Mahayana embraces Tibetan Buddhism, Chan (Zen in Japanese, Son in Korean) Buddhism, and Pure Land Buddhism (Morgan 1993). Originally, Buddhism was not concerned with life after death. The Pure Land School in India pioneered the idea of a paradise (the pure land) where those will go who, with faith, call on Buddha Amitabha. The sect was named, accordingly, Pure Land Buddhism. The sect was transmitted to China, and then developed further in Japan.

The school of Pure Land Buddhism, which became successful in northern China through the Chinese monks Tan-luan, Dao-zhuo, and Shan-dao around the sixth and seventh centuries, was introduced to Japan by the Japanese monk Hōnen and other pupils. After further elaboration by Shinran and others, various sects of Japanese Pure Land Buddhism were established.

In his book, Hōnen (1133–1212) said that Buddhism can be divided into the Path of the Sage and the Pure Land Path. Further, one cannot save one's self merely by following the Path of the Sage but must use the power of others—the thought known as "the Power of Others." Although his Chinese master, Shan-dao, advocated chanting, Hōnen did not believe that any of the chanting had any value. Instead, he developed the practice of *nenbutsu,* or chanting only the name of Buddha.

Shinran (1173–1262) further elaborated Honen's thought of the Power of Others. Moreover, he put together a conventional system that included sutra, practice, and realization, and added faith. The concept of faith refers to Amida's compassion. Shinran believes firmly that faith refers to Amida's mercy, which is given when one surrenders to another, not because of one's own power.

The basic principle of Pure Land Buddhism is the same as that of Mahayana: Life is filled with pain (or sorrow), and all beings have no content with which to interact with one another. The object of the belief is not the Absolute, but the universal truth. Europeans often say that Buddhism is philosophical, rather than religious, thought. The thought of Shakyamuni (Sha-ka in Japanese) from India was different from that of Pure Land Buddhism, because he focused more on daily life, rather than presuming the world after death.

To fully comprehend the Power of Others emphasized by Pure Land Buddhism, it is useful to know how Shinran came to develop it (Shinran and Hirota 1995). Shinran had started to notice the existence of "blind passion," which can never be resolved by one's own strict discipline. Moreover, he was interested in learning how a person could be saved from distress. Shinran had a strong tendency toward sacredness, and cultivated his sharp eye for incidents in this life. Doing this, he ended up searching for higher sacredness. Eventually, he realized that he could not escape from blind passion in his life. Shinran strongly believed that it was hypocrisy to focus only on sacredness, with one's eyes closed. This type of pain, through which one could not attain sacredness, could not be erased by conventional practices, which were misunderstood when one saw a Buddha going through strict discipline. That is to say, Shinran's thought started from the realization of the limits of his own power.

Breaking with the requirements of a traditional monk, Shinran married and had children, embarking on the life of an ordinary citizen and experiencing its joys and sorrows. Through his experiences, Shinran faced the essence of being human and established his own structure of thought. In the same way as the initiators of Pure Land Buddhism, Shinran developed the notion that all humans are foolish. He also realized that, while humans do not know the universal truth, they are obsessed with self-centered desires. Shinran's view also attained a sense of guilt. Shinran did not criticize humans in general but, rather, grieved to himself in despair about them. Shinran's thoughts on salvation contain the idea that the salvation of an evil person is greater than that of a good person (expressed in the Japanese phrase *aku-nin shō-ki*). As Shinran noted in *Tannisho*, "It is impossible for us who are possessed of blind passion to free ourselves from birth and death through any practice. Sorrowing at this, Amida made the Vow" (chapter 3). Shinran altered the significance of Amida's vow, stating, "Even a good person attains birth in the Pure Land, so it goes without saying that an evil person will."

After this despairing recognition, one can liberate one's self for the first time, and stand aloof from birth and death and at a distance from good and evil. Guided by the primal vow of Amida, people are able to live in the Pure Land of Buddha. The theory of spiritual enlightenment without breaking off blind passions was intensified by Shinran's understanding of human beings.

Ishin Yoshimoto, the initiator of Naikan therapy, was an ordinary civilian involved in business, who also indulged in calligraphic writing. He was licensed to become a monk and was well acquainted with the thought of Pure Land Buddhism. As mentioned, Shinran's view of humans is that they are too caught up with self-centered desires and are fools who do not know the truths of life. Also, humans cannot escape from their foolishness, but must depend on the wisdom of Buddha. In Naikan therapy, there are three items to be examined: what good has been received from a person (in the past), what has been done to repay that person, and what troubles and worries one has caused that person. Naikan therapy requires the patient to inspect childhood experiences according to these three items, in order to recall childhood memories correctly. By going through these items in self-examination, the patient will realize that his or her tiny existence has been supported by other people. The patient will also realize that his or her self-centered desires have created trouble. That is, a patient will have a sense of appreciation and support and will realize how much he or she has been supported by others. After freeing one's self from self-obsessed desire, one will end up with a new perspective: that of other people. This psychological development is common to the spirit of the Power of Others. The patient will decide to lead life in a natural way, and will also reach the level of the concept of "breaking out from the self." This concept is common to the "thought of the void."

Naikan Therapy: Program and Practice
The History of Naikan Therapy

Naikan therapy started as self-examination *(mishirabe)*, which is the method of self-discipline that was originally practiced in the True Pure Land sect. It detached from the religion and became much simpler. In 1941, through Ishin Yoshimoto's efforts, it developed into Naikan meditation.

The effect of Naikan on people was initially recognized among juvenile delinquents at a reform institution (Reynolds 1977). Later, it was adapted to promote mental health, and designed to be carried out at home, in school, and in the workplace. By 1968, three items of self-examination had been formalized as the basic framework of Naikan therapy. The client was instructed to examine the three items mentioned above in order: first, what the client had received from a significant person in his or her life; second, what the client had done in return for that person; and finally, what troubles or worries the client had caused that person (Murase and Johnson 1974). Gradually, Naikan therapy was adopted in medical fields as Naikan-style psychotherapy. Now, Naikan psychotherapy is applied broadly to neurotic disorders (Kawahara et al. 1995; Reynolds 1977), drug dependence (Suwaki 1979), and psychosomatic diseases (Reynolds 1977); to patients in consultation-liaison service; and to patients in terminal care. Recently, Naikan psychotherapy has even been cautiously applied in the treatment of prolonged depression or schizophrenia (Kawahara, Kimura, and Nasagawa 1993). The procedure of Naikan psychotherapy is easy to follow, brings out deep introspection, and is, therefore, considered a beneficial form of psychotherapy.

Basic Practice of Self-Inspection

The patient is instructed to recall concretely the facts of his or her life from the past to the present, according to the three items of self-examination. It is suggested that the patient carry out introspection toward others (close family members or relatives) over and over, in chronological order, according to these three items (Takeuchi 1965).

The patient will look into her- or himself according to each item for one to two hours and will be interviewed immediately after each period of introspection. The patient will carry out introspection from early morning to evening, for a total of about fifteen hours, with a brief break in between, for about seven days. The patient may introspect about his or her mother during a three-year period in childhood, from age six through age eight, for example, going through self-examination according to the three items and recalling concrete facts about his or her relationship with his or her mother. After this, the patient will be able to recollect childhood memories that were too obscure to remember at first but that have become as clear as yesterday's memories through the Naikan sessions. The patient finally realizes that old memories were buried by individual psychic reality. Thus, the Naikan sessions start with a reconfirmation of the facts of one's childhood.

After recalling these childhood facts, the patient will be able to recall positions and situations from the perspective of close relatives. Moreover, the patient will recall his or her state of mind at the same time and will be able to see him- or herself from the viewpoint of other people for the first time, thereby becoming detached from a self-centered attitude. Through this self-examination the patient ends up with self-discovery (with an objective viewpoint and realistic recognition), influenced by a sense of appreciation and support, and, later, a sense of self-reproach, which is considered an emotional transition during a Naikan session.

There are three important rules in Naikan therapy that a client needs to observe carefully. First, to avoid enhancing a tendency toward self-centeredness and a sense of aggression, the client is forbidden to introspect on the three items in reverse of the order prescribed, that is, what did one do for other people, what did one receive in return from others, and how was one troubled by others? This is called *gaikan* (external inspection). It is considered the wrong way to carry out inspection and is strictly forbidden during therapy. It is contrary to the instructions for self-inspection, which are designed to enable the client to obtain the viewpoint of others, rather than his or her own self-perspective (Egashira 1998). The interviewer has to lead the patient away from this reverse way of recalling memories.

Second, when the patient introspects according to the three items in a Naikan session, he has to recall from his actual, individual experiences, not from his imagination. Third, it is necessary to focus on the relationship between one's self and close family members or immediate relatives, not remote friends or insignificant persons in one's life. It is necessary to concentrate on significant persons, mostly encountered in early childhood, in order to utilize Naikan sessions to search the inner world of the self.

Through the self-introspection of the first and second items, the client will often start to regard family members and close relatives as others, with their own personalities, and grasp objective relationships with them. Following this realization, the patient will begin to recall the love and affection he has received from his family (particularly his mother) and close relatives. This is called "the recollection of loved experience." In other words, when the patient recalls how much he is supported by close, significant people, he feels a sense of appreciation and support from his emotional experiences with them. Eventually, the patient will recognize the existence of other people, making it possible to have eyes of reverence for them, and also enhancing the idea of recognition of others. It seems that this recognition opens up the path to self-realization.

Next, after introspecting on the third item in Naikan therapy, the patient will recollect many concrete facts about the trouble he has caused people close to him. This is called "the recollection of self-centered attitude." Associated with this third item of examination, the patient will often recall the details of episodes of lying and stealing—and any other bad behavior that he has exhibited in the past—and the trouble and worries he has caused other people. Lies and stealing are in the same category as the third item in Naikan psychotherapy. When the patient becomes aware of his self-centered attitude and self-obsessed mind, he will tend to have a sense of self-reproach. His recognition of his self-obsessed mind is equivalent to an escape from it (breaking out of the self), that is, it opens up the path to self-discovery (Tatsumi 1999).

In summary, by going through the three items of introspection in Naikan sessions, a sense of appreciation and support and a sense of self-reproach will pour out endlessly through the recollection of experiences of love and the recollection of one's self-centered attitude. The influence of these two emotions will change the patient's recognition of his present selfhood. A sense of appreciation and support and a sense of self-reproach function in the same way as the wheels of an automobile; each drives the others to reform one's self-recognition. The patient will acquire a "cardinal point of others" and succeed in breaking away from a sense of reproach, which is "breaking out from the self." It seems that the patient will reach "self-discovery" by gaining an objective view and realistic recognition.

Required Structural Setting and Mood

Usually, intensive Naikan sessions take place in a Naikan therapy room or in a private room in a hospital. One prominent characteristic of intensive Naikan is its temporary sense of concentration. Intensive Naikan has to take place in a therapeutic structural setting that enforces concentration. The Naikan procedure forbids communication from the outside or interchanges with other clients; only the interviewer can communicate with the client during the sessions. The client is often asked to sit in a corner of the room, isolated by a portable folding screen. This setting helps the client shut out his surroundings and enhances his concentration. This shut-out effect plays a big role in projecting the patient's consciousness inward.

A tender response toward the client by the interviewer (i.e., the therapist) and the use of a portable folding screen around the client give a sense of security, as if the client were embraced by his parents. The sense the client gets from the screen is that of a soft boundary between the self and the exterior world. It seems that these motherly aspects advance the recollection of love experiences and evoke a sense of appreciation.

The interviewer maintains a modest attitude toward the patient, using kind and polite words, but at the same time being firm. This attitude helps the patient see himself in a strict manner. An important element of the fatherly, therapeutic atmosphere is that the activities of the patient are limited during Naikan sessions, requiring him to focus only on recalling his memories within a limited space, shut off by the screen, except for going to bed, taking a bath, and going to the restroom.

Therapeutic Mechanism and Effects

It is important to examine the mechanisms used in Naikan therapy and their effects on the clients receiving therapy.

The therapy offers the opportunity to "retreat" and examine one's mind and life, an important process for every person to go through periodically. The involvement of religiously rooted therapeutic activities provides a sense of power of effects. Further, the religious ideas and philosophical views of the self and life provide a new perspective for dealing with the patient's self and the life surrounding him. In particular, eliminating the self-obsessive mind, learning the limitations of the self, appreciating the support of others, and living life in accordance with nature are all useful for a therapeutic, cognitive reconstruction of one's self and one's life.

Based on religious knowledge and experiences acquired through the self-examination and meditation practiced in Buddhism, many therapeutic mechanisms are incorporated into the self-improving and healing practice, without the patient's being aware of them. It is often observed that, when a client is going through the third item in the Naikan sessions (the trouble he has caused others), he recognizes his self-obsessed mind. Through self-introspection, a person will acquire the perspectives of other people, and, as a result, will discard his self-obsessed desire, which is the source of his problems (Ishida 1969).

Kawahara (1999) has analyzed in detail the psychological process that occurs therapeutically in Naikan therapy as follows: Through self-inspection according to the three items of the past chronologically, the client will obtain the "rerecognition of reality" that has occurred. Through this exercise, the client will recall the experience of being loved by others and will realize the nature of his self-centered behavior. The client will be able to see and recognize from others' perspectives and will become aware of the self-centered and self-obsessed mind that he used to have. Then, through "reexamination of selfhood," two kinds of emotions will arise: a sense of love, when he discovers that he has been loved by others, and a sense of self-reproach, when he realizes his own self-centered attitude. This process will lead to "self-discovery," which will reinforce the patient's ability to see things from others' perspectives and to minimize his own selfishness to the extent that he will almost be relieved from the self-obsessive mind. This will result in the development of a mature self, which is autonomous and filled with human nature.

Sakano (1999) has evaluated Naikan therapy from the standpoint of cognitive and behavior therapy. He remarked that "recognition of reality" is equal to the process of modeling. He also pointed out that "reexamination of selfhood" (reexamination of interpretation and signification) is equal to the process of cognitive reconstructing. That is, in his view, Naikan therapy can be understood according to the theories of recognition and behavior therapy.

However, Naikan therapy does not merely focus on cognitive enlightenment but is also associated with affective forces. The two emotional experiences described previously are very significant, and are driving forces in the development of the mind associated with self-enlightenment. In other words, Naikan therapy is not exactly the same as "ordinary" cognitive and behavior therapy, which practices confirmation, reexamination, and modification of automatic thinking and schema systematically.

Case Illustration

A case will be presented here to illustrate how the therapy is carried out and the process through which the client goes.

A thirty-year-old male client, an employee of a company, visited the clinic with the chief complaints of feeling down, irritated, and tired, and having sleeping problems. He was born the eldest son, with a younger brother. He was married, with two daughters. He started to work after graduating from industrial high school, and had a good work and performance record. However, eight months earlier, he had begun to develop problems, resulting in frequent sick leave, beginning six months before. After a physical workup, he was diagnosed as suffering from a moderate depressive episode. It was recommended that he go through Naikan therapy as an inpatient, and sessions took place as follows:

First day.   He was able to relax and started to recall his past personal life, from early childhood. Among his recollections, he remembered that, when he was in high school, he had badly criticized his mother about a lunch she had prepared for him, and made her cry.

Second day.   He was able to inspect the past more seriously than on the first day. He recalled an episode when he was in high school. He was told he needed to study harder, and became rebellious, refusing to eat the dinner his mother prepared. He also remembered that his mother took care of his children and that he showed no appreciation because he thought that she should do so, as they were her grandchildren.

Third day.   He thought of his father who arranged and paid for an elaborate wedding ceremony for him and his wife, and invited many friends to the wedding reception. However, he did not appreciate his parents until now, when he thought of these things and felt grateful to them.

Fourth day.   The interviewer (therapist) asked him to calculate how much money his parents had spent raising him. He found that his parents had spent a large amount (nearly $180,000), and was surprised by this. Even now, his mother would make coffee for him, but he never expressed his appreciation. He never paid anything back to her in return. He recalled that, about the time he started to work, he became jealous because his parents became more concerned about his younger brother, who was accepted onto a high school baseball team. He deliberately showed that he did not care about this by avoiding his home and staying out late, fooling around.

Fifth day.   He recalled one episode when, after his father's workplace was destroyed in a fire, his father became discouraged, but in spite of this, he said something that hurt his father. When his father rebuilt his workplace and held an opening ceremony to celebrate with his neighbors, the son did not attend the ceremony (as was expected of the eldest son). In the session, with tears in his eyes, he stated that he had failed to share his father's difficult feelings.

Sixth day.   He recalled many occasions when he had lied and stolen things, including cheating on an entrance examination, cheating on golf scores, lying to his family about a holiday that was really a work day and playing outside, taking money from his salary before giving it to his family so that he would have money to play around with, and so on. He showed regret that he had done many bad things in the past simply to satisfy his own selfish desires.

Seventh day.   He recalled how his wife often prepared a good lunch for him, and he failed to show his appreciation. Also, he let his wife take care of many troubling matters. He simply thought that it was a wife's responsibility and never expressed his gratitude toward her.

Explanation from the interviewer. The client was very selfish toward his immediate family members, his parents and his wife, but he was able to show consideration toward others in his workplace. In order to be well liked by his superior, he worked almost excessively hard. He was always competitive, disliking to be less accomplished than his colleagues. Recently, however, he had found it difficult to maintain his super-performance; he felt exhausted, and he began to feel inferior. Through the process of self-examination, he began to realize that he should recognize himself as an ordinary human and should not maintain such high expectations of himself in order to obtain approval from his superior; it was better for him to learn to do things at a slower pace.

Through intensive self-examination, he began to realize that he had been very selfish toward his close family members, even feeling dissatisfied with and resentful or hostile toward them, although they actually had treated him well. He became aware that all of these ungrateful views and attitudes came from within himself. He also came to understand that, in the workplace, even though he tried to gain the high regard of his superior, he did not treat his colleagues well, but with competitiveness. As a result, he became exhausted and depressed. From these self-inspections, he learned that he needed to change his attitude toward others and his views about himself. With that enlightenment, the client returned to work. Eight years later, he is living a contented new life.

Comments from a Cultural Perspective

Since Naikan therapy focuses on the cognitive correction of one's self, one's relations with others, and, most important, one's views about the nature of life, in a broad sense, it can be regarded as a unique kind of cognitive therapy. It is speculated that this form of therapy may be applicable universally, beyond Japanese clients.

However, from a cultural perspective, it is relevant to ask why Naikan therapy emerged in Japan, and why it worked well for Japanese patients. After examining Naikan therapy, Japanese psychologist Takao Murase (1976, 266) made the following comments: "Japanese guilt seems to be very closely related with the mother-son relationship, in which the fundamentally empathic and sympathetic attitude of the son toward his mother brings about guilt in him when he realizes he has done harm to his beloved mother, who may have raised her child in a rather 'morally masochistic' (devoted), self-punitive way. . . . Naikan (therapy) seems to facilitate guilt-

consciousness skillfully by reinforcing the sense of *on* (obligation), particularly the *on* (grateful obligation) regarding one's mother. . . . Thus, Naikan
therapy very effectively utilizes such basic characteristics of the Japanese
personality as strong potential guilt feelings, *on*-consciousness, the predominant significance of the mother, and specific moral values in the context of highly 'particularistic' interpersonal relationships."

American psychologist David K. Reynolds, who had a special interest in
unique therapies practiced in Japan, also commented about Naikan therapy (1980). He pointed out that Naikan's genuine purpose was to change
the client's attitude toward his past, both distant and recent. The therapy
helped the clients realize that they do not, and did not, suffer alone. The
context of the suffering was reformed by *naikan,* or self-inspection, that is,
philosophical enlightenment about the actual nature of life.

In a society characterized by intense and close interpersonal relations,
as exemplified by Japanese society, it is extremely important to learn how
to live with empathy for others. In a way, Naikan therapy is used to enhance this culturally necessary and sanctioned way of life. From the standpoint of interpersonal relationships, the Japanese family is characterized
by close mother-child relationships and devoted maternal care of the children. As a result, some children tend to be overindulged by the mother,
and enjoy being overly dependent on their parents (*amaeru* in Doi's term,
1973). They take their care for granted, without being able to appreciate
things from others' perspectives. They become self-centered and unhappy
about life if their egos are not satisfied by their surroundings in their adult
lives. In such cases, it is necessary to help them relearn reality, develop
the ability to see things from others' perspectives, and discard the self-
obsessed mind. Thus, Naikan therapy is useful for clients who need to
achieve self-recognition through the reexamination of reality. It offers an
opportunity to correct culturally induced individual psychopathology derived from a culturally shaped family background.

Finally, it should be pointed out that Naikan therapy not only utilizes
the self-examination technique that was practiced as *mishirabe* by the disciples of Pure Land Buddhism, but has adopted the ideology rooted in Pure
Land Buddhism into the therapy. As mentioned previously, according to
Shinran, the major master of Pure Land Buddhism in Japan, humans are
too caught up with self-centered desires and blind passions, and are fools
who do not know any truths of life. Also, humans need help from the wisdom of a buddha to get away from their foolishness. Through the power of
others (the thought known as the Power of Others) and the process of self-

realization, one can eliminate one's self-obsessed desire, break out from the self, and lead one's life in a natural manner. This is the basic concept of the Thought of the Void, which is valued as the ultimate goal in Pure Land Buddhism. Thus, the basic philosophical framework of Naikan therapy is the Buddhist thought that was developed and elaborated in Japan.

CHAPTER 13

Application of Proverbs in Psychotherapy: Asian Experience

Wen-Shing Tseng, Jing Hsu, Keisuke Ebata, S. Peter Kim, and Oksuk Mary Kim

Proverbs are common sayings that express certain ideas and attitudes traditionally shared by ordinary people in a society. Proverbs have long served as vehicles for the transmission of wisdom and guides of conduct that represent the cultural values of a society. Proverbs are often very short, and are symbolic and metaphoric in nature; thus, they can be interpreted in various ways on different levels, either concretely or symbolically. The interpretations of proverbs have been regarded as gauges by which various thinking and personality processes may be assessed (Bass 1957; Gorham 1956; Walsh 1966). Proverbs are often orally transmitted from generation to generation, elaborated on, screened, revised, and retained by the people in a society. Thus, in a way, they are cultural products (like myths, fairy tales, folk stories, plays, and operas), reflecting the society's basic philosophical ideas (Hsu and Tseng 1974). Proverbs are often used as folk guides on how to deal with distress or difficult situations. By examining proverbs, we can learn the culturally sanctioned coping mechanisms of a society. It is from this perspective that cultural psychiatrists are interested in studying the proverbs in different cultures.

The extent to which proverbs are used and appreciated varies greatly in different societies. It may be affected by the length of the society's history, its attitudes toward tradition, and how habitually it expresses ideas through short, familiar sayings. In Asia, proverbs are products of ancient culture. Asian people customarily use proverbs in their daily lives, particularly in times of distress, as philosophical guides to coping with their problems. Proverbs are often cited in daily conversations, in writing, in formal speech, and in folk or professional counseling. Since proverbs are commonly known, they are powerful instruments by which to convey the thoughts and meanings they contain.

Comparison of Proverbs: East and West

To understand the similarities and differences in the philosophical views of the East and West on coping with problems, common proverbs from both areas are examined and compared to each other. Given the sheer number of proverbs and no valid way to determine which are more popular, commonly used, and representative of a society, their selection for comparison is a subjective choice. To overcome this potential bias, the *World Proverbs Encyclopedia,* published by Taishiukan-shotian, Tokyo, Japan, in 1995, was used as a resource from which sixty to a hundred proverbs were chosen. China, Japan, and Korea are identified as representative societies of the East, and England, France, and Germany are identified as representative societies of the West. American proverbs were not chosen since their origins can be traced back to proverbs from England. The proverbs chosen are grouped into four categories: philosophical attitudes toward life; coping mechanisms; interpersonal adjustments; and man-woman and family relations. Within each category, the proverbs are further divided by proverbs of the same nature to allow for meaningful comparisons; however, given the small size of these samples, comparisons for purposes of statistical analysis are not made on the number of proverbs illustrated (table 1).

Similarities

It was revealed that some of the proverbs are similar across the cultural groups examined. Some of them clearly originate in the society, but disseminate to others, keeping the exact wording of the original proverbs. "All roads lead to Rome," used in Italy, England, France, and also in some Asian countries, is one such example.

Some proverbs have the same basic meaning but are expressed in different ways. Examples are "The best swimmer drowns first" (Germany), "Monkeys will fall from trees" (China), and "Even *kappa* [a legendary animal good at swimming] would drown in the river" (Japan). The virtues of persistence and diligence are expressed in various ways in different cultures. For example, "Dropping water will drill a stone" (Germany), "Sitting on a stone for three years [even the stone will warm up]" (Japan),

Table 1. Proverbs Compared: East and West

	East			West		
	China	Japan	Korea	England	France	Germany
Philosophical attitudes toward life						
Caution against the unpredictable life	2	6	4	0	0	0
Emphasis on morality, nobility	0	0	0	3	0	2
Emphasis on God, religion	0	0	0	0	4	0
Emphasis on being wise, experienced	3	2	2	1	2	4
Caution against being too successful	3	0	0	0	0	0
Emphasis on being realistic, practical	4	3	2	5	14	4
Recognition of power, gains	6	0	0	0	0	0
Emphasis on acceptance of reality or the situation	2	0	0	0	0	0
Coping methods suggested						
Controlling temper, impulses	1	3	0	3	1	2
Diligence, endurance, persistence	1	2	1	1	1	1
Taking action, even taking risks	0	0	1	4	1	1
Effective, practical	4	8	4	4	2	1
Handling situations properly	0	3	5	2	4	7
Obtaining help	0	3	1	2	1	0
Being flexible	3	0	0	0	0	0
Avoiding bad situations	2	1	2	2	0	0
Waiting for an opportunity	1	1	1	0	0	0
Interpersonal adjustment						
Reciprocal, mutual	1	2	1	0	0	1
Yielding to others	0	4	0	0	0	0
Value of friendship, harmony	3	2	4	1	0	2
Relating to others openly	0	5	1	5	0	5
Relating to others guardedly	2	1	5	0	1	1
Being careful of others' gossip	5	1	2	0	1	2
Examining the self	1	1	1	0	2	1

and "After three years, even a dog in school will learn how to bark poems" (Korea). To encourage active coping, even risk taking, it is said "To eat the inside meat you need to crack the outside shell" (Germany), "Without breaking the bone you cannot get to the marrow" (France), and "[You need to] enter into a tiger's cave to catch a baby tiger" (China).

We also know the sayings "The neighbor's cow makes more milk"

(France), "The grass is greener on the other side of the fence" (England), and "The moon is rounder in a foreign country" (China). Thus, there are many proverbs shared across cultures that are expressed in unique ways.

Differences

In examining the proverbs obtained for each category from the six societies—China, Japan, Korea, England, France, and Germany—we found numerous differences. Following are some of the findings.

Philosophical Attitudes toward Life
All three Asian societies and Germany in the West have proverbs that caution against unpredictable and unfortunate life experiences, such as "When a person is unlucky, his teeth will be stuck even by water" (China), "Knock on a stone bridge before crossing" (Japan), "Ten years' cultivation to become a monk, *amitofu* [Buddhahood is lost] in one morning" (Korea), and "The best swimmer drowns first" (Germany). However, such proverbs are not found in England or France, according to our resource.

Characteristically, proverbs that emphasize morality or nobility are found in England ("Honesty is the best policy") and Germany ("To be German is to be faithful"), but not in others. Christian morality is strongly reflected in proverbs. An emphasis on God and the church (e.g., "A person for himself, but God for every person") is noted in France, reflecting the strong Catholicism there.

Every society takes the philosophical view that things have to be realistic or practical, but in France there are more proverbs of this nature. Examples are "Fat meal, slim will" and "The clever fox does not eat the neighbor's chickens." China has proverbs that remind people of power or gain in real life. Examples are "A fly does not land on an egg without making a crack," "No one can become rich [suddenly] without illegitimate income; no horse gains weight [quickly] without grass [from a wild plain]," and "White wine makes a person's face red; shining gold makes people's minds dark." At the same time, interestingly enough, China has proverbs cautioning against being too successful or famous, such as "A person afraid becomes famous; a pig afraid gets fat" and "A big tree catches a big wind." These sayings reflect situation-oriented societies in which excessive individual success can lead to a person's becoming a target for attack by others and a source of disaster. Associated with this are proverbs that encourage accepting reality or the situation (such as "There is no banquet that does not end").

Coping Methods

In contrast to the attitudes toward life described above, coping mechanisms sanctioned by proverbs are more evenly found across cultures, except in certain areas. All societies stress the importance of coping methods that are effective and practical, but Japan has relatively more of such proverbs. Some examples are "[Prepare] a stick before falling down," "A cake [is better] made in the cake house [by specialists]," and "Replace the back with the abdomen" (sacrifice something for a more important thing). Proverbs on handling problems properly are found in most of the societies, but especially in Germany. Examples are "Good planning makes things half done" and "The sail will be smooth when there is a right wind blowing." German proverbs are among the most pragmatic and methodological in dealing with distress.

Proverbs that value the importance of taking action (even risk taking, if necessary), such as "The largest fish is in the deepest water" (England) and "To eat the inside meat you need to crack the outside shell" (Germany) are found in Korea, France, and Germany, but even more in England.

Proverbs that emphasize the usefulness of obtaining the right kind of help from others are found in Japan, Korea, and France, but most in Japan. Examples from Japan are "To encounter Buddha in hell" (meaning to be lucky and meet a rescuer in time) and "A devil gets the golden bar [as a weapon]" (meaning obtaining powerful assistance makes you stronger).

Interpersonal Adjustment

Even though the number is not strikingly large, proverbs concerning reciprocal interpersonal relations are found in all Asian societies and in Germany as well. An example from Korea is "Kind words to others return with nice words from others." Proverbs stressing the importance of yielding to others are found only in Japan, with examples such as "To lose is to win," "To lose some is to make a big gain," and "Fortune is contained in the leftovers" (not to compete with others for food).

Proverbs that emphasize the virtue of relating to others properly (with empathy) are found more in England, Germany, and Japan. Examples are "Do not check the teeth (to find out the age) of a horse given by others," from England, and "To play with the truth is to be hit by a violin on the head," from Germany. An example from Japan is "Buddha's face, three times" (meaning one should not ask for favors from others too often, because even a Buddha will lose his temper if his face is touched more than three times).

Although proverbs that warn people to be careful of others' gossip are found in most cultures, there are more in China, with examples such as "A thousand persons' saliva could drown a person" and "The sound of a bell inside a temple goes to the outside." Chinese tend to relate to others guardedly, as expressed in sayings such as "Read the hidden meaning behind the word" and "The bottom of a one-thousand-foot-deep cliff can be reached, but a person's mind cannot be reached through one-inch-thick belly skin."

Man-Woman and Family Relations

The variations among proverbs on relations between men and women, marital relations, and family relations are so great we are unable to categorize them for mathematical comparison. However, certain features are obvious. For instance, proverbs regarding men and women and marital or family relations are very scarce in Japan. It is not clear whether this is the result of the bias of the author of the *World Proverbs Encyclopedia* or whether the Japanese actually have fewer such proverbs. In contrast, China and Korea both have abundant proverbs relating to marital and family relations. Chinese proverbs emphasize the bond and commitment between spouses, the importance of family, and, at the same time, point out the potential problems among family members, reflecting the family system observed in reality (Hsu 1983). In Korea, there are many proverbs describing negative in-law relations that are not found in other societies.

The three Western societies all have ample proverbs relating to men and women. However, characteristically, proverbs from France are concerned with creating the relationship between a man and a woman, with none about marital relations.

In summary, it can be said that, although there are many similarities among proverbs, there are also clear differences among those found in different societies. Some differences are observed between Eastern and Western societies, while others are found between societies of the same region. As noted in the beginning of this chapter, proverbs, as cultural products, reflect the values and ideas that are sanctioned in societies. This comparison supports the notion that proverbs are cultural products that may vary cross-culturally or subculturally and strongly reflect the values sanctioned by each individual cultural or subcultural system. Also, proverbs are tools that can potentially be utilized for culture-relevant psychotherapy.

Applications of Proverbs in Psychotherapy

It is common in modern psychiatry to ask patients to interpret proverbs as a part of an examination of their mental status. The primary purpose is to evaluate the patients' ability to think abstractly and the appropriateness of their thinking processes. However, interpreting proverbs is subject to cultural bias (Kim, Siomopoulos, and Cohen 1977).

One of the purposes of psychotherapy is to provide guidance to patients regarding their often ill-functioning behavior patterns and suggestions about how to change their attitudes, reaction patterns, and coping styles. This is normally carried out through communication between the therapist and patient. In order to do this, the therapist may rely on analyzing the patient's emotional complex or may simply provide advice without interpretation, particularly in supportive therapy. Proverbs can be used effectively in the latter approach to convey meaning through symbolic thought. This is particularly true if the patient understands or shares the culturally transmitted traditional sayings. They are often a powerful communication tool to promote enlightenment (Zuniga 1992). If the patient is not familiar with the proverbs, they can be explained by the therapist. Through such explanation and discussion, interaction between therapist and patient is facilitated, stimulating emotional exploration (Aviera 1996). Most important, the patient can obtain a clear idea of the message contained in the proverbs. Since proverbs are short sayings with crystallized thoughts, the ideas are communicated very effectively, as expressed in the Chinese saying "One needle [punched correctly into the vessel] will show blood."

Also, proverbs are expressed without addressing a person personally and directly, minimizing any embarrassment or resistance on the patient's part. For instance, for a patient who repeatedly behaves unwisely, the therapist may use the proverb "Anybody can make a mistake, only the fool practices it." This will highlight the patient's problem without causing too much embarrassment. It will minimize the complicated work of analysis and reduce unnecessary resistance by the patient.

If there are many proverbs available, the therapist can skillfully select the appropriate ones to meet the immediate purpose. For example, if a patient is overwhelmed by problems and feeling frustrated, the therapist can choose the Chinese proverb "The mountain does not move, but you can make the road turn around." If a patient is depressed, the proverb "A shaded area can turn out to have sun" (Korea) would be appropriate. If a patient is frustrated by a minor sickness, the proverb "A vase with a crack will last longer" (France) can be used to motivate him to take good care of his health. If a patient is not enthusiastic and hesitates to start a project, the proverb "Strike while the iron is hot" is useful. If a patient keeps changing jobs for better opportunities, the proverb "To dig a well, dig only one first"

(Korea) can be used. In other words, proverbs can be utilized according to the situation. This is especially true if proverbs from other cultures are collected and used clinically. This will certainly enrich the pool of proverbs available for clinical purposes.

Asian Experience of Using Proverbs in Psychotherapy
Familiarity with Proverbs

As mentioned previously, people in Asia customarily use proverbs in their daily lives, particularly in times of distress, as philosophical guides to coping with their problems. Proverbs are often cited in daily conversations, writing, and even formal speech. Proverbs are also frequently used in folk and professional counseling. In fortune-telling, the client needs to read and interpret the saying or proverb written on the fortune-telling paper (called *chien* in Chinese, *kuji* in Japanese), such as "The sun will come out after the cloud is gone," suggesting patience and waiting for the good fortune that will come afterward, or "A premier's belly can contain a ship," suggesting that a mature and cabable person should be generous and tolerant of any problems. In other words, it is customary for clients to obtain instruction through proverbs written on fortune-telling paper (Hsu 1976). As an extension of this, it would not surprise patients to hear their therapists quoting a saying or proverb.

Because proverbs are commonly known, they are powerful instruments by which to convey the thoughts and meanings they contain. They not only provide cognitive understanding, but also stimulate emotional reaction in resonance. Because patients are familiar with the proverbs presented to them, they will automatically associate the feelings and emotions conveyed by the proverbs. For instance, mentioning the Chinese proverb "A dragon in shallow water is teased by a shrimp; a tiger on a plain, teased by a dog" would certainly convey the meaning vividly, at an emotional level, of avoiding placing yourself in a disadvantageous situation. The Korean proverb "Chili powder for eye-sickness," causing one to imagine how it would feel to put chili powder into sick eyes, strongly conveys the feeling of taking a wrong approach to a problem. The Japanese proverb "Pounding a nail into *nuka* (rice bran)" stimulates the image of a useless attempt. All these proverbs involve action and tend to provoke the imagination with a sense of action and feeling. They are powerful messages associated with emotion, communication tools that would be effective in psychotherapy.

Cultural Wisdom from Authority

As cultural products, proverbs reflect value systems that are sanctioned by cultures and can be utilized in psychotherapy. When the proverbs are used by the therapist, representing the social authority for guiding one's life, they have special meanings for the patient. People in Asia generally value the past, emphasize tradition, and respect authority. All these factors, acting together, have a greater effect on patients who are seeking guidance for their lives from their therapists.

Although in the West it is generally believed that therapists should avoid advising their patients on how to live their lives, particularly regarding major decisions, in the East, patients often expect their therapists to offer them wise advice on how to live. Offering advice through proverbs is one way of giving philosophical suggestions on how to live properly. The Japanese proverbs "A water bird leaves water behind, not mud" (meaning that one should end things in a clear-cut way, without a mess) and "Fish's mind, water's mind" (hinting that if one has empathy toward another, it will be reciprocated) and the Korean proverbs "Crying over one cup of wine" (meaning that one should not ruin a relationship over a little thing, such as a cup of wine) and "Even the bottom of a grindstone may come out" (meaning that a person should not depend on inherited power) are examples of proverbs that are often told by the elderly to their children, healers to their clients, or psychotherapists to their patients to show them how to follow cultural wisdom in leading their lives.

In contrast to formal scholarship or religious teaching, such as Confucian thought, Daoist philosophy, or Buddhist teaching, which are more or less colored by idealized philosophical values or ethical ideas, proverbs are often characterized by a practical nature. Many proverbs, such as "It does not matter if it is a black cat or a white cat; as long as it catches a mouse, it is a good cat" (China), "To speak Buddha's words into a horse's ear (is useless)" (Japan), and "After starving for more than ten days, a person is a gentleman no more" (Korea) provide lessons about how human nature needs to be practical and grounded in reality.

Interpreting Individual Complexes

One of the goals of psychotherapy is to help the patient gain insight into his own problems, including those psychological complexes arising from unconscious roots. Psychotherapy also involves the technical issue of providing interpretation in a way that is relevant for the patient, with consideration of his individual ego strengths, and that properly matches his cultural context. For patients of Asian backgrounds, whose culture emphasizes subtlety in pointing out emotionally delicate matters rather than direct communication, proverbs become useful tools for making indirect interpretations, without offending or embarrassing the patients.

This point is well illustrated by the following clinical situation. A woman brought her husband to consult a folk healer. In the presence of her husband, she spent a lot of time nagging and complaining to the healer that her husband was passive and indecisive, and not successful in his business. She asked the healer what the problem was, and how to solve it. A Western-trained family therapist following system theory might advise that a person's behavior pattern is always a result of interaction with others; a passive husband could be a response to a dominant wife. For the husband to be less passive and more decisive, the wife should behave less aggressively and be less dominant. Such direct suggestion, however, is likely to invite a strong reaction from the wife who is used to behaving aggressively toward her husband. Sensing this reaction, the folk healer invoked a less offensive approach by quoting the proverb "A woman with a tiger's tongue will make her husband not a man." Instead of pointing out to the wife that she was too aggressive and complaining, making her husband feel castrated, the healer used a proverb as a subtle, but powerful, way of conveying the point to her, without embarrassing her too much. Saving face is important to people in Asia. Providing explanations and reasoning in metaphors is one technique for dealing with this cultural requirement.

"Cultural Reframing"

Therapists often reframe a situation for their patients. "Reframing" means stating the situation differently (usually in a positive, rather than a negative, way) to help the patient gain insight into an alternate perspective. This method is commonly used in couples therapy or family therapy in the West, to minimize the complaints and resentments among family members. The method of reframing often used in therapy in Asia is the quoting of proverbs by the therapist, whether it is family or individual therapy.

The following are some examples of reframing. When a patient was devastated by frustration and became depressed, a Chinese therapist often quoted the Chinese saying "Mr. Sai's horse" *(Sai-weng zhi ma)*. The saying is related to a story about an old man, Mr. Sai, who lost his horse. His neighbors came to comfort him for his loss, but Mr. Sai said it was all right. The next day, his horse came back, but it came back with a wild horse. The neighbors came to congratulate Mr. Sai, and he said it was nothing. Several weeks later, when his son tried to ride the wild horse, the boy fell down and broke his leg. The neighbors came to express sympathy for Mr. Sai, but he said it was all right. Several years later, a war occurred, and all the young men in the village were drafted, except Mr. Sai's son, who was rejected because of his leg. All the young men died in the war, but Mr. Sai's son survived. This proverb, which reflects the philosophy of life shifting between success and failure, is often used by therapists to comfort and encourage patients in facing the vicissitudes in life. Looking at the situation in a different framework often helps us feel different about a situation and encourages us to face the problem in a different way.

Wide Range of Choices

One of the advantages of using proverbs is that there are so many, allowing a wide range of choices. This is particularly true in Asian societies, where the custom of using proverbs is prevalent. There are many proverbs with different meanings from which to choose. For example, concerning relationships within a family, the Chinese offer many proverbs emphasizing the beauty of the family, such as "One tries all tastes to discover that salt is the best, one travels around the world to realize a mother is the best" and "A child does not complain that his mother ugly; a dog does not complain that his master is poor." At the same time, there are proverbs indicating problems inherent within a family, such as "There is no chimney without [black] smoke; no pot without a dark bottom" [every household has its own private worries] or "No child is still filial after a parent has been sick for one hundred days." Similarly, the Koreans provide numerous examples, such as "Husband lying on the bed to eat, son sitting on the floor to eat, the wife standing to eat" [illustrating the hierarchy within a family], "Having three daughters could open the door to thieves" (meaning having a daughter is not good, as you will lose all things in the house to dowries, as culturally expected), and "To cut your finger or bleed for another's parent" [indicating that such a filial action is not going to be effective]. The Japanese have many sayings concerning how to view and relate to others, such as "Even a one-inch worm has a half-inch soul," "Even a thief has some reasons" [for his bad behavior], and "Even a *mago* [a pack-horse man] will look different after dressing up." Thus, there are ample proverbs from which therapists can choose, depending on what they want to emphasize, what point they want to stress at a given time in therapy.

Finally, it needs to be said that the application of proverbs in psychotherapy is not always useful. Since many proverbs refer to issues in an abstract way, there is always the possibility that they will be interpreted differently. This is particularly true when a proverb is said in a shortened or incomplete way, leaving room for various interpretations. For instance, the Japanese saying "When a dog walks around, it gets hit (by others)" can be interpreted either as cautioning one to be careful in taking action or discouraging taking any action at all. Another saying from Japan—"A loach under the willow"—may imply that a person should not be foolish enough to expect to be able to catch a loach under a willow tree next to a river each time or that a miracle may happen, and one must be patient for the arrival of opportunity. Likewise, the saying from Korea that "an axe cannot cut its own handle" can be used to warn symbolically that one is unable to criticize one's own mistake or to stress the truth that there is no danger of self-injury.

Thus, in a clinical situation, the patient may choose his own interpretation of a proverb. Without checking with the patient, the therapist will not know what subjective interpretation the patient has made. Not knowing the effect on the patient, the therapist may take the therapy in the wrong direction. This pitfall can be avoided, or at least minimized, by checking with the patient to be sure of the interpretation he is making, consciously as well as subconsciously.

General Implications for East and West

The nature and goal of psychotherapy can be understood from various perspectives. From a cultural perspective, in addition to defining cultural norms, psychotherapy can be seen as reinforcing culturally sanctioned values and coping mechanisms (Hsu 1976) or providing alternatives to culture-defined solutions (Tseng and Hsu 1979). Knowing the proverbs that exist in a particular culture as well as in other cultures will provide the therapist with a wide selection from which to choose, enabling him or her to make appropriate choices and applications.

Using proverbs from a patient's culture will probably enhance culturally sanctioned values and methods of coping; applying proverbs from other cultures will surely expand the resources for alternative approaches. For instance, for Japanese patients, the proverb "Fish's mind, water's mind"

(Japan) may be used to emphasize the need for reciprocal empathy between people according to their traditional cultures; at the same time, it may be useful to know other proverbs regarding interpersonal relations, such as "One who is too humble will be treated as a fool" (Germany) or "Renting a maid's room will result in the master's room being invaded" (Korea).

In the same way, for a British patient, the proverb "Honesty is the best policy" reinforces the values of British culture. At the same time, it may be helpful (and therapeutic) for the patient to be aware that things may sometimes be different, as reflected in the proverbs "Lying can be a convenient maneuver in life" (Japan) and "Honesty is another name for useless" (China).

Clearly there is no right or wrong in the meanings expressed in proverbs. They simply reflect the different views and values that work in certain circumstances in various cultural contexts. Nevertheless, they provide options from our own and other cultures that expand our scope of choices. This is the virtue of exchanges among different cultures, particularly those of the East and West, through cross-fertilization of ideas and values.

Proverbs are seldom used clinically by Western therapists to communicate philosophical ideas to patients. It has been noticed that they are useful for patients with Asian backgrounds, who are used to proverbs in their daily lives. Clinical work tends to point out that the use of proverbs in therapy is beneficial for certain ethnic groups, especially minorities or immigrants, who tend to have a language barrier with mainstream therapists (Aviera 1996; Zuniga 1992). It is a clinical challenge for Western therapists to learn how to utilize various proverbs in the practice of psychotherapy, not only for minorities or immigrants, but also for mainstream patients, taking advantage of the resources of other cultures and using them properly.

CHAPTER 14

An Asian Way of Healing:
The Psychology of Meditation

Suk Choo Chang

Meditation, a representative traditional approach to healing in Asia, originates in a belief in benevolence and, therefore, the fundamental rationality and purposefulness of our minds as well as our bodies. To be purposeful is to be self-healing. This is a belief that is common to all major
traditions of the East, from which issue the views on the causes of and
means of release from suffering (read, neuroses). Suffering originates when
the nature of the mind is clouded and consciousness is filled with artifacts—conflicting thoughts and feelings; release from suffering follows a
cleansing of the consciousness of the conflicting contents. In meditation,
the conflicts are allowed to develop fully to be resolved for experiential and
existential reasons.

The text below consists of three parts: personal experiences of meditation, a view of the psychology of meditation, and culture and healing.
The term "meditation" is used synonymously and, therefore, interchange-
ably, with Zen, which is a transliteration of *dhyana*. (For definitions of these
terms, see Fischer-Schreiber et al. 1994; MacGregor 1989.)

Experiences of Meditation

In the 1980s, I attended three intensive Zen training courses, each lasting
for one week, at a retreat in the northeastern United States. The purpose
was to reduce my anxiety, gain clarity of mind, and experientially learn
the psychology of meditation. I failed in my first attempt, since the drastic
change in surroundings—from my usual habitat to a novel environment

where "normal" communication was essentially prohibited, not only with the outside, but also within the retreat—was intolerable. It was not that one could not communicate, but each participant was made to understand that nonessential communication distracted him from his task. It dispersed and diverted his attention away from his inner world, the "self." What follows is based on two meditation sessions, one week each. Personal experiences are significant, especially for psychological and cultural perspectives, because they inevitably color our views. This is why, on some issues in life, we can be most objective by being most subjective and personal.

The Externals

The venue was a meditation hall situated in a pristine, mountainous countryside in a valley through which brooks run. The facility could accommodate fifty live-in students. It was austere and devoid of modern conveniences, such as radio, TV, telephone, and so forth. The students came with the bare minimum necessities of daily life, such as toiletries and sleeping bags. Two students were assigned to each small room. Since conversation was discouraged, I did not learn the names of any of the participants, including my roommate. It was a community without words. I learned that I can become more socially attentive and observant without conversation. Words can obscure as much as they can illuminate.

Daily life began at 6 A.M. and lasted until 9 P.M. Vegetarian meals were served thrice daily by assigned volunteers. I tended to overeat and often wanted to have seconds, but did not, out of embarrassment. My needs and cravings soon dissipated. Each meal lasted half an hour, and was followed by a brief rest. The balance of the day was devoted to meditation, which was divided into about ten sessions, one hour each. During the hour, fifty minutes were devoted to sitting in meditation proper, and ten minutes to standing up, stretching, or walking. Once or twice a day, there was a lecture by a teacher, usually on a past master's commendable life or an inspirational story, often from a Buddhist sutra. At times, there was chanting in unison. There was also a private interview with the master, during which one could presumably ask any question on one's mind.

For the meditation proper, the students sat in two rows, facing each other across a hall, on a shiny, well-polished wooden floor. Any loose-fitting garment was acceptable for the occasion, but we could also purchase uniforms made for meditation at cost. The total amount of sitting time could be nearly ten hours, minus the periodic stretching and walking. Some literature dwelled extensively on the technicalities of sitting—breathing, eyes (open or shut), posture. I do not recall that the master (or his assistant) ever explained those details. Perhaps they did, but I missed it. It may have been something that I was supposed to ask the master during a private interview. However, I rarely availed myself of an interview. I presumed that I knew the methods, that they were unimportant, or both. I breathed regularly and my eyes were usually shut. The most important technique may have involved the sitting posture, because we spent so much of the day sitting. The posture had to be comfortable, yet alertness-sustaining, that is, relaxed, but alert. Asians are generally accustomed to squatting, but I was impressed that all the other students (mostly native-born Americans) were able to squat all day long. I noticed only one out of fifty students sitting on a chair, possibly for some physical reason.

The Internals

My principal interest in the experience was in the psychological vicissitudes: What happened in my consciousness during the extended and intensive periods of meditation? What happened to my sensations, feelings, and thoughts, the three easily observable signs of my mental activities? Literature generally discerns two out of many approaches to meditation: concentration and meditation. In concentration, a focal point of interest is the state of one's attention: how can a person concentrate his attention? In meditation, our interest is in the mental process, especially thinking and feeling, that is, the content of consciousness. More will be said on this later, but here I took an approach that had elsewhere (Chang 1974) been called the "free association" method. I let my mind roam anywhere it would, without my conscious (ego) interference. The flow of mental content, or the stream of consciousness, was my main interest. Literature mentions two types of meditation, one with a focus (such as a visual image, sound, an idea, etc.). In the second type, the person does not focus on anything, but gives his mind maximum freedom to roam where it will: he neither avoids nor directs his thoughts. In other words, he does not let his ego interfere with his mental flow, giving utmost freedom to the self. Not interfering with our thoughts is one of the more difficult parts of meditation. The difficulties make us realize how much our thoughts are conditioned and controlled by the mores, fashions, ideologies, and theories of the time and place—the culture. Despite the struggle that must have been going on in the mind of each participant, an absolute silence prevailed in the hall.

My mind was generally blurry much of the time that I was sitting. It was like a stream flowing, with muddy water. Ideas and memories floated up, but none was pursued, and they soon faded away. I do not recall any particular idea that could be anxiety provoking. Or it may be that any idea that could have caused anxiety in my usual environment did not cause anxiety in this setting, and soon vanished. This phenomenon has been attributed elsewhere to a reversal of the stream of association from peripheral (and derivative) to more central (and basic) issues. One is an anxiogenic stream of association, the other, anxiolytic. These will be discussed later in more detail.

I was drowsy more often than not. It was an effort to simply stay awake and not slouch, to keep my posture erect. Any laggard in this respect was noticed by a roaming inspector (an assistant to the teacher/master), who would remind the slacker by tapping his shoulder with a bamboo staff that made a sharp, cracking sound. It was an embarrassment I wished to avoid.

Out of the blurry stream of consciousness consisting of any and all imaginable ideas running through my mind, three strands of ideas were more distinct and coherent. They involved sex, food, and, more persistently, past social relations. The sexual imageries and fantasies were more clinical and anatomical than sensual and erotic. I had never seen the genitals so clearly and vividly, even during my rotation through obstetrics and gynecology during my internship training. Occasionally, my mind wandered toward food. I saw the food less in terms of need, such as hunger or satiation, than in terms of aesthetics. One particular image is still vivid. It was a noodle dish called *jajangmyun,* which came with noodles covered with heavy gravy, on top of which were fresh diced cucumbers. I found myself looking at the shape of the diced cucumbers intently for some time. This was a considerable change for me, because my usual mental association of food was in terms of practical needs and values. During the meditation, however, the aesthetics superseded practical questions.

It was not difficult to understand the distinctness of the sexual and food imageries out of the endless stream of fragmentary ideas and imageries passing through my consciousness. After all, what are more basic human instincts and conditions for personal and species survival and preservation? They are questions beyond the realm of theory. They are existential issues. Another reason for the clarity of the images was a clearing of my consciousness—like the clearing of a muddy stream or the lifting of a mist over a mountain range. That is, inchoate ideas and imageries filling and clouding my consciousness were being resolved and cleared out, helping my perception. An incidental experience at that time reinforced this view. One day, during a brief recess, I went outside to refresh myself in the bracing wintry air. As I looked around at the hills, the evergreens, and the blue sky, my perception of the scene could not have been clearer and fresher. The only explanation I have is that some of the mental contents and pollutants were resolved and removed from my consciousness, so that I could see the world better. That is, it was not the world that had changed, but my consciousness that had become more transparent. If so, what were the mechanisms for this change?

An incidental experience related to my back pain was revealing. As I sat day in and day out from early morning until late at night, I kept or tried to keep my posture comfortable, but erect, so that I could stay awake and alert. However, my mind was blurry and drowsy much of the time. One of the problems with sitting so long was a discomfort in my back that required posture adjustments to relieve the muscle tension. The discomfort soon turned into pain, however, and minor posture adjustments no longer sufficed. I was curious how other participants were conducting themselves. Though I could not look around, I could sense that they all seemed to be doing well. Once, however, I heard a man shriek for a few seconds. I have no idea why. Meanwhile, my pain was intensifying, and I needed a major adjustment, such as standing up, lying down, or stretching. Of course, I could not and would not do it. Meantime, I was getting angrier and angrier, perhaps proportionately to my pain and discomfort. I had no idea what I was angry about. In response to my intensifying anger, I felt like hitting or breaking something. I would have felt good if I had, but I didn't. The pain became excruciating. It dawned on me that all my efforts at easing the pain were futile, and there was no way out. At the moment of that realization, I gave up: I resigned myself to my predicament—an insoluble problem—and the pain vanished instantly and totally. I cannot find a better word to describe the experience than "miracle."

In retrospect, my experiences are easy to explain. Because my posture was not good enough, I had tension and pain in my back. I did my best—my ego's best—to relieve the pain. However, that ego was the very source of the discomfort, tension, and pain. What released me from the pain was an instinctive, intuitive, and experiential understanding that prevailed over my intellectual subterfuge. This is what Buddhists call "overcoming one's ego." Another notable experience was an anger felt at times very strongly, but without clear object or reason. Could the object have been myself, that is, my ego, the ego that had brought me to this predicament? Only when I let go of the grip of my ego (sociocultural and personal artifacts) did my innate force for life begin to function, loosening the chains of pain and anger. It may also be noted that, during my struggle with the pain, "I" was totally absorbed with (or concentrated on) the process. This attests to the well-known fact that only after making a total commitment can a person find the meaning and value of the object of his desire and thereby free himself from his attachment. This was a novel experience for me, because normally I would have done everything I could think of to avoid the pain, with innumerable, easy ways of doing so available in modern society.

Finally, the third stream of thoughts involved recollections of my past social relations, beginning with my parents, siblings, family, colleagues, friends, and all other significant people. The recollections tended to be remorseful and wistful, for not having realized and responded to their goodwill, thereby defaulting on my social obligations. Again, this contrasted with my usual pattern of finding fault with others, rather than with myself. In other words, during meditation, I could withdraw my projection. Such an experience attests to the validity of the claim that properly conducted meditation sessions for prison inmates (for instance, in Japan) could induce such contrition for their past deeds that the prison would be filled with a collective wailing.

What does my experience tell me? How does it relate to enlightenment? I can only say that the experience gave me an intimation of what could be. It was like a glimpse of the light at the end of the proverbial tunnel. Or it may be more correct to say that the experience allowed me to sense a light emanating from within.

The view above, incidentally, does not conflict with the description by Patanjali, the author of *Yoga Sutra*, circa 300 B.C. (cited in Wood 1959), to whom "meditation is an unbroken flow of thoughts toward the objects of consciousness" to reach a "shining of the true nature of the object . . . not distorted by the mind of the perceiver."

Culture and Psychology of Meditation

Healing occurs by the principle that underlies and is common to diverse pathways, each of which is bounded by time and place. Meditation is one such approach. Thus, to understand the psychology of meditation, we need to go beyond the culturally and historically characteristic features not only of the approach, but also the observers' patterns of perception and conception. That is, our understanding of the psychology of meditation depends as much on unlearning our presumptions as it does on learning meditation.

How does meditation reduce stress and resolve conflict? There are three types of data available to help our search: historical writings by past practitioners and masters, which are usually esoteric and descriptive; modern observers' more analytical studies; and the findings of clinical applications of meditation, such as in Morita and Naikan therapy. The following have authored literature from which I have learned much: D. T. Suzuki (1949), Humphrey (1972), Wood (1959), Naranjo and Ornstein (1971), Ross (1960), Luk (1972), Thondup (2001), and Watts (1957, 1958).

Based on these authors' works, among others, and leavened by my experiences, described above, the following view on the psychology of meditation suggests itself. A practitioner (or student) places himself in a quiet setting, away from his usual environment. There will be a minimum amount of gratuitous stimuli and distraction. This means that he will be away not only from the unnecessary distractions that fill society today, but also out of the environment in which his neurosis was born and is being sustained. For many, a group setting—a community without words—may be easier and more productive than practicing alone.

The rationale for the verbal abstinence may be the following, all of which have to do with the nature of human language. Language (or words), a quintessentially human trait, has contributed to the best as well as the worst in human society. Language can clarify reality and relations with others, and it can also obscure and alienate. Neurotic conversation is a typically alienating communication. During meditation in a group without words, one becomes more attentive to others as well as to one's inner self.

Literature describes two types of meditation: concentration and free association. In one, the practitioner focuses his attention on an object, physical or mental. The following anecdote illustrates the nature of the concentration: Once upon a time in ancient India, a tournament was held to test marksmanship in archery. A wooden fish was set up on a high pole; the eye of the fish was the target. One by one, many valiant princes came and tried their skill, but in vain. Before each shot his arrow, the teacher asked him what he saw, and, invariably, each replied that he saw a fish on a pole at a great height with head, eyes, and so forth; but Arjuna, as he took his aim, said, "I see the eye of the fish," and he was the only one who succeeded in hitting the mark (cited in Humphrey 1972).

In the other approach, called the "free association" method elsewhere (Chang 1974), the student simply sits and lets his mind wander where it will, without censoring or pursuing. This may be close to what is called *shikan-taza,* or "simply sitting" (Naranjo, in Naranjo and Ornstein 1971; and T. Suzuki 1969). Based on literature on meditation, the clinical application of meditation in Morita therapy, and this writer's experiences, the following view on the psychological impact of meditation on anxiety is suggested (see also T. Suzuki 1969; Murase 1978; Murase and Johnson 1974; Reynolds 1980; and also see chapters 11 and 12 in this book).

All kinds of ideas and feelings float and stream through the mind of the person meditating, sitting motionless for a sustained period in a quiet environment, undistracted. The ideas are generally fragmentary and have little affective coloring. Much of the time, my mind was a blur, without a discernible, coherent thread of thoughts. In the blurry whirl of inchoate mental activities may be an essential mechanism of meditation. My consciousness at that point may have been comparable to a dark room in which little was visible. If a beam of light can be shown through a hole in the wall into a room, however, a person may be able to see innumerable particles floating around apparently at random. In reality, however, their movements follow exacting physical dynamics. All phenomena in nature, as well as in our minds, we believe, have reasons for being. In other words, a lead to the healing mechanism of meditation may be in the invisible mental activities occurring beneath our consciousness.

This conscious versus unconscious approach may be the most significant difference between the Western and Eastern approaches to healing. For instance, psychoanalysis, premised on a belief in the irrational human unconscious, endeavors to gain "intellectual" control of the unconscious. On the other hand, a person who believes in the basic rationality of the human psyche endeavors in meditation to allow the human psyche to fully develop—not by his intellect (ego), but by his innate mental dynamics.

The imageries of food and sex, as noted earlier, were clearer during meditation, but recollections of my social history had the strongest emotional value—feelings of remorse and regret, rather than anger and anxiety. Though the configuration of my mental processes during meditation undoubtedly had idiosyncratic elements, the basic pattern and themes were universal. Are food, sex, and the relationship of the individual to all others not universal, basic, existential issues? Their expression can vary, of course, according to a person's personal and cultural background. For a person who grew up in an environment of affluence and satiation, food may not be an issue; for someone who grew up severely repressed sexually, sexual imageries may be prominent; and for someone who lived in conflict with society, social relations may loom large.

During my meditation, hardly any idea was anxiety provoking, or those that would usually have been were not. The (relative) absence of anxiety during the course of meditation may be due to a reversal of the direction of mental association: from anxiety producing to anxiety reducing, from peripheral and symbolic to more central and substantive. This illustrates the well-known view that symbolic problems can be more anxiety provoking than practical and existential questions.

A number of concepts deriving from Buddhism can be helpful in understanding the mechanisms of the healing power of meditation. They include *toraware, arugamama,* and *sei-no-yokubō.*

Toraware connotes affliction, conflict, entanglement, preoccupation, possession, and so forth. Neurotic processes, in average, expectable circumstances and in an average, neurotic range, begin with a preoccupation, which can progress, if it is not interrupted and reversed, toward an obsession and even to a delusion and psychosis. This progression is accompanied by intensifying anxiety, and the anxiety further drives a person's association to secondary and tertiary issues, which may have only a symbolic connection to the original questions. In other words, progression (or worsening) of neurosis correlates with preoccupation with increasingly derivative questions. Meditation, if effective, reverses the process by reversing the direction of mental association on conscious as well as unconscious levels, as noted earlier. This process is further explained by the concept of *arugamana.*

Arugamama means accepting what is. We need to accept what is inevitable, because fighting against the inevitable—like the sun's rise in the east, ageing, or water seeking lower ground—is ultimately futile. At the basis of the concept is karma, which suggests that an individual's past deeds have inexorable and exacting (psychological) consequences, most notably manifesting themselves as neurosis. That is, neurosis has reasons for being. It cannot be and should not be obliterated or rationalized away, but must be understood. Neurosis is like physical pain. It tells us something about basic, underlying issues or larger, overarching issues that require attention. Therefore, it needs to be understood first, before a person is given analgesics, anesthetics, and tranquilizers. *Arugamama* is not a passive resignation and fatalism, as it is commonly misunderstood to be, but an ultimate affirmation of life (D. T. Suzuki 1949).

Sei-no-yokubō (urge to life) is an urge and drive toward health and life inherent in all living beings. It means that life is purposeful and self-healing. This is a rationale for allowing the mind to heal itself by allowing it to be free of ego interference *(arugamama)*.

How effective is the Asian approach? How widely can it be applied? If the Asian approach has developed in the context of its culture, to what extent can the technicalities separated from their matrix and underlying cultural values be applicable elsewhere? Few reports are available on its clinical application and effectiveness, and what is available requires further substantiation. For instance, T. Suzuki (1967) suggests that the meditative approach called Morita therapy, used on severely anxious patients requiring hospitalization, yielded a 70 percent improvement rate. This finding would be more useful if the criteria were clarified. More recently, Teasdale, Segal, and Williams (2003) asked about various clinical issues related to the meditative approach. On questions related to the application of meditation in various contexts and other philosophical and clinical issues, readers are referred to Bond (1986), Kim and Berry (1993), and Lee and Zane (1998).

What we need today is a framework that can accommodate and encompass both Western and Eastern experiences and values. Neither can explain the other, because they are based on different premises. On the surface, they can conflict and contradict, but, in depth, they complement. On these questions, readers are referred to Alford (1999), Bodde (1953), Chang (1988), Dumont (1966, 1970), Eisenberg (1972), Lai (1984), Montagu (1968). Rhee (1995) has long advocated for common ground, and Tseng (2001) has compiled cultural psychiatric data broadly from across cultural boundaries: Mitchell's (1988) findings on "relational" concepts in psychoanalysis and Kohut's (1984) findings on the place of "experiential" insight; Jung's (1928) psychological and Northrop's (1960) epistemological works on East and West. These works are the basis on which we can continue toward a more wholesome approach to relief from suffering and to the attainment of good health.

In this chapter, meditation, as a representative Asian approach to psychological healing, has been presented. Its healing mechanism is based on purposefulness, rationality, and the self-healing nature of the human psyche, as well as in physical healing, because of which the mental content is allowed to develop fully, according to its innate dynamics, without ego-interference. A practical problem with the Asian approach derives from its very strength—a hindrance of analytical-conceptual drive and clarification. This is where it can learn from Western experiences. Neither the Eastern nor the Western perspective can explain the other, because each is based on contrasting premises and denial of the other. Our concepts of East and West are as much projection as reality. We need an overarching theory that can encompass both. While concerted efforts have been made toward this goal in recent years, many more are needed.

V

Psychotherapeutic Experiences from Asia

CHAPTER 15

Culture-Relevant Psychotherapy in Korea: Clinical Insight

Kwang-Iel Kim

Although Western psychiatry was introduced into Korea a hundred years ago, its practice has not been a success, mainly because many patients still seek help from practitioners of traditional medicine, shamanistic rituals, faith healing, and various other folk remedies. In a psychiatric epidemiological survey of a rural community (Hwang et al. 1996), it was found that only 28.8 percent of psychotic patients were cared for in contemporary psychiatric facilities, while the remainder visited one or more of various other therapeutic facilities, such as nonpsychiatric physicians, pharmacists, asylums, Oriental herb practitioners, and practitioners of other superstitious regimens. Only 32.1 percent of nonpsychotic psychiatric patients had ever used psychiatric facilities, and only 13.1 percent were under psychiatric care at the time of the survey. Others wandered around seeking care from various therapeutic sources, including folk healers. Another community survey (Nam, Sasaki, and Kim 1992), which concerned only schizophrenic patients, revealed that only 11 percent maintained contemporary psychiatric care, while 77 percent alternated between psychiatric treatment and quasi-therapeutic regimens, such as nonmedical institutions, herb medicines, health foods, faith healing, repose, and shamanistic rituals. Twelve percent had never even visited medical psychiatric facilities. Looking at these studies, we can safely conclude that psychiatric practice in Korea has been challenged by quasi-therapeutic practices.

This difficulty can be attributed to the traditional concepts of disease held by the people and the related behavior exhibited by those who are ill. Indigenous concepts of mental illness are rooted in three traditional systems: traditional medicine, shamanism, and Daoism. Each system offers a different view of mental problems. In traditional medicine, each visceral organ is believed to have a specific (symbolic) emotional or mental function. Emotional problems and mental illness are attributed to the disharmony of the internal organs. Thus, mental illness is treated by controlling the corresponding organ. A strong somatizing tendency originates from this disease concept of projection onto the soma (K. I. Kim 1973a, 1999). In shamanism, emotional ailments or mental illnesses are believed to result from an improper relationship with the spirits (which results in spirit intrusion, soul loss, and violation of taboos). Mental illness is treated with magico-religious rituals. Poor insight into intrapsychic problems originates from projection onto the supernatural will (K. I. Kim 1973b, 1999). Finally, in Daoism, mental illness is believed to originate from excessive striving, excessive thinking, and excessive action or work. To maintain health, patients must cultivate their minds, live in harmony with their neighbors, not go against nature, not strive beyond their abilities, and rid themselves of greed. Therefore, repose, cultivation of the mind, and self-training are the key practices for patients according to Daoism (K. I. Kim 1999; Rhee 1990). Many people who are oriented toward tradition have a synthetic view of these three different traditional concepts. They believe that illnesses are caused by multiple origins. For example, when one's body is invaded by demons (shamanistic concept), one fails to control his mind and becomes greedy (Daoistic concept), and, finally, one's heart malfunctions as a result of disharmony between yin and yang (a traditional medical concept).

The illness behavior of the Korean people, in general, is characterized by several aspects: (a) multiple help-seeking behavior, (b) noncompliance, (c) preference for medical facilities that treat physical illness (strong somatizing tendency), (d) preference for magico-religious devices, (e) preference for health foods, and (f) preference for "word of mouth" advice from non-medical laypersons (K. I. Kim 1999).

Within this sociocultural background, some Korean psychiatrists have worked diligently to establish a culturally relevant psychotherapeutic approach. In this chapter, several successful psychotherapeutic approaches that are practiced in Korea at the present time will be described, together with case histories that illustrate the key idea stressed in each approach, whether traditional or contemporary. By using these examples from Korea, it is my intention to discuss how culture-relevant psychotherapy can be performed through various therapeutic modes, with the common goal of meeting the cultural needs of the patients.

Intuitive Approach and Shamanistic Healing

Analytic therapy with an insightful approach is poorly accepted among traditional Korean patients. Rather, an intuitive and projective approach is favored. This point is well illustrated in shamanistic practice. Shamanism is a primitive religious system characterized by polytheism, a proclivity for projection, and a magical approach to the human being's fortune and misfortune.

Shamans use several kinds of approaches to treat illness. The first approach is a divination in which the shaman finds the cause of illness in possession, violation of taboo, soul loss, sorcery, or object intrusion. Based on the nature and severity of the cause, a shaman will recommend one of three procedures: (1) simple praying with simple offerings (e.g., *pudakkori*, with the sacrifice of a hen or cock symbolizing that the hen or cock took the illness away); (2) *salpri*, which involves vigorous dancing by the shaman, who uses a spear and sword to act out how he will drive away the evil spirit or power from the patient's body; and (3) *goot*, a grand healing ceremony that takes sixteen hours to several days to perform twelve separate sessions, each involving the worship of the shaman's twelve gods.

Shamanism has a long history in Korea. It is rooted in traditions that are embedded in the cultural system. In a projective way, all illnesses are attributed to supernatural causes (K. I. Kim 1973b). There is no insightful approach into inner psychological problems. Instead, shamans, in the same way as fortune-tellers, use an intuitive approach. They do not directly ask their clients about their problems, but discover them by forecasting. Their talk is both short and intuitive. It is well suited for people with traditional concepts of illness and help-seeking behavior. For example, an old man from the countryside visits a clinic. The physician asks, "What is your problem?" In reply, the old man complains, "I know that you are a very able doctor. You have to find my problem by yourself. Why do you ask me?" Thus, taking a detailed history may not be a useful practice for some traditional patients, especially those from the country.

Examples of a Shaman's Approach

Case A.   Mrs. Lee, a forty-five-year-old housewife, became sick after moving into a new house. She could not sleep because of bad dreams, and was troubled by palpitations, indigestion, headaches, and worrying about the future of her family. She visited a (female) shaman, who entered into a trance state and called on a spirit for healing. In the shaman's trance state, the following interaction took place:

Shaman: "I am a spirit of your ancestor. Why did you come here?"

Mrs. Lee: "Hi."

Shaman: "You might have some trouble."

Mrs. Lee: "You are right. I'm sick and so anxious."

Shaman: "Hmm. It's very natural. I have gotten angry. You know why?"

Mrs. Lee: "I don't know."

Shaman: "You have not treated me and your parent well. You are not keen to make offerings to the ancestor. You have no filial piety. You became sick because of my anger."

Mrs. Lee: "Yeah. You are right. Because I have a hard life recently" (moved to tears).

Shaman: "I understand that. But you have to treat me as well as your parents sincerely. If you do so, you can get well. And your family will be blessed."

Mrs. Lee was happy with her visit to the shaman and got well, even though her symptoms recurred after six months. Her emotional problems originated from pressure from a moneylender to pay the debt she owed for buying the new house. The problem remained unresolved. She visited the shaman again. The shaman advised her to have a grand shamanic ritual called *goot*. In the ritual, she was choking with tears and fully ventilated her long-standing, repressed grudge against her ancestors. Eventually, it was revealed that she felt bitter against her ancestors because she felt that her misfortune and poverty were due to them. After full ventilation, she got well again.

From this case, we can learn that the shaman's intuitive and projective approach was well suited to the patient's inclination. There was no need to examine her mind intrapsychically or to work on her problem of purchasing a house that was beyond her financial ability. Her problems were simply projected into the culturally sanctioned value system, filial piety, and her repressed feelings of regret were ventilated.

Case B.   Mrs. Min, a fifty-year-old merchant, lost a great deal of money to a swindler. After that, she nearly went mad with vexation and could not sleep because of her anxiety about her future. She visited a shaman.

Shaman: "You came here for your hard time."

Mrs. Min: "You are right."

Shaman: "Who gave you it? Your husband?"

Mrs. Min: "No!"

Shaman: "Money problem?"

Mrs. Min: "That's it."

Shaman: "You were deprived of money . . . by fraud?"

Mrs. Min: "That's it."

Shaman: "How much?"

Mrs. Min: "Several billions . . ."

Shaman: "Oh! That's a large sum of money."

Mrs. Min: "Can I get back the money?"

Shaman: "My god is telling me almost impossible. Sorry."

Mrs. Min: "Oh, my God!"

Shaman: "But . . . it is very good to give up the money. If you keep the money, you'll have the misfortune to . . . die earlier or to be disabled. So, you are better to take it as the price for your escape from misfortune."

After this session, Mrs. Min's emotional symptoms disappeared. The shaman's simple approach was intuitive and effective. The shaman advised the woman to give up her hope to recover the lost money and, in exchange, gave her hope for a long life.

Intuitive Therapeutic Approach of a Psychiatrist

Dr. Se-Jong Lee is one of the most successful psychiatric practitioners in Korea. His therapeutic interview is highly intuitive, suggestive, and simple. It is not based on an established psychotherapeutic system but on an interview tactic developed by clinical experience with insight derived from shamanistic-oriented healing practice.

Two vignettes are briefly presented here as examples of Dr. Lee's brief, intuitive interviewing style, which is very similar to a shaman's (Kim and Kwak 1992).

Case C.   A forty-eight-year-old female peasant from the countryside visits the clinic for the first time.

Doctor: "Heavens! You suffer from hardships."

Patient: "That's my destiny" (begins to cry).

Doctor: "Now, why did you come here today?"

Patient: "I have a sore back."

Doctor: "Only your back? You might also have sore feet and hands and your entire body may be sore."

Patient: "You guessed right."

Doctor: "Headache is an urgent problem."

Patient: "You are a fantastic doctor."

Doctor: "I could read your troubles from your face. You are so troubled. Who gives you trouble?"

Patient: (With a sigh) "My husband."

Doctor: "Dear me! You have to pacify your husband. Don't be angry. Take my medication and calm down."

Case D.   Mrs. Pak, a forty-year-old peasant, visits the clinic for the first time.

Doctor: "You look ill-tempered."

Patient: "You are right! I am ill-tempered."

Doctor: "Now, you are not sick. Why did you come here?"

Patient: "You are right! Why am I troubled?"

Doctor: "Because of your ill temper. Take this medication continuously and calm down your mind."

In the same way a shaman forecasts, Dr. Lee intuitively taps the patient's hidden emotions in order to treat their psychological problems. The patients are gratified by such an approach.

Grafting of Traditional Medicine onto Western Psychotherapy

Many Korean patients, influenced by traditional disease concepts and the approaches of traditional medicine, somatize their emotional problems. *Hanbang* is a traditional medical system in which psychic problems are projected onto the soma (which consequently reinforces somatization). This somatization behavior of patients is frequently not in accord with the psychiatrist's expectations.

An Example of a Therapeutic Approach in Traditional Medicine

Following is a typical example of the approach of traditional medicine.

Case E.   Mr. Kim is a thirty-five-year-old white-collar worker. He has been married for five years to his present wife, with whom he has had frequent disputes as a result of conflicts between the wife and his parents. (Problems between a mother-in-law and a daughter-in-law are common.)

Mr. Kim has suffered from palpitations, insomnia, and a "vacant feeling of the stomach" for several months. He visited many physicians, and was given the same diagnosis of neurosis, which was hard for him to accept. He was sure that his nervousness and insomnia were simply the results of his worry about palpitations, indigestion, and the peculiar feeling in his stomach, and not due to "neurosis."

Meanwhile, he had several thorough examinations, and no physical illness was found. An internist advised him to see a psychiatrist. He was angry with the internist, protesting, "I am not crazy. Why do I have to see a psychiatrist?" Visiting a psychiatrist, he dwelt upon his somatic symptoms. To the psychiatrist's questions "What are you worrying about?" and "Do you have any trouble in the family or in the workshop?" he answered, "I have no problems, no worries in my family or in my workshop. I'm only worried about my indigestion and heart trouble." Upon hearing more questions from the psychiatrist, he got angry, exclaiming, "You have only to cure my heart and stomach! I am not mentally ill!" He refused psychiatric help.

Finally, he visited an herb doctor, a practitioner of traditional medicine, who readily diagnosed him with a "weak heart" after asking simple questions about his symptoms and examining his pulse. He was happy with that diagnosis. The herb doctor prescribed some herb mixture for his weak heart and applied a moxa to his upper abdominal wall. He got well after several visits. Afterward, the herb doctor advised him, "You had better control your mind well. It's very important for your health." The patient said, "Yes, doctor! You are a really noted doctor. It is fortunate that I sought your help."

From this case, we can understand the principle of the herb doctor's approach. He never asked about the patient's psychological or emotional problems. Mr. Kim was gratified with this approach because he was afraid of exploring his inner conflicts. The herb doctor first reinforced the patient's somatization by ameliorating his somatic symptoms, and later suggested that emotional problems could be the cause of the symptoms.

Dr. Lee's Theory of Mind and Therapeutic Approach

A few psychiatrists have successfully approached patients with a flexible combination of traditional medicine (such as yin-yang and hot-cold theories) and Western ideas (such as constitutional disposition/diathesis and a functional framework of the central nervous system). Pragmatic and symptom-oriented, these physicians combine medication; simple, down-to-earth dialogue; and modern technology, such as electroencephalograms (EEGs) and computerized tomography (CT) scans (Kim and Kwak 1992).

Dr. Se-Jong Lee, as mentioned previously, is one such physician. Dr. Lee (1991) developed his own theories of disease by combining the disease concepts of traditional medicine—understood and reevaluated according to the Western framework of neurophysiology—and Western psychiatry (the energy balance theory, the diathesis theory, and the hot-cold theory).

In the clinical setting, Dr. Lee's concepts of psychiatric disorders can be characterized by a symptom-oriented view and somaticism (Kim and Kwak 1992). These ideas are easily accepted by patients who are familiar with traditional medicine. In traditional medicine, the focus is not on inner psychic problems. All psychological symptoms are projected onto the dysfunction or disharmony of the internal organs, thereby reinforcing the somatization tendency.

Dr. Lee's approach gratifies and meets patients' needs. To a neurasthenic patient, he explained the cause of the illness by saying, "You are weak in physical constitution, and you are so tired because of overwork. Your brain has shrunk as a result of excessive thinking and worrying. Your strength is eighty percent of normal. You were born in a weak body. Why have you been so greedy? That is why you became sick. You have to take the medication I prescribe. After doing so, you will recover."

The patient was struck by Dr. Lee's explanation. This approach is suited to a traditional people, and provides culturally relevant psychiatric practice.

Dao and Psychotherapy

For Koreans, "Dao" is a philosophical essence derived from Buddhism, Confucianism, and Daoism in Asian society. In Dao, the ideal state of mind is "nothing" or "empty." It is a state of mind in which one accepts one's feelings, perceptions, impulses, and consciousness without any defensive distortions. Neuroses, therefore, are a state of struggle against the inner conflicts derived from distorted feelings, perceptions, and impulses. Neurotic persons can free themselves from these conflicts through acceptance, not through struggle.

An Example of Dao Healing Practice

Case F.   Mr. Chang, a forty-seven-year-old clergyman, visited an internist for a recently developed headache and palpitations. After detailed laboratory and physical examinations, the internist diagnosed hypertension and anxiety disorder and prescribed antihypertensive and anxiolytic drugs. In spite of the medication, Mr. Chang's blood pressure was still unstable, and he could not overcome his worry about having a stroke. He contacted a Dao practitioner, who advised him to undergo Daoist training. At the initial encounter, the Zen practitioner asked him his problem.

Mr. Chang: "Headache and heart throbbing. Doctor said hypertension and anxiety."

Practitioner: "What do you worry about?"

Mr. Chang: "Stroke . . ."

Practitioner: "Why?"

Mr. Chang: "My father died of stroke several years ago."

Practitioner: "Are you afraid of death?"

Mr. Chang: "That's it."

Practitioner: "That's just your trouble. Hypertension and anxiety are not the real problems. What are you fretting over? You are worrying about too much. Everybody has to die. Your fear of death is quite natural. Accept it. Don't try to struggle with it."

Mr. Chang: "Oh, I know that. But it's very hard to accept it. How can I cope with it?"

Practitioner: "You had better participate in a meditation program. In doing so, you'll be able to accept your trouble, fear of death, and then you'll be peaceful in your mind. And your hypertension and anxiety will disappear, because these came from the loss of your peaceful mind."

Mr. Chang joined the training program at a meditation center. Meditation sessions every other day and monthly lectures on mind control were the main procedures. The meditation sessions consisted of two séances. The initial thirty minutes was spent sitting in meditation; the trainees sat upright on mats holding their heads and backs straight with their hands placed one above the other in their laps. They fully relaxed their whole bodies, keeping their eyes open and mouths closed, and concentrated their mental and physical power into the lower part of their abdomens, with no thought swelling anywhere. They breathed uniformly, inhaling a little longer and stronger than exhaling, keeping consciousness alert. After that, walking in meditation followed for ten minutes. They walked in a row very slowly, holding their heads and trunks straight in an upright posture with their hands placed one above the other in front of them. In their meditation, they tried to have the true nature of their minds manifested.

After three months of training, Mr. Chang was free of fear and anxiety, even though he was still taking antihypertensive drugs.

Daoistic Psychotherapy

The research of Dr. Dong-Shick Rhee and his colleagues at the Korean Academy of Psychotherapists on the therapeutic application of Dao seems to be promising for developing a culturally relevant model of psychotherapy (J. K. Kang 1990; Rhee 1990, 1993). Their psychotherapeutic approach is not very different from Western insight-oriented psychotherapy. They unravel the nature and the origin of conflicts by way of a dynamic viewpoint. However, the method of resolution is different. The patients are advised not to refuse but rather, to accept their conflicts, and then to transcend them. Only by doing so can patients be free of the conflicts (Rhee 1993).

The practice of Dao itself is not a psychotherapeutic system, but a philosophical teaching. There are strong psychotherapeutic elements in Dao, such as the attitude, process, and methods of developing insights into one's mind. In applying the principles of Dao to psychotherapy, practitioners not only understand and treat the pathological condition, but also help patients discover and cultivate their health potential. Western psychotherapy is more concerned with the negative aspect, and is theory and verbal oriented. In contrast, Daoistic psychotherapy is more concerned with the positive aspect, and is reality and training oriented. Moreover, Western psychotherapy treats neurotic anxiety only, whereas Daoistic psychotherapy treats even existential anxiety. In this way, Daoistic psychotherapy is closer to existential psychotherapy than is Western therapy (Rhee 1990).

Among the present 2,100 psychiatrists in Korea, about 50 have been trained in the Daoistic approach and use Daoistic psychotherapy in their work. This approach, I think, is a successful and culturally relevant use of Western psychotherapy.

Imago Therapy and Tea Therapy

Other unique therapeutic approaches, imago therapy and tea therapy, were developed approximately three decades ago by psychiatrist Dr. Jong Hae Kim.

For imago therapy, Dr. Kim (1972) designed and chose various images of Buddha for meditation therapy according to the developmental stage of each patient's personality. These images are arranged in order, and the patient meditates before the Buddha image that reflects his present level of personality development. In this way, the patient learns to confront and accept his conflicts, and finally becomes free from them. This can be understood as modified meditation.

Tea therapy is a supplementary treatment method that is derived from the Buddhist tea ceremony (Kim and Rhee 1975). In the tea ceremony, there are particular rituals involving the boiling and sipping of a cup of tea. During the ceremony, which requires full concentration, one can see into one's mind and learn to accept conflicts.

Dr. Kim applied these two therapeutic approaches in supplement to usual psychiatric treatments. Unfortunately, he passed away two decades ago, and the efficacy of his therapies was not fully investigated. I speculate that these approaches would be beneficial to neurotic patients but risky for psychotic patients (because the therapies might provoke fantasies and lead to confusion of reality).

Western Psychotherapy and Korean Culture

Finally, I would like to comment on whether or not Western psychotherapy (especially analytic psychotherapy) is suitable for Korean patients. Clinical experience suggests that Western psychotherapy is useful, but only for Westernized and psychologically minded persons. Frankly speaking, many Korean psychiatrists frequently confront substantial difficulty in carrying out psychoanalytic psychotherapy on many Korean patients, especially those who are soaked in traditional values. This problem has been an object of much debate in a cross-cultural context (Chang 1998; Tseng 1999).

Two issues regarding Western psychotherapy and Korean culture will be elaborated here.

Differences in Perceptions of the World

The first issue is that there is a difference in the way Western and Eastern people perceive the outer world and the self (Chang 1988). Westerners are inductive and analytic. They also tend to be oppositional; human beings are separated from nature, and frequently nature is considered to be in opposition to humans and may even need to be conquered by humans. Westerners explore the causes behind problems, and a situation is recognized according to a cause-and-effect scheme. Because the self and the world are seen as oppositional, conflict with the outer world follows, leading to endless struggle between the self and the world. Personal inner issues are evaluated by analyzing the self and the world and searching for a resolution accordingly.

In contrast, the Easterner's perception is deductive, and harmony is highly valued. Things are recognized in harmony. Human beings are part of the universe and exist in harmony with the principles of the universe. The self and the outer world are seen as harmonious rather than oppositional, and human beings try to accommodate themselves to the world. For example, in interpersonal relationships, the self and others are not clearly differentiated. The self is perceived as "us" in the collective consciousness (Chang 1988, 1998). Rather than analyzing inner problems according to cause and effect, Easterners tend to accept things as they are.

Because of these differences in perception, Western psychoanalytic psychotherapy, which is inductive and analytic, may not be applicable to Koreans, especially those with traditional attitudes. In psychotherapeutic situations, serious resistance is often encountered when patients are faced with issues that call for insight into their inner conflicts. They easily somatize, project, and emotionalize. They also tend to respond more to intuitive than analytic approaches. Traditional medicine and shamanism, which have affected traditional concepts of illness and treatment, have no implications of analytics, inductiveness, or oppositionalism.

In traditional medicine, illness is understood as disharmony with nature, and health is understood as harmony with nature. Disharmony among the somatic organs is illness; thus the treatment is to make them harmonious. Such perceptions can result in a strong somatization tendency (K. I. Kim 1973a, 1997).

In shamanism, all the good and bad of life depend on the will of supernatural beings. The solution is to control the supernatural will. This perception brings about a strong projective tendency. There is no place for seeing through inner problems in either traditional medicine or shamanism.

Another cultural heritage, Dao, is somewhat different. Insight into internal problems is an important aspect of Dao, but eventually a solution is sought by accepting the problem as it is, rather than struggling with it (K. I. Kim 1997; Rhee 1990, 1993).

As mentioned above, I believe that different perceptions of the self and the outer world are major reasons for Korean patients' resistance to Western psychoanalytic psychotherapy.

Intellectuality versus Emotion

The second issue is intellectuality and emotion. Contemporary Western psychotherapy is intellectual and logical. Its principal approach is to make unconscious conflicts conscious. A cause-and-effect relationship is prerequisite in this process, and logical inference is required. Of course, there has been recent recognition in Western psychotherapy that without emotional resolution there is no place for logical and intellectual insight. However, many Korean patients vividly express their emotions in psychotherapeutic settings, even though repressed emotions are transformed into somatization or projection in some cases. Therefore, we have learned through psychotherapeutic experiences that approaches to these repressed emotions are far more important than the theoretical or logical approaches of psychotherapy with Koreans. It has been pointed out (Rhee 1993) that approaching "the central feeling" is the most important aspect of conflict resolution.

In fact, the shamanistic approach is directed to emotions repressed for a period of time. A patient's anger is externalized, and the patient is then soothed. In every séance in a shaman's ritual, the shaman turns into supernatural beings and talks with a patient to stimulate and provoke his repressed emotions to the level of ventilation (K. I. Kim 1973b). In some séances, shamans express vigorous hostility toward supernatural beings, parent symbols acting for the clients. In other séances, shamans deeply sympathize with clients' sorrow and soothe it for their ancestors.

In closing, it can be said that contemporary Western psychotherapy is often successful with some Koreans. However, for patients with traditional values, it is necessary and wise to modify it to fit the traditional Korean mind. Various culture-relevant psychotherapeutic approaches that have been carried out in Korea and described in this chapter seem well suited to traditional Koreans.

While human nature is universal, its manifestation is considerably different from culture to culture. In other words, the core structure and function of the human psyche are surrounded with a thick membrane of culturally influenced behavioral patterns. In psychotherapeutic situations, therapists have to unravel this cultural membrane. This process is called a culture-relevant approach (K. I. Kim 1997).

There is often a considerable difference between the public's (including the patient's) view of illness and that of modern medicine. Consequently, the patient's illness behavior often is not in accord with the physician's expectations. This is especially true in psychiatric practice.

Many Korean psychiatric patients still visit practitioners of traditional medicine and participate in shamanistic rituals, faith healing, and other quasi-therapeutic treatment modalities. This is one reason why Western psychiatry and Western medicine have not been very successful in Korea. However, some Korean psychiatrists have successfully developed and applied culturally relevant approaches to psychotherapy by using traditional therapeutic resources that are more meaningful to people in Korean culture.

CHAPTER 16

Culture and Psychotherapy in Korea: Past and Present

Suk Choo Chang

As material conditions improve and society stabilizes, there has been an increasing awareness of the need for psychological well-being. Consequently, psychology, psychiatry, and treatment have been developing rapidly. A majority of practitioners are practical and eclectic, availing themselves of various methods from diverse sources—traditional, Western, pharmacological, and others. In the development of psychotherapy, one important question has been theoretical in nature: how can the approaches born of a long Western tradition be applied to the Korean mentality, which has been imbued in thousands of years of distinct traditions, many of which lie beneath a thin layer of modernity? This question suggests that the future development of psychotherapy significantly depends on the nature and integration of the two traditions. There has been a concerted effort to better understand the issues involved, and we can look forward to the further development of psychotherapy in Korea.

The following text includes a sketch of Korean history and culture (at a level where it is a variation on the Asian themes reflected in Confucianism, Buddhism, and Daoism) and of psychotherapy in Korea, examines four case vignettes, and discusses the problems and potentials of modern psychotherapy in South Korea.

History and Culture of Korea: A Sketch

The beginning of Korea is shrouded in the mist of the remote past. Increasing findings in recent years, however, suggest human activities in the

Korean Peninsula by the Paleolithic period (forty thousand to fifty thousand years ago). The people lived in caves, used stone tools, fished, hunted, farmed, and gathered fruits, berries, and edible roots. About eight thousand years ago, in the Neolithic period, polished stone tools and pottery were in use. By seven thousand years ago, there were clearly humans present throughout the peninsula. Their societies were clan based, and the people were shamanistic, believing that every object in the world possessed a soul. By the eighth to the ninth centuries B.C., bronze implements from northeast Asia were in use, and by the fourth century B.C., the continental culture, including iron tools and writing, flowed in from China. In short, the earliest identifiable culture in Korea consisted of two principal elements and layers: the Northeast Asian complex and the continental-Sinitic (Fairbank, Reischauer, and Craig 1973; K. B. Lee 1984; P. Lee 1997; Osgood 1951).

Beginning in the first century, tribal societies began to form into kingdoms. Thus, the Three Kingdoms arose during the first and fourth centuries. By the eighth century, they were unified into the Silla dynasty (eighth to tenth centuries), which was followed by the Koryo dynasty (tenth to fourteenth centuries). The Koryo was taken over by the Chosŏn (1392–1910), the last and longest Korean dynasty. During the Chosŏn (or Yi) dynasty, Korea was invaded, occupied, and colonized by Japan (1910–1945), until its liberation at the end of World War II.

The liberation was ephemeral, however, because, in 1945, Korea was divided into the North and the South by global geopolitics beyond its control. Confusion and turmoil followed for five years, until the not surprising outbreak of the Korean War (1950–1953), in which the avowed objective for both was the reunification of the country. The war to end the division was the most destructive in the long annals of Korean history: four million people perished, and the land was razed from one end to the other. That war to unify the country was followed, sadly, by an even more impervious separation, and the two Koreas took remarkably contrasting paths of development: extraordinarily ideological and dogmatic for one, and, after a series of military dictatorships, pragmatic, laissez-faire, and mercantile for the other. Although the division and contrasting development of the two societies are as much correlates of the global geopolitical dynamics, an insight into the Korean contribution, especially the Korean "personality," will considerably enrich the usual geopolitical perspective. Whereas the ideology hardens as the economy withers in the North, in the South, despite (or some say because of) a series of dictatorships, the economy developed spectacularly during the 1980s and 1990s, until the infamous "Asian financial crisis" in 1997. One of the central causes of the crisis has been thought to be the "human infrastructure" of the economy. This human factor is also a Korean variation on the general Asian theme, on which a psychological perspective would be useful. In other words, social development in both the North and South cannot be separated from global political relations, and Korean culture and psychology. A clarification of the basic issues involved in psychotherapy in Korea will help us understand its complex nature, which includes the global environment and Korean history, culture, and psychology. In other words, psychotherapy is as much a cultural as it is a psychological problem.

Culture is a totality of humankind's legacy. As an integral whole, culture embeds and surrounds individuals from the cradle to the grave and molds their personalities into a basic and normative form, the reason for the consonance between the patterns of culture and personality.

It has been suggested that Korean culture can be seen in two layers and components, the pre-historical Northeast Asian complex and the historical continental. The former includes the "shamanistic," while the latter refers to the continental-Sinitic, as reflected in what have been called the Three Teachings—Buddhism, Confucianism, and Daoism. Since Buddhism is historically related to Hinduism, somewhat analogous to the historical relationship between Protestantism and Catholicism, Korean culture can be said to be a variation on the general "Asian" (or Eastern) civilization.

Since my focus in this chapter is more on the conscious layer of Korean psychology and culture, it dwells on the Three Teachings. The basic themes of the teachings are responses to questions on man's relation to the cosmos (Daoism); man's relation to the two realities (the illusory and the real) and the two selves (the false and the true) (Buddhism); and men's relationships to each other (Confucianism). Please see chapter 14 herein and Chang (1988); Kakar (1995); H. A. Kim (2000); L. I. C. Kim (1999); Roland (1988). For further discussion on broader cultural, psychological and philosophical issues, readers are referred to Jung (1928, 1954); Northrop (1960); and Watts (1957, 1961).

Psychotherapy in Korea

Modern psychiatry was introduced into Korea via Japan in the early twentieth century. It was largely Kraepelinian, organic, and descriptive (Chang and Kim 1973), as it was in Japan (Chang 1965). More significant contact with Western psychiatry occurred during the Korean War, through young American psychiatrists in the armed forces stationed in Korea. This psychiatry was refreshing because it opened a window not only to the technical field, but also to the cultural matrix of the dynamic Western world. After the war, a large number of Korean medical graduates went to the United States for further training. Many of them went into psychiatry, some by default, and others by choice. After their training in various aspects of psychiatry, many returned to build a new psychiatry in Korea. They and their trainees were the builders of modern Korean psychiatry.

A wide range of psychiatric treatments, including psychotherapy, has been introduced and practiced. For instance, there are Freudian, Jungian, Sullivanian, and other groups. One group, led by Rhee (1984, 1993), has been more active than others, and has a wider following. Rhee is known for his advocacy of what he calls Dao-oriented psychotherapy, in which concepts from Buddhism, Confucianism, and Daoism are liberally combined with psychoanalytic and philosophical concepts from the West. A majority of the practitioners are eclectic and practical, however, using whatever means and views are available—biological, psychological, Eastern, or Western. In psychotherapy, however, the analytical approach drew particular interest. The reasons for this, one may suggest, are more cultural than technical. Western psychotherapy presented, if implicitly, a refreshingly novel way of looking at life for a society and consciousness that had been imbued and weighted down with thousands of years of tradition.

As the Koreans became more familiar with analytic, especially psychoanalytic, approaches, a number of questions arose, including "How can the therapeutic approaches born of Western tradition be applicable to Korean patients reared in ages-old tradition? How can the two, with their contrasting premises on life, be reconciled?" Some said they are not applicable. Others found no difficulty in applying the analytic approach to Korean patients (Cho 1999b; Rhi 1999; K. I. Kim 1984). Still others suggested that the difficulties are due to ignorance of the nature of both the Asian and Western traditions because, they claim, most basic, analytic concepts have been prefigured in Asian traditions, namely, the Three Teachings (Rhee 1984, 1993; Kang 1989; Rim 1999).

For theoretical debates on psychotherapy, it will be useful to begin with a glimpse of the actual practice of psychotherapy. The following four vignettes are my abstractions and translations of four cases, case A by Cho (1999a), and the remainder by Rhi (1986).

Four Case Vignettes

Case A.   Mrs. A, a thirty-nine-year-old woman, was referred because of her anxiety by the psychiatrist who had been treating her twelve-year-old son. Her symptoms began following a panic attack she had had one day eight years before, when she was taken to an emergency room, medicated, and referred to the psychiatric clinic. In addition to the anxiety, she had marital difficulties and problems with her son's behavior, including his hypochondriasis, fear of heights, separation anxiety, and undue craving for physical closeness to his mother. Mrs. A's mother, M, left home during her teens, because M was mistreated by her stepmother, and went to Seoul, where she worked as a waitress in a restaurant. While working, she met a man who wanted her to bear him a son. When she bore a daughter, however, he was disappointed and deserted her. Thus, she brought up A (our patient) as a single mother.

After high school, Mrs. A wanted to go to college but was unable to do so, for financial reasons. Instead, she took a graphic design course and obtained a job, overcoming severe competition. At the job, she felt discriminated against because of her insufficient education. While working, she met two men with whom she became involved. However, she was rejected by both because their parents disapproved of her background. She married her third choice, with whom many conflicts soon developed. He was afflicted with a considerable inferiority complex, was abusive, and had difficulties holding a job. She knew little about his background, except that he had grown up in a poor household under an abusive father.

The above extract is from the early part of a long-term treatment program (fifty-five sessions by the time of this report, and still going well). That it has been going well for an extended period is, in my view, due to the analytical approach being used. That is, there are two reasons, among others, in traditional Korea that make extended psychotherapy such as this case difficult: gender separation and hierarchic social relations. In such situations, psychotherapy tends to become educational (as in teacher-student relations) and moralistic (as in parent-children relations). This makes it difficult to sustain a long-term male-female psychotherapeutic relationship in the modern sense of psychotherapy because the relationship can deteriorate and become too intense or congealed. What an analytical approach provides, if only implicitly, in such traditional Korean circumstances, is separateness of and equality between the therapist and the patient. In other words, the analytic approach can provide certain novel regulatory social mechanisms. More will be said on this later.

Case B.   Mrs. B, a twenty-seven-year-old married mother of two, came for treatment with a one-month history of depression and suicidal thoughts. The loss a month before of a considerable sum of money in an ill-conceived investment was the immediate precipitant. In addition, she had been suffering from marital conflict. Her husband was the youngest of five siblings and twelve years older than the patient. He was "a truly filial son, as Confucian teaching advocates." He took his meals with his mother, and had his wife and children eat separately. His mother was so pathologically controlling that her daughter-in-law (the patient) was restricted from going out of the house. The patient pleaded with her husband to live away from his mother's house, but he responded, "If you cannot live with her, I have no choice but to divorce you." With the therapist's support, the patient became more assertive, and her husband more flexible. By the eighth session, their marital relations had improved, and the patient's depression eased.

As in the case above (Mrs. A), family conflict is a common reason for consultation, and problems are usually seen in terms of family problems. This is inevitable in a society where "social harmony" is the ideal and where couples stay together despite sometimes intolerable conflict. In traditional Korea, the family member who suffers most is the daughter-in-law, at the hand of the mother-in-law. This situation has changed greatly already because of rapid urbanization, which makes it financially difficult to keep a large family physically together. To characterize the son's behavior as "truly filial and Confucian" is a common and convenient rationalization.

Case C.   Mrs. C, a thirty-one-year-old woman, complained of chest discomfort, labored breathing, numbness and trembling of the hands, poor sleep, weakness, and guilt feelings toward her husband for her difficulty in doing housework. She had been anxious and depressed since the birth of her child. She also had strained relations with her parents-in-law. She had grown up very attached to her own mother. Her husband was the oldest son of the head family of a clan, which has a great symbolic meaning in a traditional Korean family, giving him considerable privilege and responsibility. For instance, he was expected to be responsible for major clan events, such as memorial services for ancestors. Though men are responsible, the more practical work—such as preparing the feast for a large gathering—goes to the women, in this case to our patient. However, she felt incapable of meeting the family's needs. With the therapist's support, she spoke with her parents-in-law, who fortunately understood her predicament and relieved her of many of her duties. This case, incidentally, is an illustration of somatization, a common condition in Korea, whereby mental conflict is easily converted into somatic symptoms.

Case D.   Mrs. D, a fifty-one-year-old housewife, complained of hot flashes, headaches, poor sleep, generalized muscle pain, excessive dreams, and anxiety. Physical findings were noncontributory. The patient had married the oldest son of a *yangban* (traditionally landed, often hereditary, upperclass) family from a part of South Korea where the honor and decorum associated with family name and status have been rigidly defended. The family was financially comfortable. A source of Mrs. D's conflict was her new daughter-in-law, who had married her oldest son. The daughter-in-law was from a Christian family, while Mrs. D's family was steeped in tradition, especially Confucian. There was an understanding, before the marriage, that the daughter-in-law would relinquish her affiliation with the church after her marriage. She did not keep her promise, however. Instead, she and her husband often avoided important family affairs, such as ancestral memorial services. This was intolerable to Mrs. D, who had expected to be able to relegate her own burdens and responsibilities to her incoming daughter-in-law and have a more leisurely old age, basking in the thought that she had accomplished her mission in life, a hope that seemed unrealizable.

Culture and Psychotherapy in Korea

The vignettes above show little that is peculiarly "Korean" (or Asian), suggesting a universality of basic human predicaments. There are certain cultural (or surface) features of which we need to be reminded, however, lest they mislead observers, especially when we are rendering Korean social and human drama into English. In this quest, the issues relating to the form and norm of social relation have priority. This is because the issues expressing traditional cultural values as the norm of social relations can conflict with the Western mode of social relations. These are some characteristic features in psychotherapy in Korea as well as in other Eastern societies. However, these issues are generally hidden or lost in the process of translation, as will be shown below.

The model of traditional social relations in Korea is hierarchic and deferential, in contrast to the egalitarian and assertive Western norm. The significance of these models derives from the fact that each (Eastern and Western) has complexly woven psychological and philosophical (and theological) rationales, which contribute to the form of psychopathology, and also to the (conscious and unconscious) criteria for mental health and personality.

Take "hierarchy," to begin. The Asian social hierarchy, in intent and theory, is based on "virtue." This should not be forgotten, even though, in practice, social relations in Korea are as much power based. (For the problem of social hierarchy in Asia, readers are referred to Dumont 1966, King and Bond 1985, and Bodde 1953.)

In Korean social relations, deference and reciprocity, not self-assertion, are the norm in average circumstances. In upbringing, children are taught to think more in terms of their obligations than their social rights. That is, between two persons (A and B), if A finds B more "virtuous," A will be more respectful of B, and psychologically hierarchic relations will follow. The traditional psychological ideal ("egolessness") and the social ideal of "harmony" are consonant values. On these points, readers are referred to chapter 14 in this book.

Such hierarchic sensibilities are weakening, it is said, as Korean society modernizes and democratizes. However, it is important to question to what depth such change is occurring. While equality in a legal sense is essential to modern society, we should recognize not only reality, but the need to recognize moral hierarchy. The point is that legal equality and moral hierarchy exist in practice, but not in theory. The Korean language illustrates some of the issues above. In Korean, the question of "hierarchy" has a great effect on lexicon and grammar (Chang 1988). This is one of the basic cultural issues directly relevant to social psychology and psychotherapy, but it is hardly visible through the English-language perspective because, in the process of translation, all such matters are automatically deleted to conform to English-speaking sensibilities.

It is these cultural characteristics that contribute to the shaping of various psychological symptoms and personality and to psychotherapeutic relationships. For instance, the relationships inevitably take a hierarchic form, most clearly illustrated in the language the therapist and the patient use with each other: they both use deferential language, usually omitting the first-person pronoun ("I"). The therapeutic ambience that is created is difficult to convey in English.

It has been said that some people and certain ethnic groups tend to convert their psychological problems into physical (or somatic) complaints. Indeed, many do so, most notably, maltreated daughters-in-law, as well as the poor and uneducated. However, a principal reason for their somatization is that they are culturally and socially inhibited in verbalization. We commonly say, for instance, in developed, especially American environments, that the poor and uneducated are not very suitable for psychotherapy. This view suggests that somatization may be less the patient's, and more the therapist's, problem.

The major Asian traditions, on an intellectual level, are highly introspective. This introspection, in addition to the norm of deference, can facilitate psychotherapy, except for the following reasons. (1) A normally hierarchic social relationship, together with a belief (conscious or unconscious) in human relatedness and interdependence, can easily lead the therapeutic relationship to one that is similar to the relationship between parent and child or teacher and student. This is understandable because otherwise, the relationship can become too involved and even congealed, making "therapy" impossible. In other words, an egalitarian relationship may be a necessary condition for modern, insight-oriented psychotherapy, such as psychoanalysis. (2) Another problem in psychotherapy is the traditional separation of the sexes. The problem of gender relationships is universal, and one with which we are still grappling. Involved in the problem are much wider cultural issues. One can only say that the Korean version of the problem requires far more studies than are currently available.

Culture shapes the way we look at the world and life. This is true with the way we perceive and classify psychiatric illness. An anxiety is a condition that is so pervasive that it is a nodal point in psychopathology, the illumination of which will shed a great deal of light into our mental lives. In Korea (and elsewhere in Asia), anxiety tends to be expressed in the social sphere as "social" anxiety as defined in DMS-IV (American Psychiatric Association, 1994). Further, whereas in the usual American social anxiety, the patient is afraid of being embarrassed by others, in the Korean type, the fear is often reversed, as that of embarrassing others (see S. H. Lee 1993 and a review article by Chang 1996). Viewing such forms of social anxiety as culture-bound is itself culture-bound, since the expression of psychopathology follows psychodynamic principles, whatever they may be. However, the ways we conceptualize and label them are eminently local and temporal, that is, they are cultural products (see Prince 1991; Chang 1999). Finally, it may be noted that, in modern psychotherapy, especially analytical, the treatment is conducted principally through an intense social relationship, whereas the traditional Korean approach, born of a culture that believes the entangling karmic chain to be the cause of suffering, is conducted by separating the person from all others.

In conclusion, a rapid development in psychotherapy is meeting an increasing need for psychological health in South Korea. A basic question that must be asked is how to adjust, reconcile, and harmonize the traditional approach and ethos with those from the West. In this respect, much still needs to be done.

CHAPTER 17

The Historical Trends of Psychotherapy in China: Cultural Review

Wen-Shing Tseng, Sing Lee, and Lü Qiuyun

China is a vast society, with an ancient history, a large, heterogeneous population, and a huge land area. It would be enlightening to examine how the Chinese people in the past have sought, and presently seek, psychological help, either through folk, indigenous, or modern, professional methods, when they encounter psychological problems. This chapter attempts to reveal the trends of psychotherapy, defined in broad terms, that have occurred in this society of 1.3 billion people, in order to gain some insight into the psychological healing obtained from a cultural perspective.

It is apparent that the development of psychotherapy as well as successful treatment outcomes are influenced not only by medical knowledge and professional theories, but also by social and cultural factors. For instance, the acceptance of psychotherapy in a society can be obstructed by political ideology. This was true in Germany during the Nazi era, Russia during Stalin's time, and China during the Cultural Revolution. The extent to which psychotherapy will prevail is also influenced by economic systems. In Scandinavian societies, for example, medical practice is heavily oriented toward socialism. Because of the emphasis on community-related health programs, it is difficult for individually focused psychotherapy to prevail (Kelman 1964). This phenomenon is also witnessed in the United States, where the insurance system determines the patterns of psychotherapeutic practice. That is, the service is available only for those who can afford it or whose insurance covers it. Further, the cultural environment within a society itself will also contribute to the fate of psychotherapy. Psychoanalysis never flourished in Old Vienna, where it originated. However, analytically oriented psychotherapy became popular in the New World, where changing society and creating one's own life were valued in the pioneer atmosphere (Schick 1973). How cultural factors affect psychotherapy and the kinds of cultural adjustments that are needed to provide effective therapy are common concerns that deserve attention not only from a scientific point of view, but also from a practical perspective. In this chapter, the situation in China will be examined to reveal how various forms of healing practices have been used in the past and present and how psychotherapy took its own course under the influences of social, political, economic, and cultural factors.

Folk Healing Practices from Premodern Times

The art of psychotherapy will be defined broadly here to include various forms, from indigenous, folk healing practices to contemporary, professional psychotherapy. It has been pointed out that the orientation of healing practices for psychological problems encompasses a broad spectrum, which includes the supernatural, natural, somato-natural, medical, philosophical, and psychological (Tseng 2001, 557–560). Following that order of orientation, let us review first the healing practices that are basically oriented toward the supernatural or the natural and have prevailed from premodern times.

Shamanism

"Shamanism" is used here as a generic term referring to the indigenous healing practice in which the healer enters a dissociated and possessed state. It is basically oriented toward the belief in a supernatural power that can be utilized for the resolution of problems. It is speculated that the geographic heartland of shamanism is central and northern Eurasia, with widespread diffusion to Southeast Asia and the Americas. This folk practice was prevalent in China in the past, particularly in the north and in the southern coastal areas. Through a religious ceremony, a shaman can work himself or herself into a trance state in which he or she is "possessed" by a god. The shaman enters into an ecstatic trance that enables him or her to link up with the supernatural and work through its powers. The client can then consult the supernatural through the shaman for instructions on dealing with his or her problems.

The causes of problems are usually interpreted according to folk concepts such as loss of the soul, sorcery, spirit intrusion, or violation of taboos. The disharmony with nature that is the basis of the concept of feng shui (geomantic belief) is often interpreted as the cause of problems by Chinese shamans. Coping methods suggested are usually magical in nature, including prayer, the use of charms, performance of extraction, exorcism, or other therapeutic, ritual ceremonies. The goal of the healing practice is to resolve the client's problems. Utilizing supernatural powers, acting as an authority figure, making suggestions, and providing hope are among the main healing mechanisms provided by the shaman.

The shaman, in the same way as other supernaturally oriented indigenous healers, often performs a special ceremony to impress the people in the community that he or she is blessed with supernatural powers. For instance, a shaman may use a specially designed instrument with which to injure his or her body to show that there are no ill effects, or undertake a dangerous action to demonstrate that he or she is protected by a supernatural power and comes to no harm. In an anthropological study of shamanism in Taiwan, Kleinman and Sung (1979) concluded that, in most cases, indigenous practitioners "must" heal, because the treatment of disease plays a small role in the care of the disorders that are usually treated successfully. He raised the possibility of a placebo effect in the shaman's treatment of severe, acute, and life-threatening or chronic diseases. Given that individuals and families who seek such help usually share the explanatory models of the shamans, a powerful placebo effect is likely to contribute to treatment successes, especially for chronic illnesses that do not have specific biomedical cures.

The practice of shamanism has been discouraged in modern China and is presently prohibited by the government in mainland China because it is supernatural and not scientific and could bring harm to people. However, it is still practiced in rural areas in a semisecret way. In Hong Kong and, especially, Taiwan, the practice is still observed, although recent empirical studies are wanting.

Divination

Divination refers to the act of trying to foretell the future or the unknown by occult means. It relies on mysterious, magical, or religious methods. Since the interpretation of divine instruction is usually provided by the diviner (or an interpreter), the interaction between the diviner or the interpreter and the client becomes an important variable.

The practice of divination as a way of dealing with psychological problems is observed around the world and has a wide range of methods. Some are very simple, others more complicated (Tseng 2001, 527–530). In ancient China, turtle shells or the bones of big animals were burned during divination ceremonies, and divine instruction was interpreted through the cracks made from the heat. Later, an elaborate divination system called *chien* was developed.

To obtain answers to questions about their lives, some Chinese visit temples for divination. After a sincere prayer to the god of the temple, the person will ask for divine instruction, which is provided through a fortune stick that the person selects. There is a fortune paper corresponding to the number on the stick with an answer written on it. This practice is called *chien* drawing in Chinese.

In *chien* drawing, the client asks for a divine answer to a specific question (such as whether it is good or bad to move, change jobs, or get married to a particular candidate under the present circumstances, and so on). There is usually a set of *chien* (which could number twenty-five, fifty, or a hundred, for example) from which a special stick is picked at random by the client. The *chien* (divine instruction) contain predesigned answers for each category of issues about which clients may inquire, such as moving, changing jobs, family problems, treatment for sickness, and interpersonal conflict.

To understand the psychological effects operating in divination, J. Hsu (1976) studied the *chien* drawing practiced by the Chinese in Taiwan. Analyzing the preset answers, she found that they were designed to reflect culturally sanctioned resolutions to certain problems. For instance, in an agricultural society, moving is usually discouraged; in cases of family or marital conflict, the client is often advised to be patient and try to resolve the conflict with harmony; lawsuits are discouraged; if current medical treatment is not satisfactory, it is suggested that the client seek other therapy. In other words, *chien* is designed as an institutional way of reinforcing culturally sanctioned coping methods.

The divine answer is written in the form of an ancient poem or in language that is difficult for a layperson to understand, and the client therefore needs to consult *chien* interpreters in the temple. The interpreters are usually educated elders who are experienced in life. Thus, a single "counseling transaction" actually takes place between the interpreters and the divining person.

The basic therapeutic operation is performed to provide an instructive answer for the problems presented. These answers fall on a spectrum of "luckiness." If the *chien* is a good one, the instructor may advise the client to avoid unexpected misfortunes. In the case of a bad *chien*, ways of avoiding trouble are recommended. Thus, the transaction is psychologically helpful to the client in finding a definite way to address his problems. Naming effects are among the healing mechanisms operating in divination. It is assumed that human life is regulated by the supernatural. It is the basic goal of the person seeking help to find the proper way to comply with the universe through "divine" instruction. This manner of counseling is still actively observed among people of different age groups in Taiwan and Hong Kong. It is officially discouraged in mainland China because, like shamanism, it is supernatural and considered potentially harmful to people.

Fortune-telling

The system of reference shifts from the supernatural to the natural in the practice of fortune-telling. Based on the concepts of microcosm and macrocosm, fortune-telling is based on the belief that human life and behavior are parts of the universe. The nature of problems is usually explained in terms of an imbalance of vital forces or disharmony with the natural principles that rule the universe. The objective of the practice is to help the client find out how to live compatibly with nature and adjust to the environment more harmoniously.

Fortune-telling can be divided into several types according to the sources of information used. Astrology involves the belief that a person's life is correlated to and influenced by the movement of the stars; thus, their movement becomes the essential source of information for predicting one's life course. The Chinese use an ancient record of universal change, the *Oracle of Change (Yi-jing)*, for fortune-telling. A person's date and time of birth and the number of strokes in the Chinese character for his or her name are the information needed to calculate his or her fortune.

Physiognomy is based on the assumption that there is a close correlation between the mind and the body and that one's character, life, and fortune can be read by examining one's physical features. It is assumed that a person is born with a certain predisposition, which shows in his physical appearance and will lead him to manifest certain behavior patterns. A physiognomist tries to help a client understand his own character and behavior patterns, learn how to make good use of his talents and, at the same time, make up for his shortcomings.

Although the basic assumption underlying fortune-telling is that every person has a predetermined course in life, this "fate" is not absolutely unchangeable, but may be subject to modification. Thus, the purpose of fortune-telling is to find a way to adjust one's fortune.

As in psychotherapy or counseling, it is important to note that the interaction between the fortune-teller and the client is a significant variable. Also, it is not so much what fortune is found from the available information, but how the information is interpreted and used by the fortune-teller in counseling the individual client that is most critical. Clearly, the fortune-teller can make projective interpretations in order to "counsel" the client. This phenomenon is similar to what is often observed in the practice of divination.

Even though the basic orientation shifts from a supernatural to a natural one, and the sources of the practice are the rules of nature, the therapeutic operation, like divination, is still characterized by offering folk-natured interpretation and providing concrete guidance for a client in making choices. Because the practice is based on the concepts of microcosm and macrocosm, complying with the fundamental rules of nature is its basic goal. Thus, it is based on the Eastern philosophy that is richly expressed in the ancient *Oracle of Change* and elaborated in its extreme by Daoist thought: seek to comply with the rules of nature.

In Hong Kong, where much of life is based on past custom, people are still very concerned with feng shui, and for any special event, such as moving into or building a new building, it is generally the custom to consult a feng-shui master for guidance. Families frequently consult a fortune-teller for problems of health and questions regarding household prosperity, corporations, for business growth. This practice is also observed in Taiwan, but is discouraged in mainland China, although to a lesser extent than shamanism and divination.

Meditation Exercise: *Qigong*

The practice of meditation is not psychotherapeutic work in a strict sense. However, many people who practice meditation or meditation-related exercise claim that they obtain considerable benefits from it, such as improving their body-mind condition and promoting good mental health. Such practices may therefore be considered a form of folk psychotherapy, if we define psychotherapy broadly as an activity to promote a healthy mind.

We know that yoga originated in India. In China, one kind of meditation is called *qigong*, which, in Chinese, literally means the exercise of "vitality" *(qi)*. It is aimed at regulating the force of vitality through the practice of meditation-related physical exercise. It was practiced by the Chinese in the past and is still practiced today, attracting the interest of many Westerners.

According to the clinical observations of C. Y. Wu (1997), a psychiatrist who is also a *qigong* master, the practice of *qigong* can help a person obtain tranquility of mind, diminish psychosomatic problems, and improve psychological conditions, particularly in the areas of self-image and self-confidence. She speculated that the mechanisms of support, suggestions, and provision of hope all work on the person. However, she also warned that some practitioners, particularly those with the premorbid personality traits of hysteria or borderline personality disorder, may develop mental complications from the practice of meditation, such as minor or major psychiatric disorders, including various forms of psychoses. This has been confirmed in a sizeable number of observational and controlled studies of *qigong*-induced mental disorders in China (S. Lee 1996; Lin and Kuo 1991). The mechanisms for such intriguing psychopathologies are unclear, but there is a need for careful clinical screening and instruction prior to practice.

Whether yoga or *qigong*, the practice of meditation has a somato-natural orientation. Meditation or meditation-related exercise seeks the therapeutic effects of regulating body-mind relations and vitality, and obtaining tranquility. The unspoken goal of the practice is harmony with nature. As Wu (1997) pointed out, the practice of mediation does not involve language interaction between the master and the practitioners. It is well suited for some Asian people, who are not used to communicating and expressing their psychological problems. Meditation can also be carried out either in a group or individually, at any time, without the need of a master once the technique is learned. Therefore, it is practical, especially in view of the limited psychotherapeutic resources in China.

Lay Counseling by the Elderly

In addition to special folk-counseling practices, such as divination and fortune-telling, in the past and even now, to some extent, many Chinese utilize the lay counseling available in their community. This is particularly true in rural areas, where the elderly of a village still have some authoritative power and influence over the lives of the people. Whenever there are severe problems within a family or between a couple, or conflict between families, the head of the village is consulted for advice. Although he is an ordinary person, he is usually respected or, at least, regarded as a person with authority who will look into the matter fairly and make suggestions objectively for resolution of the conflict. The suggestions are mostly based on common sense and are often didactic in nature. However, the power of authority works in such a way that it affects the clients who seek resolution of their problems. As a long-time member of the community, the head of the village often has detailed information on the background of the clients and their families, and is able to offer appropriate solutions. Needless to say, the suggestions are often culture-oriented ones. Since the head of the village is not professionally trained, only experienced in life, his suggestions for coping with problems are nonspecific in nature. However, they are available when they are needed. Thus, their value cannot be ignored.

Transient Early Development in the Era of the Republic

Chinese traditional medicine was the most well developed in the ancient past, and is still actively practiced in contemporary China and the rest of the world, including the United States (Barnes 1998). It is characterized by its own unique system of theory and practice (Tseng 2001, 151–155) and is strongly oriented toward the concept of the close relationship between body and mind, emphasizing the importance of maintaining the health of the mind in order to regulate the body. Stated differently, mind-body dualism is not a guiding principle. Thus, in contrast to modern medicine, there is only fragmented knowledge of psychiatric disorders as defined in the modern classification systems, and there is no formal practice of psychotherapy (Tseng 1973b). There is little knowledge on how to deal specifically with certain emotional problems through psychological treatment (Xu 1997).

During the end of the Qin dynasty and the early stages of modern China, many scholars were given the opportunity to go abroad and to study new sciences in the West. This included general medicine as well as psychiatry. It was during this time that psychotherapeutic concepts and practice were introduced from the West into China. Formal psychiatric facilities were developed for severely ill psychiatric patients, but there were far fewer outpatient clinics for less severe patients. There were signs of interest in developing psychotherapy in modern China, and a society of psychotherapy was even established. However, repeated civil wars within China and the invasion of Japan before and during the Pacific War of World War II created massive turmoil and destruction of social life in China. All psychiatric services were seriously interrupted, as was the movement toward psychotherapy. The practice of psychotherapy almost disappeared entirely during these several decades, while people were preoccupied with their struggle for survival.

Destruction and Creation around the Era of the Great Leap Forward
Antipsychotherapy Trend

When the civil war ended shortly after World War II and China was taken over by the Communist government, the focus was on rebuilding the nation, with an emphasis on socialism. There was an anti-Western atmosphere to the times. Individually focused psychotherapy was considered the product of Western capitalism and was criticized as unsuitable in a socialist country. The analytic concept of the unconscious and the sex-oriented theory of personality development were also considered unsuitable. Psychotherapy was severely criticized during the early period of communism and faced heavy suppression during the Cultural Revolution in particular, when any tradition, establishment, or product from the West was subject to criticism and destruction.

Politically Implemented Community Workers

The special social system developed in Communist China is still in effect today. It was a tight community system under the leadership of a local political committee. In the city, it was called the "street committee"; in rural areas, the "village committee." This social organization sent a committee member to visit each household periodically, to provide services for practical living needs, including physical and emotional needs. At the same time, the committee member ensured that each family was following the rules that had been set by the government. To use a Western term, this unique "social worker" was a member of the community, selected for his or her political background, often being a loyal Party member, who provided care, and, at the same time, regulated the lives of every community member and family in his or her defined area, either a block of streets in the city or a village in the country. In this manner, the community was both cared for and tightly regulated at the same time.

The committee member provided various needed services. In addition to taking care of daily life matters, including behavior, the member also supervised medical care. This may have included the supervision of psychiatric care for mentally disordered patients as well as counseling for psychological problems encountered by any individual or family. In other words, the committee member replaced the old system, in which the head of the village provided counseling for emotional problems for any person in the community who was judged to need it. Needless to say, the new service was heavily colored by the political ideology behind it.

Group Meetings for Political Thought Reform

Religion and superstition were radically opposed during the early stages of Communist China. Professional Western-psychotherapy was opposed, and divination, fortune-telling, and all other superstition-related healing practices were prohibited. Instead, a new form of mental work was developed. People from the same working unit, either a manufacturing plant, school, or farming village, were expected to meet periodically. They discussed the teachings of Chairman Mao and how to apply them in daily life. Criticisms and suggestions were encouraged, and pressure from the group was maximally utilized. The group was characterized by a political tone and served as an instrument for political thought reform. Thus, in a way, it offered politically based, group "rational-emotive" therapy in a work setting.

Rapid Integrated Therapy

A specific mode of therapy for neurasthenic patients, the so-called rapid integrated therapy, was developed by Chinese psychiatrists in China during the 1960s. At that time, China was vigorously pursuing the Great Leap Forward. According to Mao's political ideology, people were encouraged to use all means, including traditional or indigenous methods, to obtain rapid economic expansion and improvement. In order to reach the target of social achievement, every member of the society was mobilized to participate in economic production. However, in the area of mental health, neurasthenic patients were identified nationally as one of the major patient populations that was not able to participate fully in social production. Rapid integrated therapy for patients with neurasthenia ("weakness of nerves") was developed in response to political demands in these social-political circumstances.

The therapy was characterized by a combination of various therapeutic procedures. Educational group therapy was coupled with individual counseling, physical exercise therapy (including *qigong* exercise), and any needed somatic therapy, such as herb, acupuncture, or drug therapy. Thus, it was referred to as "integrated" treatment. Patients, in small, organized groups, were treated as outpatients in a short-term course of therapy (usually four weeks) for rapid improvement. Therefore, it was called "rapid" therapy. It was claimed that the therapy was useful for treating neurasthenic patients, and the program grew throughout the nation.

According to Chinese psychiatrists (C. P. Li 1997), this form of therapy was effective for several reasons. Neurasthenia was originally considered by patients to be a chronic disorder. However, this pessimistic view was corrected through instruction in group therapy. The nature of the disorder was explained and the possibility for improvement emphasized in the introductory teaching, so that patients were motivated and activated for recovery. Many neurasthenic patients (mostly students and intellectuals) tended to be overinvolved in mental work in their daily lives, lacking adequate physical activities. By participating in the therapy, which emphasized a balance of mental and physical activities, they normalized their life patterns. The therapy included instruction and group activities, integrated with needed somatic therapy. Group activation and regulation of the daily life activities of the mentally exhausted person were recognized as the mechanisms for therapy.

However, no matter what mechanisms were claimed to be useful, it is clear that this mode of therapy was a product of the time, and the prevailing social atmosphere and political ideology functioned as the main force behind its effectiveness. When the Cultural Revolution started in 1966, creating extensive social turmoil, this therapy was disrupted and then discontinued. Recently, this therapy has been reactivated and practiced under the new name of "enlightment-practice psychotherapy" (*wu-jian* psychotherapy) (C. T. Li 1998, 822–828). Apparently, it focuses on cognitive therapy, with an emphasis on actual practice, without the use of sociopolitical force.

Renewed Interest in Psychotherapy after the Open Door Era
Renewed Interest in Psychotherapy

Since the end of the Cultural Revolution, China has undergone rapid market reform and opened itself to Western influence and ideas, including those of psychotherapeutic theory and practice. As Li and colleagues (1994) pointed out, while there is a great need for psychotherapy, there is a lack of formal psychotherapeutic skills within the Chinese medical profession. During the Cultural Revolution, all established systems suffered destruction, under the excuse of building a new system. All high-level education was discarded, and qualified medical care was interrupted for several decades of social chaos and internal conflict. Most medical practices were neglected, including the practice of psychotherapy. There was a great lack of professional workers after this period of political turmoil, including psychiatrists and related mental-health workers. The nation was in need of recovery from this professional vacuum.

Rapid Spreading of Morita Therapy

It was within this social and professional setting that the knowledge and skills of various modern psychotherapists were introduced into China. These included Morita therapy from Japan. Even though Morita therapy was originally developed as a unique psychotherapy (please refer to chapter 11 herein), it should be pointed out that, like Naikan therapy (please refer to chapter 12 herein), it never became a mainstream mode of psychotherapy, even in Japan. Actually, the trend toward these therapies was fading, to some extent. However, surprisingly, once Morita therapy was introduced into China, it spread quickly and, at least for a while, became a popular mode of psychotherapy. There were several reasons for this interesting phenomenon. As Cui (1997) pointed out, the basic philosophy behind Morita therapy, namely, Zen (Chan in Chinese) Buddhism was originally developed in China. Thus, it involved a familiar concept for Chinese laymen and was easy to accept and use in therapy. The practice was simple and easily performed by psychiatrists, even without intensive knowledge of psychotherapy. This suited the situation among Chinese psychiatrists after the disruption of professional training during the Cultural Revolution. Finally, and perhaps most important, the Morita therapy foundation offered financial assistance for its practice in China, a practical reason that could not be ignored.

New Demand for Psychotherapeutic Service

After the inhibition of (Western) psychotherapy ceased, psychotherapy became prevalent in China, like a dry sponge that had started to absorb water. Numerous counseling and psychotherapy clinics began to appear in general and psychiatric hospitals. The number of patients seeking psychotherapy increased, and there was a demand for more trained psychotherapists. This was a remarkable phenomenon, in contrast to the trend in many other societies, both in the East and West, where biologically oriented psychiatry was becoming the mainstream of psychiatry and emphasis on psychotherapy was declining.

There are several reasons for this new interest in psychotherapy. First of all, China has experienced great socioeconomic improvement recently, and the old problems of struggling for a living are gradually ending for most people. Many have begun to be concerned with the quality of their lives, including their emotional lives. Thus, there is a great demand for therapy to improve their mental health. Further, many patients are not satisfied with the biological psychiatric approach and being treated merely with medication. They are, so to speak, thirsty for psychological treatment.

In spite of the comments made by some Western researchers in the past, indicating that Chinese patients tend to somatize their problems and are less likely to work on their problems at a psychological level, the reality is that the Chinese people are very psychologically oriented. Even a layperson knows the wisdom that it is better to work on the mind than on the body. This is reflected in the everyday saying *Gong-xin-wei-shang,* which literally means "It is superior to work on the heart (mind)." This saying originated from knowledge of military strategies, which indicated that a psychological attack (on an enemy) is superior to a physical attack. Clinicians need to understand that patients present somatic complaints in the early stages of therapy merely because they are following a cultural pattern of presenting somatic complaints. Patients are often ready to work on psychological and emotional issues, as long as the therapist is skillful enough to guide them to do so (Tseng 1975).

Clinical experiences with Chinese patients has revealed that the patients' dynamic complex is relatively transparent and easy to understand by the analytically oriented therapist. In other words, many Chinese patients are not only eager to receive psychotherapy, but it is easy to carry out dynamic psychotherapy with them, as their problems are less defensively covered up (Tseng 2002).

The rapid and uneven social, economic, and cultural changes occurring in contemporary China have contributed to the considerable stress observed in marital and family systems. Young couples prefer to choose their own mates rather than have their marriages arranged by their parents, as was the custom several decades ago. With improvements in the quality of life, people have begun to be concerned about the emotional aspects of marital life. The phenomenon of the extramarital affair is gradually increasing, and the rate of divorce has doubled two or three times over the past two decades ago, even though, in contrast to Western societies, the overall rate of divorce is still very low. However, maintaining harmonious and satisfactory marital relations is becoming a major concern. Under the official "one couple, one child" family policy, the size of the family has been greatly reduced, and learning how to raise a single child is a major concern for parents. This change in the family system is particularly significant because it is in such contrast to the traditional emphasis on the value of a large family. Thus, a common concern among mental-health workers is how to provide marital and family therapy. Further, special attention is being given to providing marital and family therapy that is relevant to Chinese people (J. Hsu 1995). Family therapy can also be a means of studying Chinese culture itself. For example, Ma et al. (2002) identified several themes from the treatment of anorexia nervosa in Hong Kong through a multiple-case-study approach. They found that self-starvation in Chinese families is an expression of love and control, a combination of the anorexic daughter, family loyalty, and the powerlessness of the mother. These themes shed insight on how women in Hong Kong embody the conflicting transformation of its culture.

Finally, because of the increasing recognition of the magnitude of the problem of suicide and attempted suicide in China (Lee and Kleinman 2000), the last decade has witnessed substantial interest in developing crisis intervention and telephone counseling hotlines (Ji 1995).

Concern for Culture-Relevant Psychotherapy

While the practice of psychotherapy is rapidly increasing, there is also an increased concern with developing psychotherapy suitable for the Chinese (Cheng, Cheung, and Chen 1993; Cheng, Baxter, and Cheung 1995). To provide culture-relevant psychotherapy, Tseng (1995) has made suggestions in the areas of technical adjustment, theoretical modification, and philosophical reorientation. He has pointed out that, in addition to a series of technical adjustments, there is a need to modify certain theories to make them congruent with the Chinese mind. These include the basic concepts of the self, ego boundary, and interpersonal relations. There are several issues involved in coping with problems that deserve careful consideration from a cultural perspective, including suppression versus uncovering, conservativeness versus aggression, and harmony versus conflict (Tseng 1995).

Aware of the need for culturally suitable psychotherapy, some Chinese psychiatrists have already started experimenting with culture-oriented psychotherapy. For instance, Chinese Daoist cognitive psychotherapy has been advocated and tried by a group of clinicians (Young 1997). They claim that using Daoist philosophy as an indigenous cognitive therapy is useful for Chinese patients suffering from generalized anxiety. Change is slow at first, but effective over the long term (Zhang et al. 2002).

Empirical Validation

As Chinese psychiatrists recognize the need for psychotherapy, some of them have carried out empirical research that has assessed the efficacy of psychological interventions, often versus nontreatment or drug therapy. In the past decade, an increasing number of such studies can be found in Chinese literature. For example, Jin et al. (2001) compared drug therapy versus psychotherapy in the treatment of depression. In accordance with Western studies, the effects of drug therapy and psychotherapy were comparable, but psychotherapy was superior to drug therapy in preventing relapses as well as improving cognitive and social functions. Zhang et al. (2000) assessed the usefulness of "comprehensive" psychotherapy in dysphoric patients with coronary heart disease. This was composed of a mixture of support, relaxation training, and cognitive restructuring. With respect to negative emotions, physical functions, and quality of life, patients who received psychotherapy did better than those who did not. Although these empirical studies are of both academic and clinical interest to Chinese psychiatrists, their effect on clinical practice in China is limited at present.

Final Comments

Several remarks can be made from this review of the trends of psychotherapy in China. It is clear that, in Chinese society, there have been, and probably always will be, multiple healing systems, whether folk or modern. Each different healing practice provides certain functions and services for the society as a whole (Tseng 1978). It should also be pointed out that geographical and subcultural differences have created many variations among Chinese living in mainland China, Hong Kong, Taiwan, and overseas.

Historically in China, social and political factors, as well as the severe circumstances of war, greatly affected psychotherapy. Now, with the Chinese facing rapid sociocultural change, it is a challenge for clinicians to provide mental health care to meet their changing psychological needs.

A major public health challenge is determining how to provide services for such a huge population, almost one-fifth of the world's population, in the midst of rapid market reforms. Clearly, it is impossible to provide an adequate number of mental health workers for the population from within the community, particularly in a limited time (Tseng et al. 2001). This problem is heightened by the official discouragement of any form of supernaturally oriented folk healing practices, particularly religion-related ones. While access to these practices by laypeople is hindered, the effect of the previous network of politically oriented "social workers" in the community is fading. Providing professionally trained counselors or psychotherapists despite widespread stigmatization and professional endorsement of a biological model of mental illness is an acute demand and a problem, as well. Not surprisingly, the lack of professional counselors and psychologists has popularized telephone hotlines as a convenient form of psychological intervention in many parts of China (Xie, Weinstein, and Meredith 1996).

Although empirical studies are lacking, the psychotherapeutic function of traditional healing methods can hardly be denied. As Barnes (1998) illustrated in her study of the indigenization of traditional Chinese healing in Boston, acupuncture and other Chinese healing practices are readily psychologized to become forms of psychotherapy. Because there are so few professionally trained psychotherapists, it is worth exploring how these methods can be enhanced in China to provide indigenous forms of psychotherapy that provide financial incentives for practitioners.

Beyond this, developing culture-relevant psychotherapy is an important matter (Tseng, Lu, and Yin 1995). It will take time for clinicians to experiment with various forms of therapy and, through clinical experiences and empirical evidence, to prove their clinical as well as cost effectiveness. However, one thing is clear: the Chinese in general are very interested in working on their mental health issues through psychological therapy, and there is a great demand for psychotherapeutic services.

CHAPTER 18

Integration and Application for Therapy

Wen-Shing Tseng

This book has presented many important issues regarding culture and psychotherapy. It has stressed that psychotherapy cannot be competently practiced without knowledge of the impact of culture on therapy (chapter 1). Psychotherapy is subject to the historical, social, medical, and even political backgrounds of the society in which it is undertaken (chapters 15–17). The nature and kinds of psychopathology may change in association with cultural changes, and therapy needs to be modified in order to manage the changing nature of psychopathology (chapter 3). Culturally relevant and competent psychotherapy requires an understanding of the culturally patterned ethnic personality of the patient and the nature of unique psychopathology he or she manifests (chapter 2). Based on this understanding, culturally geared, unique treatment models and therapeutic approaches will emerge (chapters 11–14).

As indicated in the beginning of this book, the impact of culture on psychotherapy can be examined from multiple perspectives, including technical, theoretical, and philosophical dimensions (Tseng 1995). A review of the literature, however, reveals that most past studies of culture and psychotherapy have concentrated primarily on the technical adjustments needed for culturally suitable psychotherapy. Few scholars or clinicians have examined culture and psychotherapy on theoretical or philosophical levels. It has been the aim of this book to fill this vacancy by focusing on theoretical and philosophical issues, and to indicate their implications for the East and West. Two efforts have been made in this regard. One has been an in-depth examination of the parent-child relationships and conflicts described in cultural products and the solutions sanctioned by various cultures (chapters 4–7). The other has been to elaborate on the traditional thoughts and philosophies embedded in Eastern culture that have had significant impact on the goals of therapy and the way in which therapy is carried out (chapters 8–10).

Comparative Characteristic Features of East and West

This book has described and compared the differences in Eastern and Western approaches to the healing of the mind at the conceptual, philosophical, and methodological levels. These differences will be summarized briefly in this section on the basic views of the world, human nature, the self, personal development, the fundamental perception of suffering and ways of resolving problems, and the essential mode of therapeutic process that is advocated. Highlighting the differences between East and West will help us to understand the differences that exist in these two cultures and to reflect on how culture influences the art of psychotherapy. However, a caution is in order. For the sake of contrast, the diverse ways of healing are described in an extreme, dichotomized manner; in reality and in clinical practice, they are not polarized to that degree. Therefore, overgeneralization should be avoided, and each situation should be examined with caution.

Concerning Worldview

The Asian considers human beings to be a part of the universe. The relationship between an individual and the outer world needs to be harmonious, rather than oppositional. As illustrated in Daoist teaching, the essence of life is to follow the Way that is observed by the universe. It stresses that humans need to try to accommodate themselves to the world and harmonize with universal principles (chapter 9). In the Buddhist view, man arises from nature and therefore will get along most effectively by collaborating with nature, rather than trying to master it (chapter 10). This is in sharp contrast to the contemporary Western (scientific) view, which believes that humans should challenge nature and, if not conquer the world, at least try to control it.

Human Nature

To the Asian, human nature is naturally benevolent (rather than evil), and the goal of life is to cultivate this benevolence. This view is highlighted in Confucian thought (chapter 8). The Western (or Christian) concept of original sin is unheard of among Eastern people. Asians view instinct and desire as natural parts of the self; it is necessary to regulate them, but they are not seen as primitive or evil.

About the Self (or Ego)

Boundaries and relations with others.   In interpersonal relationships, Asian people do not clearly differentiate the self and the others, and the self is perceived as "us" in the collective consciousness (Chang 1988, 1998). Self-centeredness is considered the reason for problems (or pathology), and egolessness is viewed as a solution to problems, as stressed in Naikan therapy in an extreme way (chapter 12).

Passion and desire.   According to Buddhism, problems arise from a person's blind passions. The ideal goal is to free one's self from such lusty desires (chapter 10). The Daoist Way is to reduce desire—a very difficult concept for Westerners and even contemporary Asian people to follow, with their preoccupation with achieving material success and fulfilling their need for enjoyment (chapter 9).

Personal Development

Universally, each individual has to go through his own personal development, not only biologically, but psychologically, in a sequential manner. In general, the parent-child (particularly mother-child) relationship is critical. Nevertheless, there are variations in how an individual grows within different cultural contexts (Tseng 2001, 787–791). It has been illustrated (chapters 4–7) that the mother-son relationship is more significant in personality development among Asian people, and the father-son relationship among Westerners, in forming an emotional complex.

Mother-son complex.   Asian family values encourage an intense parent-child relationship, and the early stage of development is characterized by a very close mother-son relationship. This is reinforced by the absence of the father figure in domestic life and Eastern child-rearing practices.

Not only does a close emotional relationship exist between mother and son, but, as illustrated in Indian legend, a Hindu mother expects her son to plan his life around her and see her as the center of the universe—referred to as the Ganesha complex (chapter 5). The son is so close to and idealizes his mother in such a way that he has difficulty accepting the "ugly" side of women (his spouse), as related in myths and folk stories concerning the taboo of a man looking at his spouse in special circumstances (when she is in an "ugly" form) (chapter 6). The intense mother-son relationship may even cause the son to want to murder his mother—known as the Ajase complex (chapter 4). Thus, the extreme closeness of the mother and son in the East can cause many emotional complexes, even in the pre-Oedipal stage, which are unfamiliar to scholars in the West.

Father-son complex.   In contrast to the mother-son complexes in the East, many Western myths and folk stories highlight a triangular parent-child complex relating to the phallic stage (Tseng and Hsu 1972). The Greek story of Oedipus was utilized by Sigmund Freud, the founder of psychoanalysis, as the core of his theory of psychopathology relating to neuroses. Perhaps the intensity of the parent-child conflict during personal development can be attributed to the emphasis on man-woman relationships (including husband-wife relations) over parent-child relations and the stress on individual independence and growth in Western societies.

Interpersonal Relations

Culture needs to be comprehended on different levels, such as the ideal, the actual, the stereotypical, and the deviant (Tseng 2001, 34–35). This is particularly true in terms of interpersonal relations. Ideally, Asian people are enculturated with the value of harmony in interpersonal relationships. However, in reality, this virtue may not always be followed, particularly when there is gross conflict with others.

In contrast, Western people are enculturated with the idea that a person should fight for his own rights and assert and defend himself. At the same time, it is considered desirable to "love your neighbors" (as advocated in Christianity) and to consider every person as equal (as stressed in the concept of democracy).

Nature of Suffering

It is a Western philosophical assumption that life should be happy and enjoyable, without any problems or suffering. If problems or suffering occur, it is necessary to resolve or remove them. This is the basic attitude of psychoanalysis, which is a product of the West.

For the people in the East, as reflected in extreme Buddhist thought, life itself is suffering. Poverty, sickness, unhappiness, and death are all a part of life (chapter 10). It is inevitable for a person to encounter suffering, and, when he does, it is natural to face and accept it. This is the core of Eastern therapy, exemplified by Morita therapy (chapter 11).

Patterns of Problem Solving

Resolving problems.   The basic premise of Western psychotherapy is the philosophical assumption that a person's life should be happy and enjoyable; if it is not, the problems preventing happiness should be eliminated and resolved. Psychoanalytic work aims to resolve unresolved complexes. Behavior therapy seeks to modify (or recondition) nonadaptive behavior. The thrust of cognitive therapy is to correct nonfunctional (or incorrect) views about the self or life. Thus, the basic aim of psychotherapy is to solve problems.

Accepting problems.   In contrast, Eastern healing practices stress a different path for dealing with problems. Rather than analyzing inner problems according to cause and effect and trying to resolve them, it is recommended that people accept them as they are. This philosophy of acceptance is stressed in Morita therapy (chapter 11). In Daoism, "doing nothing" is the best way to do things, in keeping with the course regulated by the universe (chapter 9).

Mode of Therapeutic Process

Logical and instructional.   Western psychotherapy is founded on logic and carried out under a therapist's guidance. Even in psychoanalysis, the therapist helps the patient obtain insight, even though the therapist is supposed to only passively participate in the therapeutic process. In behavior therapy, the patient is given a standard set of therapeutic activities to follow.

Intuitive and experiential.   In contrast, some Eastern psychotherapy takes a more intuitive approach, as illustrated in the Korean examples of culture-relevant therapy (chapter 15). Enlightenment through experience is valued in Naikan therapy (chapter 12) and, similarly, in Zen meditation (chapter 14). These approaches cannot be programmed or standardized, but require the actual experience of self-enlightenment.

Suggestions for Clinical Applications

Finally, the purpose of this book is not so much to examine psychotherapy from the perspective of the East as opposed to the West, but to learn how to perform psychotherapy in a cultural context, within the broad spectrum of variations found in comparisons between the two cultures. In other words, the major concern is how to adjust to and carry out culturally relevant, suitable, competent, and effective psychotherapy in accordance with the cultural background of the patient. This culturally relevant approach is attempted here, from the standpoint of technical adjustment, theoretical modification, and philosophical reorientation, three aspects that need to be considered in depth for culturally competent psychotherapy (Tseng 1995).

Technical Adjustment

Orientation toward psychotherapy.   From the beginning of the therapeutic relationship, it is important for clinicians to be aware that patients and their families may have different levels of understanding of and orientations toward psychotherapy, and various expectations about receiving treatment, that may or may not be congruent with those of the therapist. Beyond their individual backgrounds, these differences can relate to the medical and social history and to their views, beliefs, and experiences of the society from which they come (chapters 15 and 17). Some consider it natural and desirable help-seeking behavior to contact psychiatrists when they have psychological problems, and to obtain psychotherapy; others consider it disgraceful to seek help from psychiatrists and useless to obtain "talk therapy." It is crucial for the clinician to find out the patient's and his family's orientation and knowledge toward therapy, and to carry out treatment accordingly, including providing guidance and education when necessary.

Therapist-patient relationship.   Every society defines the proper relationship between a superior and subordinate, such as a therapist and patient. In a culture that stresses authority, the therapist will be expected to act authoritatively in performing therapy. In contrast, when equality is valued, it is more desirable for the therapist to relate to the patient in a more or less democratic way. Otherwise, the therapy will not fit cultural expectations of the therapist-patient relationship and will hinder the therapeutic process.

Communication and explanation.   A crucial aspect in therapeutic work is the communication between the healer and the client. This is particularly true when the therapist and the patient do not share the same language or culture. In such intercultural therapy, an important issue is overcoming the language barrier. However, even when the therapist and the patient share a common language, caution is still needed, as the meaning behind the words and values expressed in language need careful attention and clarification. The therapist must be skilled in selecting, training, and guiding the interpreter when one is required (Tseng 2003).

The therapist needs to be able to explain, interpret, and guide patients through the process of therapy. Carrying out these therapeutic activities to reach the goals of therapy requires a certain level of professional skill. One technique is to use proverbs to explain and guide. It is useful from a cultural perspective to know various proverbs and how to use them properly (chapter 13).

Explanations of illness.   In the process of therapy, a competent therapist should know the patient's own recognition and explanation of his problems from the standpoint of "illness," in contrast to the therapist's understanding and interpretation from the standpoint of "disease." Even though the terms are similar from a semantic point of view, they are used differently to distinguish between the views of the patient and those of the therapist, which may or may not be the same (Tseng 2001, 159–161).

In general, the patient's illness view may include supernatural, natural, and medical-psychological dimensions, while contemporary physicians tend to focus on medical, psychological, and social aspects. Understanding the patient's view of illness will help the therapist to conduct proper therapy. The patient's own explanations of illness will be subject to his social and cultural backgrounds, which may be influenced by the history of his society and the traditional medicine it practices (chapters 15 and 17).

Cognition and experience.   A unique aspect among therapies carried out in the East and West is that most Western therapy values the rational, cognitive approach to understanding the nature and cause of problems and how to deal with them. In contrast, some Eastern therapies stress the importance of actual experience, without cognitive understanding. This is illustrated in the practice of meditation (chapter 14). Thus, there are two extremes of approaches that can be used in treating patients. Selecting an appropriate approach for a particular patient is a matter of clinical judgment and choice.

Theoretical Modifications

Body and mind.   Even though, by definition, psychotherapy aims to treat a patient's psychological problems, dealing with the problems expressed through the body is a concern that cannot be ignored. The dichotomy between body and mind is a product of Western culture. However, many people, whether from the East or the West, may express problems synthetically through both the mind and the body. It is generally observed that many people in the East are used to manifesting and communicating their problems through their bodies, even though the problems are psychological. This tendency of "somatization" among Eastern people deserves careful interpretation (chapter 2). In the past, Western therapists considered somatization a less developed way to express problems. From a cultural perspective, this hierarchical view of mind and body needs to be challenged. There are different explanations for the tendency toward somatization (Tseng 1975). One is that it is more acceptable to the culture to communicate problems indirectly, through the body, rather than directly, through verbal and psychological expressions. Thus, the theory of body and mind needs to be revised from a cultural perspective.

Self and ego boundaries.   The psychoanalytic division of the "self" into the id, ego, and superego is useful for understanding human psychology. However, this theoretical concept of the self must be challenged from a cross-cultural point of view (Tseng 2001, 787–788). From an Asian cultural perspective, the boundaries of the "self" do not end with the id, the ego, and the superego, but often extend into and merge with the surrounding society in a concrete sense (including interrelation and interaction with people, such as immediate family, friends, neighbors, and members of society at large) and, abstractly, into culture (including ways of thinking, attitudes, and value systems). In this psychosocial view, the structure of the "self" can be expanded into sociocultural layers, and the boundaries of the self as an individual may become blurred for persons from various cultures (F. L. K. Hsu 1973). This view has been echoed and restated in a slightly different way (Chang 1988), namely, the idea of the self was experienced, defined, and used among the cultures of the world between two conceptual poles. At one extreme, the self as individual was emphasized as independent and separate from the social group. At the other extreme, the self was viewed as integrated with the whole. The former idea of the self is dominant in Western tradition; the latter is characteristic of the East (chapter 16). In terms of therapy, it is necessary to understand the psychology of the self within this spectrum, appreciating that the ego boundaries can be clear and limited or blurred and expanded among people in various cultures.

Individuality and collectiveness.   Similarly, human behavior can be regarded, examined, and comprehended from the perspectives of individuality and collectiveness in the West and East, respectively. In a culture that stresses individuality, a person's thoughts, decisions, and actions can be based primarily on what an individual wants; in contrast, in a culture that emphasizes collectiveness, an individual needs to consider his responsibility toward and the potential effect of his thoughts and behavior on the group (whether his family or community).

Personality development.   The theory of personality development describes how an individual grows through different stages sequentially, with specific tasks to accomplish on the way to maturity and adulthood. It is very useful to understand an individual's stages of development. However, the theory of personality development needs cross-cultural modifications. For example, clinical experiences by cultural psychiatrists from divergent cultural backgrounds have indicated that the major themes emphasized in each stage of psychosocial development (Erikson 1950) warrant cross-cultural revision.

For instance, in the oral stage, it is more important for children in societies with inadequate living conditions, in which people struggle for daily survival, to obtain a sense of security rather than to establish basic trust, as originally described. This is the current situation in many societies, including parts of Asia.

It has been pointed out that, in association with the prolongation of the oral stage, many Asian children are permitted a sense of dependence and indulgence in the muscular-anal stage, while the emphasis on autonomy is delayed. Asian people in rural or agricultural settings are less strict about anal discipline through toilet training, whereas there is greater stress on controlling behavior through shame (Tseng and Hsu, 1969).

Many cultures do not stress initiative during the locomotor-genital stage. Instead, more emphasis is given to collaterality, that is, living with others harmoniously and interdependently, and not "sticking out" from the group. This is exemplified by people living in small island societies with limited resources, such as Micronesia, where mutual dependency and collaterality are vital. This is still true in some Asian societies, in which living according to the benefit of the group and the community is strongly emphasized.

In addition to the major theme in each stage of development, the pace of shifting from one stage to the next needs consideration from a cross-cultural point of view. For instance, how long a child is permitted to stay in the oral stage may be determined by child-rearing patterns, including the way in which the infant is viewed and cared for. In many contemporary Western societies, there is a great emphasis on growing up fast. However, many Eastern societies have a more relaxed attitude. Small children are allowed to remain "babies," indulged by their parents, grandparents, and siblings, with no pressure for them to move into the next stage of development.

However, the pace after that can change rather abruptly. Among some Asian people, diligence is stressed for youngsters in the latency period, with the inculcation of the desire to achieve, a drastic shift in developmental requirements from the earlier stages of indulgence. Following this, the stage of puberty and adolescence is relatively prolonged and the entry into young adulthood delayed for Asian children (Bond 1991; Tseng 1995).

Thus, it is necessary to consider cross-cultural adjustments to psychosocial development as it was originally proposed. Although the basic concept of development by stages is universally applicable, the main themes emphasized in each stage and the pace of the transition from stage to stage are subject to cross-cultural revision (Tseng 2001, 788–791).

Parent-child complex. Freud's developmental theory focused on the psychosexual aspects of individual development. Since it concerns biological instinct, it is regarded as universally applicable. However, inasmuch as each individual has a unique developmental course, it is reasonable to speculate that the drive that emerges in each developmental stage may be subject to variations. In particular, scholars have pointed out that the intensity of the triangular parent-child relationship conflict that occurs in the phallic stage, called the Oedipus complex, will depend on the sexual attitudes that exist in the environment. It will also be subject to variations based on the family system and structure within the society.

Based on his field study of the Trobriand Islands, Malinowski (1927) reported that, in a matrilineal society, where family lineage is traced from mother to daughter (rather than from father to son, as in a patrilineal system), the relationship between the son and the mother's brother (maternal uncle) is more intense than between the son and his own biological father. Also, in the matrilineal family system, the bond between brother and sister is an important one. Malinowski reported that in such a society, a boy tends to have dream wishes of the death of his brother—his potential rival subject. Thus, based on the family system, the persons involved in the triangular relationship will vary.

In chapters 4–7 of this book, parent-child relations are elaborated in detail through an analysis of cultural products from the East. It has been pointed out that there are not only different types of parent-child complexes, but different solution patterns proposed for them by the culture. This certainly illustrates that the theory of the parent-child conflict, regarded as the core of psychopathology and the focus of psychotherapy, needs broad cultural expansion beyond the original parent-child complex described by psychoanalysts based on their clinical observations in Western societies.

Defense mechanisms and coping.   Similar to developmental theories, the theory of defense mechanisms developed by psychoanalysts has made a significant contribution to clinicians and behavior scientists in terms of the in-depth understanding of human psychology. Various defense mechanisms have been identified (Vaillant 1986) and categorized hierarchically (Vaillant 1971). In principle, the concept of defense mechanisms is considered universally applicable. However, there is a rising call for cross-cultural study and possible revisions of presently recognized defense mechanisms that are conceptualized and utilized clinically by Western scholars (Tseng 1995). The concern is whether there is any particular set of defense mechanisms that might be more or less frequently used by people of particular cultural groups and whether there are any unique defense mechanisms that are applied in certain cultures (and not described in the present list of defense mechanisms derived from experiences in the West) (Tseng 2001, 790–792).

For example, a "passive-aggressive" coping pattern is generally considered "immature" by contemporary Western psychiatrists (Gabbard 1995), whereas this coping behavior may be considered an "adaptive" coping mechanism in many non-Western societies. This is particularly true in relations with authority figures. Direct confrontation (especially with administrative authority figures) is viewed as "unwise" behavior.

A defense mechanism often used in China was illustrated several decades ago when the well-known Chinese writer Lu Xun portrayed an imaginary individual, Ah-Q, in a short story. He used Ah-Q's behavior ("passive-aggressive rationalization") as a reflection of the Chinese way of dealing with problems. Politically, it was used to criticize the Chinese way of dealing with Westerners' invasive and insulting behavior in China at the time the story was written. However, Ah-Q's spirit has been consciously recognized among the Chinese since then as a means of understanding some characteristics of Chinese behavior. In fact, in developing a personality inventory for the Chinese, the behavior cluster of Ah-Q's coping patterns was incorporated into other clusters in the questionnaire (chapter 2); it was found to be one of the characteristic personality traits revealed in the survey. In other words, "passive-aggressive rationalization" is a common defense mechanism utilized by the majority of ordinary Chinese, and therefore can be listed as one of their "frequently used" (if not "mature") defense mechanisms, rather than a neurotic one, as it was previously categorized.

Differences have been pointed out in the defense mechanisms of suppression and repression among cultures commonly using them (F. L. K. Hsu 1949). Based on his behavioral observation of two groups of people from four cultures, Hsu claimed that suppression was used more as a defense mechanism by the Chinese and Japanese in the East, while repression was used more by the Americans and Germans in the West. This view is awaiting empirical investigation for confirmation. However, it should be mentioned that suppression of desire is generally considered a less desirable coping mechanism by Western therapists, whereas it is viewed as an adaptive coping pattern by Eastern therapists. To suppress an individual's desire and to comply with social rules to benefit the group is considered "mature" behavior in a society that emphasizes collectiveness.

In summary, many psychiatric theories were originally developed in the West with the belief that they addressed the "basic" nature of human psychology and were "universally" applicable. However, with the improvement of cultural psychiatry, scholars have begun to challenge this belief. Certainly, there is a need to expand and revise theories that originated in the West in order to apply them to the East as well. Such theoretical modifications will result in a more culturally appropriate understanding of human behavior and more culturally competent therapy.

Philosophical Reorientation

Acceptance versus conquering.   Viewing life in an optimistic way, as happy and enjoyable, and considering that any obstacles should be removed or resolved, is often counterproductive. Life is often not as satisfactory as one might wish. A person can become sick, or fail in work or in marriage, and will grow older, and die eventually. In the vast scheme of things, a person is only a tiny existence in the universe. Assuming that all problems can be resolved and all obstacles eliminated can itself be a potential problem. It is useful to comprehend the limitations of a person's ability to deal with problems. This is particularly a comfort for those who have difficulty resolving the problems facing them. In contrast, taking an almost fatalistic view of life, trying to accept things as they are, will reduce the opportunity to resolve certain problems that can be worked out. It is desirable to work on problems, to make an effort to achieve one's goals, and to try to reach one's maximum potential, leaving the final results to the rules of nature (chapters 11, 12).

A competent therapist should know how to adjust and modify the therapeutic modality and approach to suit patients' needs. Such adjustment and modification involve many considerations, such as cultural dimensions and the individual's strength and stage of personal development (Tseng and Streltzer 2001). It is generally considered that, while a person is young and full of energy and ambition, it is advantageous to actively deal with problems, to develop one's maximum potential, and to seek achievement (in a Western sense). When a person has passed the middle stage of life, it is desirable to learn how to accept limitations and live according to the rules of nature (in the Eastern way).

Normality and maturity.   The concept of "normality" can be examined and approached by professional definition, mathematical means, assessment of function, and sociocultural definition (Offer and Sabshin 1974).

Definition by sociocultural perspective can be made according to commonly held concepts and usually takes the prevailing view of the society concerned or is expressed in comparison with the model or mean personality of a particular ethnicity or society. However, there are great variations within a single group with regard to a so-called ethnic or national personality. It is necessary to know the more characteristic or representative personality from ethnic or national perspectives (chapter 2).

Closely related to the concept of normality is a society's view of "maturity." The concept of maturity is often utilized in carrying out therapy, and as a goal of therapy. However, "maturity" is not easily defined and is seldom described objectively. An attempt has been made from multiple perspectives to describe what we mean by psychological maturity. Needless to say, the concept and definition of maturity will vary according to cultural perspectives.

Soul and spirituality.   Finally, the concepts of soul and spirituality have not been elaborated by most psychiatrists and mental health workers, who have, in fact, shied away from them in the past. However, it has become clearer to contemporary clinicians that it is important to focus on, address, appreciate, and utilize the patient's concern about matters of the soul and spirituality as a part of psychotherapeutic work, as folk therapists have done since ancient times (chapter 1). These matters cannot be dismissed as supernatural and superstitious issues, as was done by some clinicians in the name of "science." It is a real part of life for many people to stress the importance of the soul and spiritually; and as long as that is true, they should not be ignored, but incorporated into therapy and utilized for the healing of the mind.

In summary, beyond the need for technical adjustments of therapeutic skills and approaches and theoretical modifications for understanding human behavior and the nature of psychopathology, there is a need for the philosophical reorientation of the therapist, in order for therapy to be applied more meaningfully and effectively from cultural perspectives.

Exchange and Supplementation

It is obvious that Eastern and Western psychotherapy, even though they share the common goal of healing the mind, have certain fundamental differences (and, in the extreme, are at opposite poles). They may differ in the technical aspects of therapy. They may differ in terms of basic theories applied to various issues, including personality development and human behavior. They may also differ in their ultimate goals, which are basically derived from different philosophical views of life. The goal of therapy in the West is to eliminate or resolve problems, while in the East it is to accept things as they are, in compliance with nature.

Even though these two approaches appear different and even contradictory, existing at extreme ends of a spectrum, they may actually be seen as supplementary to each other, following the yin-yang theory that originated in the ancient text of the *Yi-Jing* (Oracle of change) (chapter 9). Examining therapy in the East and in the West will certainly expand our knowledge of therapy and broaden our views on how to carry out treatment in a greater variety of ways, on the technical, theoretical, and philosophical levels.

Both Eastern and Western approaches to the healing of the mind have their own strengths and weaknesses, and each can learn from the other. They can supplement and expand our views about human nature and our theories about the nature of problems and can provide broader and more comprehensive ways of dealing with them. An exchange of knowledge, theories, views, and experiences will increase our insight and improve our practice of psychotherapy by helping us reach the optimal state of the middle ground, the golden mean emphasized in Daoist philosophy.

Glossary

The origin of a word is indicated by (C) for Chinese, (E) for English, (I) for Indian, (J) for Japanese, or (K) for Korean. For words of Chinese origin, the pinyin transliteration is used and, if applicable, is followed by the Wade-Giles translation in parentheses. Simplified Chinese characters are used for Chinese words.

Ah-Q (C) 阿Q—the name of the main character in a well-known novel by Lu Xun, 鲁迅, who illustrates the passivity and defensiveness of Chinese of the period

Ah-Q mentality (C) 阿Q精神—the mentality shown by Ah-Q, whose spirit is characterized by passive-aggressive rationalization

Ajase (I) **complex**—the early emotional complex arising from the relationship between mother and son; named by a Japanese psychiatrist after the legendary Indian story of Prince Ajatasatru

Ajatasatru (I) 阿闍世—a prince in Indian legend who illustrates the Ajase complex (literally, "committing an action that causes guilt even before the birth")

aku-nin shō-ki (J) 悪人正機—literally, "even an evil person will have salvation"

amae (J) 甘え—dependent-indulgent love between parent and child

Ama-goshi (J) 歧过し—the title of a Japanese movie, meaning "crossing a place called Ama"

Amida (I); Amitofu (C) 阿弥陀佛; Amitabul (K); Amidabutsu (J)—the name of Buddha

arugamama (J) 有るがまま—acceptance of what is

"Bai-she-zhuan" (C) 白蛇传—Chinese folk story of a white serpent

Buddha (I)—name given to Siddhartha Gautama, an Indian prince and the founder of Buddhism; literally, "the Enlightened One"

"Cai-Lou Pei" (C) 采楼配 (Matching at the bouquet tower)—title of a Chinese opera

Chan (C) 禅; Sŏn (K); Zen (J)—transliteration of *dhyana* (Sanskrit); *see also* Zen

Chaotuo xinlizhiliao (C) 超脱心理治疗—transcendental psychotherapy

chien (C) (抽)签 (J. *kujibiki*)—fortune-telling paper

Chosŏn (K) 朝鲜—the last Korean dynasty, 1392–1910; also known as Yi dynasty

Chun-Qiu (C) 春秋—literally, Spring and Autumn, referring to the period of Chinese history characterized by warring states, 770–476 B.C.

Confucius—*see* Kong-Zi (C)

danshūkai (J) 団集会—group therapy meeting

Dao (C) 道—Literally, "the Way," referring to the principle governing the universe. The concept is identified with Daoisim but came to be used in a more generic sense broadly referring to not only Daoistic but also Confucian and Buddhistic ideals in Korea. It has moral and psychological connotations. *See also* Tao

Daode-jing (C) 道德经—*Oracle of Morals,* a book written by Lao-zi

Dao jiao (C) 道教—Dao religion; indigenous religion developed in China by borrowing some concepts from Daoism

Daoism (E) 道学—school of Dao philosophy

Dao-zhuo (C) 道綽 (J. Dou-shaku)—Chinese monk who stressed that people have to go through painful lives

Da-xue (C) 大学—the *Great Learning,* one of the four books of Confucius

Edo (J) 江戸—ancient name of the Japanese capital, Tokyo, before the Meiji Restoration

engawa (J) 縁側—an open corridor or veranda, between a house and the outside

Fen-He Wan (C) 汾河弯—*The Fen-River Bay,* a Chinese opera

fumon (J) 不問—no question, or no asking questions

gaikan (J) 外観—external inspection

Ganesha (I) (*also* Ganesa)—a deity in a legendary Hindu story; son of the deity Devi

giri (J) 義理—duty

gong-an (C) 公案 (K. Kong-an; J. Ko-an or mondo 问答)—a Zen training method; a question or puzzle assigned by the master to student to resolve to attain enlightenment

gong-xin-wei-shang (C) 攻心为上—literally, "it is superior to work on the heart," i.e., psychological warfare is better than a direct physical attack

goot (K)—a shamanistic ritual

han (K) 恨—unresolved grudge

hanbang (K) 汉方—Korean word for traditional Chinese medicine

Han dynasty (C) 汉朝—Chinese dynasty, 206 B.C.–A.D. 220

Han Wu-di (C) 汉武帝—Han emperor who ruled during the apogee of the Han dynasty (141–87 B.C.)

haragei (J) 腹芸—literally, "belly game"; i.e., playing without showing one's real feeling and thoughts in social relations

he (C) 和—harmony

Hōnen (J) 法然—Japanese monk who came to learn Buddhism from master Shan-dao in China during the Tan dynasty

Hong-zong-lie-ma (C) 红鬃烈马—*A Fiery Horse with Red-Colored Mane;* a Chinese opera

Hsueh Jen-gui (C)—*see* Xue Ren-gui

huan pu gui zhen (C) 还朴归真—literally, "returning to the simple state of self and belonging to the innocent truth of life"

hua tou (C) 话头—head-word

hwabyung (K) 火病—literally, "fire (anger) sickness" (in Korea fire and anger are homophones); refers to sickness that follows long-suppressed anger and resentment

ie (J) 家—house, household, or family

in-nen (J) 因缘—interconnected chain of causality; closely related to Buddhistic concept of karma; *see also* karma

Issun-bōshi (J) 一寸法师—One-inch Boy; a boy in Japanese folklore

kappa (J) 河童—a Japanese legendary animal that excels in swimming

karma (I)—a Buddhist belief that all phenomena are interrelated and interdependent

Kojiki (J) 古事记—record of early history of Japan; literally, "record of ancient things"

Kong-zi (Kong-tse) (C) 孔子—Confucius

Koryo (K) 高丽—Korean kingdom between tenth and fourteenth centuries

Lao-zi (Lao-tse) (C) 老子—legendary master of Daoist thought

li (C) 礼—etiquette; one of the central Confucian concepts, roughly meaning rites, customs, morality, the rules governing human relations

li er bu hai (C) 利而不害—doing things that benefit self without harming others

Lun-yu (C) 论语—the *Analects;* one of the four books of Confucius

Lu Xun (C) 鲁迅—pen name of Zhou Shuren (1881–1936), a writer commonly considered to be one of the greatest figures in twentieth-century Chinese literature

mabiki (J) 間引—thinning of a rice field; also, infanticide

Mahayana (I) 大乘佛教 (J. Daijou butsukyou)—Great Vehicle Buddhism; also called Great Way Buddhism; one of the Hindu Buddhist schools

Meng-zi (Meng-tse) (C) 孟子—Mencius; a major disciple of Confucius; also the name of one of the four books of Confucius

miko (J) 巫女—a female shaman

mishirabe (J) 身检べ—self-examination or internal inspection; synonymous with *naikan*

mizuko (J) 水子—water child; i.e., an aborted child
Momo-tarō (J) 桃太郎—Peach Boy; the name of a boy in Japanese folklore
Morita Shōma (J) 森田正馬—the founder of Morita therapy

naikan (J) 内観—internal inspection or self-examination
naikan ryōhō (J) 内観療法—introspection therapy or self-inspection therapy
nenbutsu (J) 念佛—chanting the name of Buddha
nirvana (I) 涅槃—a state of liberation or enlightenment that frees one from
  suffering, death and rebirth, and all other worldly bonds; literally, "extinction"
"Niulang and Zhinü" (C) 牛郎与织女 (The oxherd and the weaving lady)—a
  Chinese legend that describes an oxherd married to a fairy lady from the sky;
  later separated and allowed to meet each other only on the seventh day of the
  seventh month
nuka (J) 米糠—rice bran

on (J) 恩—moral obligation

pudakkori (K)—one kind of healing procedure that may be suggested by a
  shaman by sacrificing a hen or a cock
Pure Land Buddhism (E) 净土佛教—a school of Buddhism that believes in the
  existence of a pure land as the ultimate place to go after obtaining
  enlightenment

qigong (C) 气功—a Chinese style of meditation
Qin dynasty (C) 秦朝—Chinese dynasty (221–206 B.C.) established by Emperor
  Qin
Qing dynasty (C) 清朝—the last dynasty in China (1644–1911)
Qin Shi-huang (C) 秦始皇—the ancient Chinese emperor who united China,
  established the Qin dynasty (221–206 B.C.), and built the Great Wall

ren (C) 仁—benevolence in human relationships
ren-ai (C) 仁爱—benevolence or kindheartedness
ren-qing (C) 人情—interpersonal favor; human feeling

Sai-weng zhi ma (C) 塞翁之马—Mr. Sai's horse; a Chinese saying referring to a
  story of an old man, Mr. Sai, whose fortune shifts between good and bad after
  losing, then gaining a horse
salpri (K)—vigorous dancing by a shaman with a weapon to expel evil
sei no yokubō (J) 生の欲望—urge for life
Shakyamuni (I) 释迦 (J. Sha-ka)—Gautama, the founder of Buddhism
Shan-dao (C) 善导 (J. Zen-do)—the Chinese monk considered the second founder
  of the school of Pure Land Buddhism

Shang, or **Yin** (C) 商,殷—the ancient dynasty (ca. 16ᵗʰ-century B.C.–1066 B.C.) that came between the Xia (Hsia夏) dynasty and the Zhou (周) dynasty

shao si qua yu (C) 少思寡欲—reduce the thought and minimize the desire

shenjing shuairuo (C) 神经衰弱—weakness of the nervous system

shinkeishitsu (J) 神経質—neurotic temperament

Shinran (J) 親鸞—one of the Japanese monks who promoted the development of Pure Land Buddhism in Japan

shun qi zi ran (C) 顺其自然—following nature

Silla (K) 新罗—name of the kingdom in Korea during the eighth to tenth centuries

Siva (I) (*also* Shiva)—the name of a deity, the father of Ganesa and the husband of the deity Devi

sunao (J) 素直な —plain mind; i.e., innocent, good, docile, gentle, pliable, and so forth

Sun Wu-kong (C) 孙悟空—a Buddhist name given to a monkey in the *The Western Journey,* meaning a monkey who became enlightened about being nothing

taijinkyōfushō (J) 対人恐怖症—interpersonal relation phobia

Tan-luan (C) 昙鸾 (J. Don-ran)—a Chinese monk who was concerned with attaining the Daoistic way of eternal life

Tang (C) 唐(J. Toh)—Chinese dynasty, 618–907

Tannishō (J) 叹异抄—a Japanese Buddhist book

Tao (K) 道 (C. Dao)—Korean concept of a philosophical essence synthetically derived from Buddhism, Confucianism, and Daoism; *see also* Dao

Taoism (K) 道学—Korean term for Daoism; *see* Daoism

tatemae to honne (J) 建前と本音—public principle versus real intention; real feeling and thought different from outward expression

te (K) 德 (C. de)—virtue

Theravada (I) Buddhism 小乘佛教 (J. Shoujou butsukyou)—one of the schools of Hindu Buddhism

ting xue (C) 听雪 (J. cho setsu; K. chung sul)—listening to the falling snow

toraware (J) 捕われ—obsessive preoccupation; a basic Buddhists concept, referring to undue craving or undue attachment

Tseng-tsi (C)—*see* Zeng-zi

Urashima-tarō (J) 浦島太郎—a fisherman in Japanese folklore

wa (J) 和 (C. he)—the harmony that needs to be maintained within a group

wei er bu zheng (C) 为而不争—to do without competing with others

Western Journey (E) 西游记 *Xi-You Ji*—Chinese story of a trip westward along the Silk Road to obtain Buddhist books from India

wu wei (C) 无为—nondoing; Daoistic teaching for not overdoing things;

unmotivated, unintentional, spontaneous action that, being completely devoid of premeditation and intention, is wholly appropriate to a given situation

Xian (C) 西安 (J. Sei-an)—the name of the ancient capital of China; literally, "western peace"

Xuan-zi (C) 玄子—an ancient Chinese scholar who advocated that humans are by nature evil

Xue Ding-shan (C) 薛丁山—the name of Xue Ren-gui's son in a Chinese opera

Xue Ren-gui (C) 薛仁贵—the main character (a general) in a Chinese opera

Xu Xian (C) 许仙—the name of a man in the Chinese opera *The White Serpent*

yangban (K) 兩玉王—two upper classes in traditional Korea

Yao, Shun (C) 尧, 舜—legendary sage-kings, 24th–23rd c. B.C.

Yi-jing (C) 易经—*Oracle of Change;* the most ancient Chinese divination text, describing the rules of change in the universe

yin-yang (C) 阴阳—the concept of the positive-negative dual forces that exist in the universe

yi rou shen gang (C) 以柔胜刚—To win the hardness by the softness

Yoshimoto Ishin (J) 吉本一信—the founder of Naikan therapy

Yu-Huang Shang-di (C) 玉皇上帝—the Jade Emperor; the highest god in heaven

yuki-onna (J) 雪女—snow women; a Japanese legend about a snow-ghost woman who married an ordinary man

zazen (J) 坐禅—sitting meditation

Zen (J) 禅 (C. Chan; K. Sŏn)—a school of Mahayana Buddhism that became the principal school of Buddhism in Korea and Japan

Zeng-zi (Tseng-tsi) (C) 曾子—one of Confucius' disciples

Zhan-Guo (C) 战国—the Warring States period, 475–221 B.C.

zhi he chu xia (C) 知和趋下—knowing how to achieve harmony by accepting a subordinate position, without competing and having conflict with others

zhi zu zhi zhi (C) 知足知止—knowing how to be satisfied and to stop at proper time

Zhong-yong (C) 中庸—*Doctrine of the Mean;* one of the four books of Confucius

Zhou dynasty (C) 周朝—an ancient Chinese dynasty, ca. 1066–221 B.C.

Zhou-yi (C) 周易—*Oracle of Change of the Zhou Dynasty; see Yi-jing*

Zhuang-zi (Chuang-tse) (C) 庄子—a major follower of Lao-zi in Daoist thought

References

Abel, T. M., and Metraux, R. 1974. *Culture and Psychotherapy.* New Haven, Conn.: College and University Press.

Abraham, K. 1913. *Dreams and Myths: A Study in Race Psychology.* New York: Journal of Nervous and Mental Health Publishing Company.

Alford, C. F. 1999. *Think No Evil: Korean Values in the Age of Globalization.* Ithaca, N.Y.: Cornell University Press.

American Psychiatric Association. 1994. *Diagnostic and Statistical Manual of Mental Disorders.* 4th ed. Washington, D.C.: American Psychiatric Association.

Anderson, C. A. 1999. Attributional style, depression, and loneliness: A cross-cultural comparison of American and Chinese students. *Personality and Social Psychology Bulletin* 25:482–499.

Aviera, A. 1996. "Dichos" therapy group: A therapeutic use of Spanish-language proverbs with hospitalized Spanish-speaking psychiatric patients. *Cultural Diversity and Mental Health* 2 (2): 73–87.

Balint, M. 1952. *Primary Love and Psychoanalytic Technique.* London: Tavistock.

Balmary, M. 1979. *L'Homme aux Statues. Editions Grassel et Fasquelle* (Chōzō no otoko: Furoito to chichi no kakusareta ayamachi), trans. Hiroshi Iwasaki. Tokyo: Tetsugaku Shobō, 1988.

Balswick, J. O., and Peek, C. W. 1975. The inexpressive male: A tragedy of American society. In *Human Life Cycle,* ed. W. C. Sze, 497–504. New York: Jason Aronson.

Barnes, L. L. 1998. The psychologizing of Chinese healing practices in the United States. *Culture, Medicine and Psychiatry* 22 (4): 413–443.

Barrett, P. T.; Petrides, K. V.; Eysenck, S. B. G.; and Eysenck, H. J. 1998. The Eysenck Personality Questionnaire: An examination of the factorial similarity of P, E, N, and L across 34 countries. *Personality and Individual Differences* 25:805–819.

Barrett, T. H. 1993. China's religious tradition. In *The World's Religions: Understanding the Living Faiths,* ed. P. B. Clarke, 176–196. Pleasantville, N.Y.: Reader's Digest.

Bass, B. M. 1957. Validity studies of a proverb personality test. *Journal of Applied Psychology* 41:158–160.

Benedict, R. 1946. *The Chrysanthemum and the Sword.* Trans. M. Hasegawa. Tokyo: Sekaishisō, 1948.

Ben-Porath, Y. S., and Waller, N. G. 1992. "Normal" personality inventories in clinical assessment: General requirements and the potential for using the NEO Personality Inventory. *Psychological Assessment* 4:14–19.

Binitie, A. A. 1985. The Oedipus complex in Nigeria: Observations in Benin. *Nigerian Journal of Clinical Psychology* 1:21–25.

Bion, W. R. 1962. *Learning from Experience.* London: Heinemann.

Bodde, D. 1953. Harmony and conflict in Chinese philosophy. In *Studies in Chinese Thought*, ed. A. F. Wright, 19–80. Chicago: University of Chicago Press.

Bond, M. H. 1991. *Beyond the Chinese Face: Insights from Psychology.* Hong Kong: Oxford University Press.

———, ed. 1986. *The Psychology of the Chinese People.* Hong Kong: Oxford University Press.

Bose, G. 1948. A new theory of mental life. *Samiksa* 2:108–205.

———. 1949. The genesis and adjustment of the Oedipus wish. *Samiksa* 3:222–40.

———. 1950. The genesis of homosexuality. *Samiksa* 4:66–85.

Butcher, J. N. 1996. Understanding abnormal behavior across cultures: The use of objective personality assessment methods. In *International Adaptations of the MMPI-2: A Handbook of Research and Applications*, ed. J. N. Butcher, 3–25. Minneapolis: University of Minnesota Press.

Butcher, J. N., and Williams, C. L. 1992. *Essentials of MMPI-2 and MMPI-A Interpretation.* Minneapolis: University of Minnesota Press.

Campbell, R. J. 1996. *Psychiatric Dictionary.* 7th ed. New York: Oxford University Press.

Caudill, W., and Lin, T. Y., eds. 1969. *Mental Health Research in Asia and the Pacific.* Honolulu: East-West Center Press.

Chang, P. C. 1969. *The Collection of Chinese National Opera.* Taipei: Taiwan Zonghua Book Co. (in Chinese).

Chang, S. C. 1965. The cultural context of Japanese psychiatry and psychotherapy. *American Journal of Psychotherapy* 19 (4): 593–606.

———. 1974. Morita therapy. *American Journal of Psychotherapy* 28:208–221.

———. 1988. The nature of the self: A transcultural view. *Transcultural Psychiatric Research Review* 25:169–203.

———. 1996. Review of S. H. Lee, *Fear of Social Relations. Journal of Anxiety* 2:58–60 (in Korean).

———. 1998. An effective analytical psychotherapy in cross-cultural context. *American Journal of Psychotherapy* 52:229–239.

———. 1999. The United States and East Asia: The diagnosis of anxiety, an obstacle to collaborative works. *Transcultural Psychiatry* 36:119–121.

Chang, S. C., and Kim, K. I. 1973. Psychiatry in South Korea. *American Journal of Psychiatry* 130:667–669.

Char, W. F. 1977. Motivations for intercultural marriages. In *Adjustment in Intercultural Marriage*, ed. W. S. Tseng, J. F. McDermott Jr., and T. W. Mareetzki, 33–40. Honolulu: Department of Psychiatry, University of Hawai'i School of Medicine.

Chasseguet-Smirgel, J. 1964. Feminine guilt and the Oedipus complex. In *Female Sexuality*, ed. J. Chasseguet-Smirgel. Ann Arbor: University of Michigan Press.

Cheng, A. T. A. 2001. Case definition and culture: Are people the same? *British Journal of Psychiatry* 179:1–3.

Cheng, L. Y.; Cheung, F. C.; and Chen, C. N., eds. 1993. *Psychotherapy for the Chinese*. Hong Kong: Department of Psychiatry, Chinese University of Hong Kong.

Cheng, L. Y. C.; Baxter, H.; and Cheung, F. M. C., eds. 1995. *Psychotherapy for the Chinese: II*. Hong Kong: Department of Psychiatry, Chinese University of Hong Kong.

Cheng, T. A. 1995. Neuroses in Taiwan: Findings from a community survey. In *Chinese Society and Mental Health*, ed. T. Y. Lin, W. S. Tseng, and E. K. Yeh, 167–175. Hong Kong: Oxford University Press.

Cheung, F. M. 1985a. An overview of psychopathology in Hong Kong with special reference to somatic presentation. In *Chinese Culture and Mental Health*, ed. W. S. Tseng and D. Y. H. Wu, 287–304. Orlando, Fla.: Academic Press.

———. 1985b. Cross-cultural considerations for the translation and adaptation of the Chinese MMPI in Hong Kong. In *Advances in Personality Assessment*, ed. J. N. Butcher and C. D. Spielberger, 4:131–158. Hillsdale, N.J.: Lawrence Erlbaum Associates.

———. 1989. The indigenization of neurasthenia in Hong Kong. *Culture, Medicine and Psychiatry* 13:227–241.

———. 1995a. *Administration Manual of the Minnesota Multiphasic Personality Inventory (MMPI) Chinese Edition*. Hong Kong: The Chinese University Press.

———. 1995b. Facts and myths about somatization among the Chinese. In *Chinese Society and Mental Health*, ed. T. Y. Lin, W. S. Tseng, and E. K. Yeh, 156–166. Hong Kong: Oxford University Press.

———. 1996. The assessment of psychopathology in Chinese societies. In *Handbook of Chinese Psychology*, ed. M. H. Bond, 393–411. Hong Kong: Oxford University Press.

———. 1998. Cross-cultural psychopathology. In *Comprehensive Psychiatry*. Volume 10: *Sociocultural and Individual Differences*, ed. C. D. Belar, 35–51. Oxford: Pergamon.

———. 2000. Deconstructing counseling in a cultural context. *The Counseling Psychologist* 28:123–132.

———. 2002. Cultural considerations in use of psychological tests in clinical assessment. Invited address presented in division 6 of the 25th International Congress of Applied Psychology, July 8–13, Singapore.

Cheung, F. M.; Conger, A.; Hau, K. T.; Lew, W. J. F.; and Lau, S. 1992. Development of the Multi-Trait Personality Inventory (MTPI): Comparison among four Chinese populations. *Journal of Personality Assessment* 59:528–551.

Cheung, F. M.; Leung, K.; Fan, R. M.; Song, W. Z.; Zhang, J. X.; and Zhang, J. P. 1996. Development of the Chinese Personality Assessment Inventory. *Journal of Cross-cultural Psychology* 27:181–199.

Cheung, F. M.; Leung, K.; Zhang, J. X.; Sun, H. F.; Gan, Y.; Song, W. Z.; and Xie, D.

2001. Indigenous Chinese personality constructs: Is the four-factor model complete? *Journal of Cross-cultural Psychology* 32:407–433.

Cheung, F. M., and Song, W. Z. 1989. A review of the clinical applications of the Chinese MMPI. *Psychological Assessment* 1:230–237.

Cheung, F. M.; Song, W. Z.; and Zhang, J. X. 1996. The Chinese MMPI-2: Research and applications in Hong Kong and the People's Republic of China. In *International Adaptations of the MMPI-2: A Handbook of Research and Applications*, ed. J. N. Butcher, 137–161. Minneapolis: University of Minnesota Press.

Cheung, F. M.; Zhao, J. C.; and Wu, C. Y. 1992. Chinese MMPI profiles among neurotic patients. *Psychological Assessment* 4:214–218.

Chien, C. P. 1999. The cognitive group therapy for panic disorder patients in Taiwan: Commonality with Morita therapy. Presented at the Fourth International Congress of Morita Therapy. Tokyo, Japan.

Chinen, A. B. 1989. *In the Ever After: Fairy Tales and the Second Half of Life*. Wilamette, Ill.: Chiron Publications.

Cho, D. Y. 1999a. *Freud and Korean Literature* Seoul: Ilchogak (in Korean).

———. 1999b. Psychotherapy case conference. *Seoul Review of Psychiatry* 1:70–95 (in Korean).

Cole, J. 1982. *Best-loved Folktales of the World*. New York: Anchor.

Costa, P. T., Jr., and McCrae, R. R. 1992. Normal personality assessment in clinical practice: The NEO Personality Inventory. *Psychological Assessment* 4:5–13.

Costantino, G.; Malgady, R. G.; and Rogler, L. H. 1986. Cuento therapy: A culturally sensitive modality for Puerto Rican children. *Journal of Consulting and Clinical Psychology* 54:639–645.

Courtright, P. 1986. *Ganesa*. New York: Oxford University Press.

Cui, Y. H. 1997. The examination and experiences of Japanese Morita therapy practiced in China. In *Chinese Mind and Therapy,* ed. W. S. Tseng, 508–525. Beijing: Beijing Medical University and China Xie-He Medical Joint Publishers (in Chinese).

Doi, T. 1973. *The Anatomy of Dependence*. Tokyo: Kodansha International.

———. 2001. *Tsuzuki "amae" no kozō* (The anatomy of dependence revisted). Tokyo: Kōbundō.

Draguns, J. G. 1996. Abnormal behavior in Chinese societies: Clinical, epidemiological, and comparative study. In *The Handbook of Chinese Psychology,* ed. M. H. Bond, 412–428. Hong Kong: Oxford University Press.

Dumont, L. 1966. *Homo Hierarchicus*. Chicago: University of Chicago Press.

———. 1970. *Religion, Politics and History in India: Collected Papers in Indian Sociology*. Paris: Mouton.

Edmunds, L., and Dundes, A. 1995. *Oedipus: A Folklore Casebook*. Madison: University of Wisconsin Press.

Egashira, Y. 1998. Naikan-ryōhō no chiryō kisei ni kansuru kōsatsu no kokoromi —ninchi-shinrigaku no kakudo kara miru (Therapeutic mechanism of Naikan therapy from the angle of cognitive psychology). In *Naikan-ryōhō no rinshō-riron to sono ōyō* (Theory and practice of Naikan psychotherapy), ed. R. Kawahara, 183–191. Tokyo: Shinkō Igaku Shuppan.

Egnor, M. 1984. The ideology of love in a Tamil family. Ms. Hobart and Smith College.

Ehrlich, M. P. 1986. Taoism and psychotherapy. *Journal of Contemporary Psychotherapy* 16 (1): 23–38.

Eisenberg, L. 1972. The *human* nature of human nature. *Science* 176:123–128.

Erickson, M. T. 1993. Rethinking Oedipus: An evolutionary perspective of incest avoidance. *American Journal of Psychiatry* 150 (3): 411–416.

Erikson, E. H. 1950. *Childhood and Society.* 2d ed. New York: Norton.

Fairbank, J. K.; Reischauer, E. O., and Craig, A. M. 1973. *East Asia: Tradition and Transformation.* Cambridge: Harvard University Press.

Fischer-Schreiber, I.; Ehrhard, F-K.; Friedrichs, K.; and Diener, M. S., eds. 1994. *The Encyclopedia of Eastern Philosophy and Religion: Buddhism, Hinduism, Taoism, Zen.* Boston: Shambhala.

Frank J. D. 1961. *Persuasion and Healing: A Comparative Study of Psychotherapy.* New York: Schocken Books.

Freud, S. 1908. Creative writers and day-dreaming. In *Complete Psychological Works of Sigmund Freud,* vol. 9. London: Hogarth Press, 1959.

———. 1922. New introductory lectures on psychoanalysis. In *Standard Edition of the Complete Psychological Works of Sigmund Freud,* 22:3–182. London: Hogarth Press, 1966–1973.

———. 1930. *Civilization and Its Discontent.* Trans. and ed. James Strachey. New York: Norton, 1961.

Fromm, E.; Suzuki, D. T.; and DeMartino, R., eds. 1960. *Zen and Psychoanalysis.* New York: Harper and Row.

Gabbard, G. O. 1995. Psychoanalysis. In *Comprehensive Textbook of Psychiatry,* 6th ed., ed. H. I. Kaplan and B. J. Sadock, vol. 1. Baltimore: Williams and Wilkins.

Gabrenya, W. K., Jr., and Hwang, K. K. 1996. Chinese social interaction: Harmony and hierarchy on the good earth. In *The Handbook of Chinese Psychology,* ed. M. H. Bond, 309–321. Hong Kong: Oxford University Press.

Gan, Y. Q. 1998. Health, personality traits, and unique pathways to psychological adjustment: Cultural and gender perspectives. Doctoral dissertation, The Chinese University of Hong Kong.

Ganzarain, R. 1988. Various guilt within the Ajase complex (trans. K. Okonogi). *Japanese Journal of Psychoanalysis* 32 (2): 93–102.

Gao, G.; Ting-Toomey, S.; and Gudykunst, W. B. 1996. Chinese communication process. In *The Handbook of Chinese Psychology,* ed. M. H. Bond, 280–293. Hong Kong: Oxford University Press.

Gorham, D. 1956. A proverbs test for clinical and experimental use. *Psychological Reports* 2:1–12.

Guggenbuhl-Craig, A. 1971. *Power in the Helping Professions*. Trans. K. Higuchi and S. Ankei. Osaka: Sogensya, 1981 (in Japanese).

Guo S. M. 1999. *Laozi jiujing shuoliao shenme* (What did Laozi actually say?). Beijing: Huawen Chubanshe.

Guralnik, D. B., ed. 1980. *Webster's New World Dictionary of the American Language*. 2d ed. Cleveland, Ohio: William Collins.

Hamilton, E. 1969. *Mythology*. Boston: Little, Brown, 1998.

Han, S. C. 1991. *Korean Folk and Fairy Tales*. Elizabeth, N.J.: Hollyn International.

Hathaway, S. R. 1943. *The Minnesota Multiphasic Personality Inventory*. Minneapolis: University of Minnesota Press.

Hearn, L. 1904. Yuki-onna (The snow woman). In *Kwaidan: Stories and Studies of Strange Things*. Rutland, Vt.: Tuttle, 1971.

Heuscher, J. E. 1963. *A Psychiatric Study of Fairy Tales: Their Origin, Meaning and Usefulness*. Springfield, Ill.: C. Thomas Charles.

Hsu, F. L. K. 1949. Supression versus repression: A limited psychological interpretation of four cultures. *Psychiatry* 12:223-242.

———. 1953. *Americans and Chinese: Passage to Differences*. Honolulu: University Press of Hawai'i, 1981.

———. 1973. Psychosocial homeostasis (PSH): A sociocentric model of man. Presented as a William P. Menninger Memorial Lecture at the annual meeting of the American Psychiatric Association, May, Honolulu.

Hsu, J. 1976. Counseling in the Chinese temple: Psychological study of *chien* drawing. In *Culture-bound Syndromes, Ethno-psychiatry and Alternative Therapies*, ed. W. P. Lebra, 210-221. Honolulu: University Press of Hawai'i.

———. 1983. Asian family interaction patterns and their therapeutic implications. *International Journal of Family Psychiatry* 4 (4): 307-320.

———. 1995. Family therapy for the Chinese: Problems and strategies. In *Chinese Society and Mental Health*, ed. T. Y. Lin, W. S. Tseng, and E. K. Yeh. Hong Kong: Oxford University Press.

Hsu, J., and Tseng, W. S. 1972. Intercultural psychotherapy. *Archives of General Psychiatry* 27:700-705.

———. 1974. Family relations in classic Chinese opera. *International Journal of Social Psychiatry* 20 (3/4): 159-172.

Huang, D. D., and Charter, R. A. 1996. The origin and formulation of Chinese character: An introduction to Confucianism and its influence on Chinese behavior patterns. *Culture Diversity and Mental Health* 2 (1): 35-42.

Huh, C. H. 1995. Empathy and Confucian *jen*. In *Psychotherapy East and West*, ed. D. S. Rhee, 466-469. Seoul: Korean Academy of Psychotherapists.

Humphrey, C. 1951. *Buddhism*. Harmondsworth, Middlesex: Penguin Books.

———. 1972. *Concentration and Meditation*. Baltimore: Penguin Books.

Hwang, S. H.; Hong, J. P.; Bae, J. N.; Yang, B. K.; Rhi, B. Y.; Cho, D. Y.; Kim, Z. S.; Woo, J. I.; Kwon, J. S.; and Cho, M. J. 1996. The utilization of health service by psychiatric patients in the Yonchon area of Kyunggi Province. *Journal of Korean Neuropsychiatric Association* 35:900–909 (in Korean).

Ilechukwu, S. T. 1999. Oedipal anxiety and cultural variations in the incest taboo: A psychotherapy case study in the Nigerian setting. *Transcultural Psychiatry* 36 (2): 211–225.

Ishida R. 1969. Naikan-analysis. *Psychologia* 12:81–92.

Ito, H., and Sederer, L. I. 1999. Mental health services reform in Japan. *Harvard Review of Psychiatry* 7 (4): 208–215.

James, W. 1890. *The Principles of Psychology.* New York: Dover, 1950.

Ji, J. L. 1995. Hotline for mental health in Shanghai, China. *Crisis* 16 (3): 116–120.

Jilek, W. G. 1982. *Indian Healing: Shamanic Ceremonialism in the Pacific Northwest Today.* Surrey, BC, Canada: Hancock House.

Jin, Z. B.; Chang, Y. S.; Sun, B. R.; and Liu, Y. J. 2001. A comparative study of drug and psychotherapy in the treatment of depressive disorder. *Chinese Journal of Clinical Psychology* 9 (1): 56–57 (in Chinese).

Johnson, A. W., and Price-Williams, D. 1996. *Oedipus Ubiquitous: The Family Complex in World Folk Literature.* Stanford, Calif.: Stanford University Press.

Jonanson, G. 1991. *Psychotherapy in the Spirit of Tao-te Ching.* New York: Bell Tower.

Jumsai, M. L. M. 1977a. *Thai Folk Tales: A Selection out of Gems of Thai Lit.* 3d enlg. ed. Bangkok: Chalermnit Press.

———. 1977b. *Thai Ramayana.* 3d ed. Bangkok: Charlermnit Press.

Jung, C. 1928. The relation between the ego and the unconscious. In *Jung,* ed. J. Campbell, 70–138. New York: Viking, 1971.

———. 1954. Psychological commentary. In *The Tibetan Book of the Great Liberation: On the Method of Realizing Nirvana through Knowing the Mind,* ed. W. Y. Evans-Wentz, xxix–lxiv. London: Oxford University Press, 1969.

Kakar, S. 1978. *The Inner World: A Psychoanalytic Study of Childhood and Society in India.* Delhi and New York: Oxford University Press.

———. 1982. *Shamans, Mystics and Doctors: A Psychological Inquiry into India and Its Healing Tradition.* New York: Alfred A. Knopf.

———. 1987. Psychoanalysis and anthropology: A renewed alliance. *Contributions to Indian Sociology* 21:85–88.

———. 1995. Modern psychotherapies in traditional cultures: India, China, and Japan. In *Psychotherapy East and West,* ed. D. S. Rhee, 79–85. Seoul: Korean Academy of Psychotherapists.

Kakar, S., and Ross, J. M. 1987. *Tales of Love, Sex and Danger.* London: Unwin Hyman.

Kang, J. K. 1990. The Eastern Tao and Western psychotherapy: Similarities and differences. In *Proceedings of Conference for Celebrating Dr. Dongshick Rhee's 70th Birthday,* ed. Korean Academy of Psychotherapists, 53–73. Seoul: Hana.

Kang, S. H. 1989. The Confucian Tao and Western psychotherapy. Presented at the 33d Meeting of the American Academy of Psychoanalysis, Captiva Island, Florida.

Kasahara, Y. 1974. Fear of eye-to-eye confrontation among neurotic patients in Japan. In *Japanese Culture and Behavior*, ed. T. S. Lebra and P. L. Lebra, 396–406. Honolulu: University Press of Hawai'i.

Kawahara R. 1999. Naikan-ryōhō no gihō to chiryō-kōka (Therapeutic techniques and effectiveness of Naikan therapy). In *Shinri-ryōhō no honshitsu—Naikan ryōhō o kangaeru* (The essence of psychotherapy: From the standpoint of Naikan therapy), ed. R. Kawahara, Y. Higashi, and Y. Miki, 3–14. Tokyo: Nihon Hyōronsha.

Kawahara R.; Kimura H.; and Nagasawa H. 1993. Sentensei-utsubyō ni taisuru shūchū-naikan-ryōhō (Naikan therapy for prolonged depressions). *Japanese Journal of Clinical Psychiatry* 22:343–348.

Kawahara R.; Nakamura J.; Tashiro S.; and Itou T. 1995. Shinkeishō ni taisuru shūchū-naikan-ryōhō (Intensive Naikan therapy for neurotic patients). *Journal of the Japanese Naikan Association* 1:51–59.

Kelman, H. 1964. Psychotherapy in Scandinavia: An American viewpoint. *International Journal of Social Psychiatry* 10 (1): 64–72.

Kida, K. 1977. On Kosawa's "Two kinds of guilt feelings." *Gendai no Esupuri* 115 (in Japanese).

Kim, H. A. 1995. Tao-oriented psychoanalysis. In *Psychotherapy East and West: Integration of Psychotherapies*, ed. Korean Academy of Psychotherapists. Rev. ed. of proceedings of the 16th International Congress of Psychotherapy, Seoul, Korea.

———. 2000. Personal communication.

Kim, J. H. 1972. Research about imagogeny, revelation of Uroimago and image therapy. *Neuropsychiatry* 11:25–30.

Kim, J. H., and Rhee, K. G. 1975. Theoretical foundation of tea therapy. *Neuropsychiatry* 14:75–78.

Kim, K. I. 1973a. Traditional concepts of illness in Korea. *Korea Journal* 13 (1): 12–18.

———. 1973b. Shamanistic healing ceremonies in Korea. *Korea Journal* 13 (4): 41–47.

———. 1978. The Oedipus complex in our changing society: With special reference to Korea. *Journal of Korean Neuropsychiatric Association* 17 (1): 97–103 (in Korean). [Abstracted by S. C. Chang in *Transcultural Psychiatric Research Review* 16 (1979): 58–60.]

———. 1984. *Psychoanalysis and Korean Culture*. Seoul: Siinsa (in Korean).

———. 1997. Traditional therapeutic resources in psychiatric practice in Korea. *Mental Health Research* 16:151–156.

———. 1999. Culture and illness behavior in South Korea. *Transcultural Psychiatry* 36:65–77.

Kim, K. I., and Kwak, S. G. 1992. Culture-relevant psychiatric practice in Korea: Case study of a clinic. *Journal of Korean Neuropsychiatric Association* 31:648–671.

Kim, L. I. C. 1999. Personal communication.

Kim, S. P.; Siomopoulos, G.; and Cohen, R. J. 1977. Verbal abstraction and culture: An exploratory study with proverbs. *Psychological Reports* 41:967–972.

Kim, U., and Berry, J., eds. 1993. *Indigenous Psychologies: Research and Experience in Cultural Context*. Newbury Park, Calif.: Sage.

Kimura O. S. 1982. *Nihonjin no taijinkyōfushō* (Japanese anthrophobia). Tokyo: Keso Shobō.

King, A. Y. C., and Bond, M. H. 1985. Confucian paradigm of man: A sociological view. In *Chinese Culture and Mental Health*, ed. W. S. Tseng and D. Y. H. Wu, 29–42. Orlando, Fla.: Academic Press.

Kitanishi, K. 1999. Tōyōteki tetsugaku to Morita ryōhō to Naikan ryōhō (Asian philosophy and Morita therapy and Naikan therapy). *Seishin igakushi kenkyū* (Psychiatric research), 2:60–65.

Kitanishi, K.; Fujimoto, H.; and Toyohara, T. 1992. Treatment results and objects in Morita therapy institute over twenty years. *Morita ryōhōshitsu kiyō* 14:2–7 (in Japanese).

Kitanishi, K., and Nakamura K. 1989. Psychotherapy for chronic depressions. *Seishin igaku* 31:255–262 (in Japanese).

Kitanishi, K.; Nakamura, K.; Miyake, Y.; Hashimoto, K.; and Kubota, M. 2002. Diagnostic consideration of Morita *shinkeishitsu* and DSM-III-R. *Psychiatry and Clinical Neurosciences* 56:603–608.

Kitayama, O. 1985. Pre-Oedipal "taboo" in Japanese folk tragedies. *International Review of Psychoanalysis* 12:173–186.

———. 1991. The wounded caretaker and guilt. *International Review of Psychoanalysis* 18:229–240.

———. 1994. Japanese tragic legends and a maternal prohibition. *Research Bulletin of Educational Psychology* (Faculty of Education, Kyushu University), 39:7–16 (in Japanese).

———. 1998. Transience: Its beauty and danger. *International Journal of Psychoanalysis* 79:937–953.

Klein, M. 1946. Notes on some schizoid mechanisms. *International Journal of Psychoanalysis* 27:99–110.

———. 1952. Notes on some schizoid mechanisms. *International Journal of Psychoanalysis* 27:99–110. Republished in *Developments in Psycho-Analysis*, ed. M. Klein, P. Heimann, S. Isaacs, and J. Riviere, 292–320. London: Hogarth Press.

Kleinman, A. 1977. Depression, somatization and the "new cross-cultural psychiatry." *Social Science and Medicine* 11:3–10.

———. 1982. Neurasthenia and depression: A study of somatization and culture in China. *Culture, Medicine and Psychiatry* 6:117–190.

———. 1986. *Social Origins of Distress and Disease: Neurasthenia, Depression and Pain in Modern China.* New Haven, Conn.: Yale University Press.

Kleinman, A., and Sung, L. H. 1979. Why do indigenous practitioners successfully heal? *Medical Anthropology* 13B (1): 7–26.

Kluckhohn, C. 1951. Values and value orientations. In *Toward a General Theory of Action*, ed. T. Parsons. Cambridge: Harvard University Press.

Knoblauch, D. L. 1985. Applying Taoist thought to counseling and psychotherapy. *American Mental Health Counselors Association Journal* 7 (2): 52–63 (special issue).

Kohut, H. 1971. *The Analysis of Self.* Madison, Conn.: International Universities Press.

————. 1984. *How Does Analysis Cure?* Chicago: University of Chicago Press.

Kondo, K. 1976. The origin of Morita therapy. In *Culture-bound syndromes, Ethnopsychiatry, and Alternate Therapies*, ed. W. Lebra, 250–258. Honolulu: University Press of Hawai'i.

Kora, T. 1938. The problem of so-called neurasthenia. *Seishin shinkeigaku zasshi* 42: 755–796 (in Japanese).

————. 1965. Morita therapy. *International Journal of Psychiatry* 1:611–640.

Korean Academy of Psychotherapists. 1995. *Psychotherapy East and West: Integration of Psychotherapies*. Rev. ed. of the proceedings of the 16th International Congress of Psychotherapy, Seoul, Korea.

Kosawa, H. 1932. Two kinds of guilty conscience—the Ajase complex. *Journal of Japan Psychoanalytical Association* 1 (4): 5–9 (in Japanese).

————. 1953. Final version of the Ajase story. Translator's afterword in *Japanese version of "Neue Folge del Verlesungen zur Einfuhrung in die Psychoanalyse, 1932."*

Kroeber, A. L., and Kluckhohn, C. 1952. *Culture: A Critical Review of Concepts and Definition*. Papers of the Peabody Museum of Archaeology and Ethnology, 47. Cambridge: Harvard University.

Krühl, M. 1979. *Freund sein Vater*. Munich: C. H. Beckesche Verlag. Trans. Setsuo Mizuno. Tokyo: Shisakusha, 1987.

Kwan, V. S. Y.; Bond, M. H.; and Singelis, T. M. 1997. Pancultural explanations for life satisfaction: Adding relationship harmony to self-esteem. *Journal of Personality and Social Psychology* 73:1038–1051.

Lai, W. 1984. Symbolism of evil in China: The *kung-chia* myth analyzed. *History of Religion* 123 (4): 316–343.

Lebovici, S. 1988. Fantasmatic interaction and intergenerational transmission. *Infant Mental Health Journal* 9 (1): 10–19.

Lebra, T. S., and Lebra, W. P., eds. 1974. *Japanese Culture and Behavior: Selected Readings*. Honolulu: University Press of Hawai'i.

Lebra, W. P., ed. 1972. *Transcultural Research in Mental Health*. Volume 2 of *Mental Health Research in Asia and the Pacific*. Honolulu: University Press of Hawai'i.

————. 1974. *Youth, Socialization, and Mental Health*. Volume 3 of *Mental Health Research in Asia and the Pacific*. Honolulu: University Press of Hawai'i.

————. 1976. *Culture-bound Syndromes, Ethnopsychiatry, and Alternative Therapies*. Honolulu: University Press of Hawai'i.

Lee, E. 1997. *Working with Asian Americans: A Guide for Clinicians*. New York: Guilford Press.

Lee, J.; Lei, A.; and Sue, S. 2001. The current state of mental health research on Asian Americans. *Journal of Human Behavior in the Social Environment* 3:159–178.

Lee, K. B. 1984. *A New History of Korea*. Trans. E. Wagner with E. J. Shultz. Cambridge: Harvard University Press.

Lee, L. C., and Zane, N. 1998. *Handbook of Asian American Psychology*. Thousand Oaks, Calif.: Sage.

Lee, P. 1997. *The Sources of Korean Tradition*. New York: Columbia University Press.

Lee, S. 1994. The vicissitudes of neurasthenia in Chinese societies: Where will it go from the ICD-10? *Transcultural Psychiatric Research Review* 31:153–172.

———. 1996. Cultures in psychiatric nosology: The CCMD-2-R and international classification of mental disorders. *Culture, Medicine and Psychiatry* 20:421–474.

———. 1998. Estranged bodies, simulated harmony, and misplaced cultures: Neurasthenia in contemporary Chinese society. *Psychosomatic Medicine* 60:448–457.

———. 1999. Diagnosis postponed: Shenjing Shuairuo and the transformation of psychiatry in post-Mao China. *Culture, Medicine and Psychiatry* 23:349–380.

Lee, S. H. 1993. *Fear of Social Relations*. Seoul: Ilchogak (in Korean).

Lee, S. J. 1991. *"Shin-kyung-sung" iran?* (What is "nervos?": Yin-Yang theory of brain function). Daejon: Kwanggaeto (in Korean).

Lee, S., and Kleinman, A. 1997. Mental illness and social change in China. *Harvard Review of Psychiatry* 5:43–46.

———. 2000. Suicide as resistance in Chinese society. In *Chinese Society: Change, Conflict and Resistance,* ed. E. J. Perry and M. Selden, 221–240. London: Routledge.

Leung, P. W. L., and Lee, P. W. H. 1996. Psychotherapy with the Chinese. In *Handbook of Chinese Psychology,* ed. M. H. Bond, 441–456. Hong Kong: Oxford University Press.

Leung, V. S. K. 1999. Influence of individual-level factors on communication: Self-other perceptions. Undergraduate thesis, Department of Psychology, The Chinese University of Hong Kong.

Li, C. P. 1997. The invention and review of rapid integrated therapy: Examination from sociocultural, times, and clinical experiences. In *Chinese Mind and Therapy,* ed. W. S. Tseng, 380–387. Beijing: Beijing Medical University and China Xie-He Medical Joint Publisher (in Chinese).

Li, C. T. 1998. Wu-Jian psychotherapy. In *Medical psychology,* ed. C. T. Li, 822–828. Beijing: Beijing Medical University and China Xie-He Medical Joint Publisher (in Chinese).

Li, M. G.; Duan, C. M.; Ding, B. K.; Yue, D. M.; et al. 1994. Psychotherapy integration in modern China. *Journal of Psychotherapeutic Practice and Research* 3 (4): 277–283.

Lidz, T. 1989. Personal communication.

Lidz, T., and Lidz, R. 1989. *Oedipus in the Stone Age*. Madison, Conn.: International Universities Press.

Lin, M. H. 1939. Confucius on interpersonal relations. *Psychiatry* 2:475–481.

Lin, T. Y. 1989. Neurasthenia revisied: Its place in modern psychiatry. *Culture, Medicine and Psychiatry* 13 (2): 105–129.

Lin, T. Y.; Tseng, W. S.; and Yeh, E. K., eds. 1995. *Chinese Societies and Mental Health*. Hong Kong: Oxford University Press.

Lin, Y. L., and Kuo, B. Y. 1991. *Qigong piancha suo zhi jingshen-zhanai 21 li fenxi* (Analysis of 21 cases of psychiatric illness occurring as complications of qigong). *Chinese Journal of Mental Health* 5 (3): 109.

Lin, Y. T. 1948. *The Wisdom of Laotse*. Trans., ed., and with an introduction and notes by Lin Yutang. New York: Modern Library.

Liu, S. H. 1993. The psychotherapeutic function of the Confucian discipline of *hsin* (mind-heart). In *Psychotherapy for the Chinese*, ed. L. Y. Cheng, F. Cheung, and C. N. Chen, 1–17. Hong Kong: Department of Psychiatry, The Chinese University of Hong Kong.

Liu, X. G. 1999. An inquiry into the core value of Laozi's philosophy. In *Religious and Philosophical Aspects of the "Laozi,"* ed. M. Csikszentmihalyi and P. J. Ivanhoe, 211–237. Albany: State University of New York Press.

Lu, L. 1995. The relationship between subjective well-being and psychosocial variables in Taiwan. *Journal of Social Psychology* 135:351–357.

Lu, L., and Shih, J. B. 1997. Personality and happiness: Is mental health a mediator? *Personality and Individual Differences* 22:249–256.

Luk, K. Y. 1972. *The Secrets of Chinese Meditation*. New York: Samuel Weiser.

Ma, J. L. C.; Chow, M. Y. M.; Lee, S.; and Lai, K. 2002. Family meaning of self-starvation: Themes discerned in family treatment in Hong Kong. *Journal of Family Therapy* 24:57–71.

MacGregor, G. 1989. *Dictionary of Religion and Philosophy*. New York: Paragon House.

Maeda, S. 1998. *Genkokeie* (Toward primal scene). Kyoto: Hakujisha (in Japanese).

Malinowski, B. 1927. *Sex and Repression in Savage Society*. New York: International Library.

Marsella, A. J., and Pederson, P. B., eds. 1981. *Cross-cultural Counseling and Psychotherapy*. New York: Pergamon.

Maslow, A. H. 1968. *Toward a Psychology of Being*. 2d ed. New York: Van Nostrand.

McCrae, R. R.; Costa, P. T., Jr.; and Yik, M. S. M. 1996. Universal aspects of Chinese personality. In *The Psychology of the Chinese People*, ed. M. H. Bond, 189–207. Hong Kong: Oxford University Press.

McCrae, R. R.; Yik, M. S. M.; Trapnell, P. D.; Bond, M. H.; and Paulhus, D. L. 1998. Interpreting personality profiles across cultures: Bilingual acculturation and peer-rating studies of Chinese undergraduates. *Journal of Personality and Social Psychology* 74:1041–1055.

Mehler, M. S., and Furer, M. 1968. *On Human Symbiosis and the Vicissitudes of Individuation*. New York: International University Press.

Mei, Y. P. 1967. The status of the individual in Chinese social thought and practice. In *The Chinese Mind: Essentials of Chinese Philosophy and Culture*, ed. C. A. Moore, 323–339. Honolulu: University Press of Hawai'i.

Meier, C. 1949. *Ancient Incubation and Modern Psychotherapy*. Trans. S. Akiyama. Tokyo: Chikuma Shobō, 1986 (in Japanese).

Mitchell, S. A. 1988. *Relational Concepts in Psychoanalysis: An Integration*. Cambridge: Harvard University Press.

Molino, A., ed. 1998. *The Couch and the Tree: Dialogues in Psychoanalysis and Buddhism*. New York: North Point Press.

Montagu, M. F. A., ed. 1968. *Man and Aggression*. London: Oxford University Press.

Morehead, D. 1999. Oedipus, Darwin, and Freud: One big, happy family? *Psychoanalytic Quarterly* 118:347–375.

Morgan, P. 1993. Buddhism. In *The World's Religions: Understanding the Living Faiths*, ed. P. B. Clarke, 148–171. Pleasantville, N.Y.: Reader's Digest.

Mori, M. 1994. *Lo-shi to Sou-shi* (Lao-zi and Zhuang-zi.). Tokyo: Kodansha (in Japanese).

Morita, S. 1921. Shinkeishitsu oyobi shinkeisuijaku-shō no ryōhō (The treatment of shinkeishitsu and neurasthenia). In *Morita Shōma zenshū* (Collected essays of Shōma Morita), ed. T. Kora, 1:231–506. Tokyo: Hakuyōsha, 1974 (in Japanese).

———. 1922. Seishinryōhō kōgi (Psychotherapy lecture). In *Morita Shōma zenshū* (Collected essays of Shōma Morita), ed. T. Kora, 1:509–638. Tokyo: Hakuyōsha, 1974 (in Japanese).

———. 1926. Shinkeisuijaku-shō oyobi kyōhaku-kannen no konchihō (The treatment of neurasthenia and obsession). In *Morita Shōma zenshū* (Collected essays of Shōma Morita), ed. T. Kora, 2:71–282. Tokyo: Hakuyōsha, 1974 (in Japanese).

———. 1928. *Essential Nature and Treatment of Nervousness*. Tokyo: Hakuyōsha (in Japanese).

———. 1934. Nikki shidō (Diary guidance). In *Morita Shōma zenshū* (Collected essays of Shōma Morita), ed. T. Kora, 4:83–84. Tokyo: Hakuyōsha, 1974 (in Japanese).

———. 1974. The therapeutic results of special therapy for *shinkeishitsu*. In *Morita Shōma zenshū* (Collected essays of Shōma Morita), ed. T. Kora, 3:67–71. Tokyo: Hakuyōsha (in Japanese).

Murase, T. 1976. Naikan therapy. In *Culture-bound Syndromes, Ethnopsychiatry, and Alternate Therapies*, ed. W. Lebra, 259–269. Honolulu: University Press of Hawai'i.

———. 1977. Naikan chiryō to Morita chiryō (Naikan therapy and Morita therapy). In *Gendai no Morita ryōhō* (Modern Morita therapy), ed. K. Ohara, 454–468. Tokyo: Hakuyōsha (in Japanese).

———. 1978. Naikan ryōhō (Introspection therapy). In *Gendai seishin igaku taikei* (Handbook of modern psychiatry), 5:215–229. Tokyo: Nakayama Shobō.

Murase, T., and Johnson, F. 1974. Naikan, Morita and Western psychotherapy. *Archives of General Psychiatry* 31:121–128.

Murphy, H. B. M. 1982. Sexual neuroses and the Oedipus complex theory: India, Laos, and the Celebes. In *Comparative Psychiatry*, H. B. M. Murphy, 269–275. Berlin: Springer-Verlag.

Nakamura, H. 1948, 1949. *Ways of Thinking of Eastern People*. 2 vols. Tokyo: Misuzu (in Japanese).

———. 1970. *Genshi bukkyō* (Original Buddhism). Tokyo: NHK Books (in Japanese).

Nam, J. H.; Sasaki, Y. J.; and Kim, K. I. 1992. Pathway of help-seeking behavior of schizophrenics in Korea. *Mental Health Research* 11:231–270.

Naranjo, C., and Ornstein, R. E. 1971. *On the Psychology of Meditation*. New York: Viking.

Nishizono, M. 1986. Book review. *Kikan seishinryōhō* (Japanese journal of psycho-therapy), 12 (1): 70–71 (in Japanese).

———. 1988. Psychiatric service and psychotherapy in Japan. In *Psychotherapy in Japan, Asia, and North America,* ed. M. Nishizono and J. Yamamoto, 13–44. Tokyo: Kobundō (in Japanese).

———. 1994. Japanese psychotherapy: Modern psychoanalysis and its cultural relevance. In *Psychotherapy East and West,* ed. D. S. Rhee, 296–305. Seoul: Korean Academy of Psychotherapy.

———. 2000. Some trends of psychotherapy in Japan. *Journal of Morita Therapy* 11 (1): 3–11.

Nishizono, M., and Yamamoto, J., eds. 1988. *Nihon, ajiya, kita-america no seishinryōhō* (Psychotherapy in Japan, Asia, and North America). Tokyo: Kobundo.

Northrop, F. S. C. 1960. *The Meeting of East and West.* New York: Macmillan.

Obeyesekere, G. 1981. *Medusa's Hair.* Chicago: University of Chicago Press.

———. 1984. *The Cult of Pattini.* Chicago: University of Chicago Press.

Offer, D., and Sabshin, M. 1974. *Normality: Theoretical and Clinical Concepts of Mental Health.* 2d ed. New York: Basic Books.

Okonogi, K. 1967. Some comments on psychoanalysis in Japan. *Journal of Japanese Psychoanalytic Society* 7:297.

———. 1978. The Ajase complex of the Japanese (1): The depth psychology of the moratorium people. *Japan Echo* 5 (4): 88–105 (in Japanese).

———. 1979. The Ajase complex of the Japanese (2). *Japan Echo* 6 (1): 104–118 (in Japanese).

Osgood, C. 1951. *The Koreans and Their Culture.* New York: Ronald Press.

Otero, S. 1996. "Fearing our mothers": An overview of the psychoanalytic theories concerning the *vagina dentata* motif F547.1.1. *American Journal of Psychoanalysis* 56 (3): 269–288.

Pedersen, P. 1999. Culture-centered interventions as a fourth dimension of psychology. In *Multiculturalism as a Fourth Force,* ed. P. Pedersen, 3–18. Philadelphia: Brunner/Mazel.

Pedersen, P. B.; Lonner, W. J., and Dragun, J. G. 1976. *Counseling across Cultures.* Honolulu: University Press of Hawai'i.

Pedersen, P. S. 1977. Asian personality theory. In *Current Personality Theories,* ed. R. J. Corsini, 367–397. Itasca, Ill.: Peacock.

Prince, R. H. 1991. Transcultural psychiatry's contribution to international classification systems: The example of social phobia. In *Environment and Psychotherapy,* ed. A. M. Ghardrian and H. E. Lehmann, 55–72. New York: Springer.

Rank, O. 1914. *The Myth of the Birth of the Hero: A Psychological Interpretation of Mythology.* Trans. Drs. F. Robbins and S. E. Jelliffe. New York: Journal of Nervous and Mental Disease Publishing Company.

Reynolds, D. K. 1977. Naikan therapy: An experiential view. *International Journal of Social Psychiatry* 23:252–263.

———. 1980. *The Quiet Therapies: Japanese Pathways to Personal Growth.* Honolulu: University Press of Hawai'i.

Rhee, D. S. 1984. Assimilation of Western psychotherapy in Asia: The Korean case. *Jungshin chiryo* (Korean journal of psychotherapy), 1:41–46.

———. 1990. The Tao, psychoanalysis and existential thought. *Psychotherapy and Psychosomatics* 53:21–27.

———. 1993. The Tao and empathy: An East Asian interpretation. *Korean Journal of Psychotherapy* 7:7–19 (in Korean).

———. 1995. The Tao and Western psychotherapy. In *Psychotherapy, East and West: Integration of Psychotherapies.* Seoul: Korean Academy of Psychotherapists.

Rhi, B. Y. 1986. Confucianism and mental health in Korea. In *The Psycho-cultural Dynamics of the Confucian Family: Past and Present,* ed. W. H. Slote, 249–271. Seoul: International Cultural Society of Korea.

———. 1999. *Shadow: Our Inner Dark Partner.* Seoul: Hangilsa (in Korean).

Rim, H. D. 1999. The future of psychotherapy: An Eastern perspective. In *Analytic Western Psychotherapy and Asian Culture.* Proceedings of the 9th Scientific Meeting of the Pacific Rim College of Psychiatrists, October, Seoul.

Roland, A. 1988. *In Search of Self in India and Japan: Toward a Cross-cultural Psychology.* Princeton, N.J.: Princeton University Press.

Ross, N. W. 1966. *Three Ways of Asian Wisdom.* New York: Simon and Schuster.

———, ed. 1960. *The World of Zen.* New York: Vintage.

Rothbaum, F.; Rosen, K.; Ujiie, T.; and Uchida, N. 2002. Family system theory, attachment theory, and culture. *Family Process* 41 (3): 328–350.

Rothbaum, F.; Weisz, J.; Pott, M.; Miyake, K.; and Morelli, G. 2000. Attachment and culture: Security in the United States and Japan. *American Psychologist* 55 (10): 1093–1104.

Rubin, J. 1998. *Psychoanalysis and Buddhism: Towards an Integration.* New York: Plenum Press.

Sakano Y. 1999. Ninchi-kōdō ryōhō karamita naikan-ryōhō (Naikan therapy from the viewpoint of cognitive behavior therapy). In *Shinri-ryōhō no honshitsu—Naikan ryōhō o kangaeru* (The essence of psychotherapy: From the standpoint of Naikan therapy), R. Kawahara, Y. Higashi, and Y. Miki, 47–59. Tokyo: Nihon Hyōron-sha.

Schick, A. 1973. Psychotherapy in old Vienna and New York: Cultural comparison. *Psychoanalytic Review* 60 (1): 111–126.

Schneider, B. H.; Karcher M. J., and Schlapkohl, W. 1999. Relationship counseling across cultures: Cultural sensitivity and beyond. In *Multiculturalism as a Fourth Force,* ed. P. Pedersen, 167–190. Philadelphia: Brunner/Mazel.

Schrut, A. H. 1994. The Oedipus complex: Some observations and questions regarding its validity and universal existence. *Journal of the American Academy of Psychoanalysis* 22 (4): 727–751.

Schulte, W. 1964. *Studien zur heutigen psychotherapie.* Heidelberg: Quelle and Meyer.

Shinran. 1966. *Kyō gyō shin sho* (A collection of papers on Buddhism teachings, training, and beliefs). Ryūkoku Translation Series, vol. 5. Kyoto: Ryūkoku University, 1966.

Shinran S. and Hirota D. (head translator). 1995. *The True Teaching, Practice and Realization of the Pure Land way*. Kyoto: Hongwanji International Center (in Japanese).

Sinha, T. C. 1966. Psychoanalysis in India. In *Lumbini Park Silver Jubilee Souvenir*. Calcutta: Lumbini Park.

Smith, H. 1958. *The Religions of Man*. New York: Harper and Row.

Souci, D. S. 1999. *In the Moonlight Mist: A Korean Tale*. Honesdale, Pa.: Boyds Mills Press.

Spiegel, J. 1988. Kachikan to taido no hikaku (Comparison of value systems and attitudes). In *Nihon, ajiya, kita-america no seishin-ryōhō* (Psychotherapy in Japan, Asia, and North America), ed. M. Nishizono and J. Yamamoto, 122–137. Tokyo: Kobensha.

Sue, S., and Morishima, J. K. 1982. *The Mental Health of Asian Americans: Contemporary Issues in Identifying and Treating Mental Problems*. San Francisco: Jossey-Bass.

Sun, H. F., and Bond, M. H. 2000. Interactant's personality and status as determinants of Influencer's choice of tactics. In *Management and Organizations in China*, ed. J. P. Li, A. Tsui, and E. Weldon, 283–302. New York: Macmillan.

Sunardjo, H. 1975. *Ramayana*. Jakata: Djambatan.

The Sutra of Contemplation of Infinite Life (Kan muryo ju kyo). 1984. Kyoto: Ryūkoku University Translation Center.

Suwaki, H. 1979. Naikan and Danshūkai for the treatment of Japanese alcoholic patients. *British Journal Addiction* 74:15–19.

Suzuki, D.; Fromm, E.; and De Martion, R. 1960. *Zen Buddhism and Psychoanalysis*. New York: Harper and Row.

Suzuki, D. T. 1949. *Essays in Zen Buddhism*. New York: Grove Press.

———. 1956. *Zen Buddhism*. Ed. William Barrett. New York: Doubleday.

———. 1973. *The Kyō gyō shin sho: A Collection of Passages Expounding the True Teaching, Living, Faith and Realizing of the Pure Land*. Kyoto: Shinshū Ōtani-ha.

Suzuki, T. 1969. *Experiential Treatment of Neurosis*. Tokyo: Seishin Shobō, 1976 (in Japanese).

Suzuki, T., and Suzuki, R. 1979. A follow-up of neurotic patients treated by inpatient Morita therapy. *Seishin shinkeigaku zasshi* 81:665–678 (in Japanese).

Tabora, B., and Flaskerud, J. H. 1994. Depression among Chinese Americans: Review of the literature. *Issues in Mental Health Nursing* 15:569–584.

Tang, N. M., and Smith, B. L. 1996. The eternal triangle across cultures: Oedipus, Hsueh, and Ganesa. In *The Psychoanalytic Study of the Child*, ed. A. J. Solnit, P. B. Nerbauer, S. Abrams, and A. S. Dowling, 51. New Haven, Conn.: Yale University Press.

Takeuchi, K. 1965. On "Naikan" method. *Psychologia* 8:2–8.

Tatsumi N. 1999. Jiga-hattatsu-ron kara naikan ryōhō o kangaeru (The consideration of Naikan therapy from the viewpoint of ego development). In *Shinri-ryōhō no honshitsu—Naikan ryōhō o kangaeru* (The essence of psychotherapy: From the standpoint of Naikan therapy), ed. R. Kawahara, Y. Higashi, and Y. Miki, 17–31. Tokyo: Nihon Hyōronsha.

Teasdale, J. D.; Segal, Z. V., and Williams, J. M. G. 2003. Mindfulness training and problem formulation. *Clinical Psychology: Science and Practice* 10:157–160.

Thondup, T. 2001. *Boundless Healing: Meditation Exercises to Enlighten the Mind and Heal the Body.* Boston and London: Shambhala.

Tocqueville (de), A. D. 1835. *Democracy in America,* vol. 2. Trans. Henry Reeve; rev. and ed. P. Bradley. New York: Vintage, 1945.

Tong, P. K. K. 1969. Understanding Confucianism. *International Philosophical Quarterly* 9:518–532.

Torrey, E. F. 1986. *Witchdoctors and Psychiatrists: The Common Roots of Psychotherapy and Its Future.* New York: Harper and Row.

Tseng, W. S. 1973a. The concept of personality in Confucian thought. *Psychiatry* 36 (2): 191–202.

———. 1973b. The development of psychiatric concepts in traditional Chinese medicine. *Archives of General Psychiatry* 29:569–575.

———. 1975. The nature of somatic complaints among psychiatric patients: The Chinese case. *Comprehensive Psychiatry* 16:237–245.

———. 1978. Traditional and modern psychiatric care in Taiwan. In *Culture and Healing in Asian Societies: Anthropological, Psychiatric and Public Health Studies,* ed. A. Kleinman, P. Kunstadter, E. R. Alexander, and J. L. Gale, 311–328. Cambridge, Mass.: Schenkman.

———. 1995. Psychotherapy for the Chinese: Cultural adjustments. In *Psychotherapy for the Chinese: II,* ed. L. Y. C. Cheng, H. Baxter, and F. M. C. Cheung, 1–22. Hong Kong: Department of Psychiatry, Chinese University of Hong Kong.

———. 1997. Overview: Culture and psychopathology. In *Culture and Psychopathology: A Guide to Clinical Assessment,* ed. W. S. Tseng and J. Streltzer, 1–27. New York: Brunner/Mazel.

———. 1999. Culture and psychotherapy: Review and practical guidelines. *Transcultural Psychiatry* 36:131–179.

———. 2001. *Handbook of Cultural Psychiatry.* San Diego, Calif.: Academic Press.

———. 2002. *Culture and Psychotherapy.* Popular Series, 10. Beijing: Beijing Medical University Publisher (in Chinese).

———. 2003. *Clinician's Guide to Cultural Psychiatry.* San Diego, Calif.: Academic Press.

———, ed. 1997. *Chinese Mind and Therapy.* Beijing: Beijing Medical University Press and China Xie-He Medical Joint Publishers (in Chinese).

Tseng, W. S.; Ebata, K.; Kim, K. I.; Krahl, W.; Kua, E. H.; Lu, Q. Y.; Shen, Y. C.; Tan, E. S.; and Yang, M. J. 2001. Asian mental health: Improvement and challenges. *International Journal of Social Psychiatry* 47 (1): 8–23.

Tseng, W. S., and Hsu, J. 1969–1970. Chinese culture, personality formation and mental illness. *International Journal of Social Psychiatry* 16 (1): 5–14.

———. 1972. The Chinese attitude toward parental authority as expressed in Chinese children's stories. *Archives of General Psychiatry* 26:28–34.

———. 1979. Culture and psychotherapy. In *Perspectives on Cross-cultural Psychology*, ed. T. A. Marsella, R. G. Tharp, and T. J. Ciborowski, 333–345. New York: Academic Press.

———. 1991. *Culture and Family: Problems and Therapy.* New York: Haworth.

Tseng, W. S.; Lu, Q. Y.; and Yin, P. Y. 1995. Psychotherapy for the Chinese: Cultural consideration. In *Chinese Societies and Mental Health,* ed. T. Y. Lin, W. S. Tseng, and E. K. Yeh, 281–294. Hong Kong: Oxford University Press.

Tseng, W. S., and McDermott, J. F., Jr. 1975. Psychotherapy: Historical roots, universal elements, and cultural variations. *American Journal of Psychiatry* 132:378–384.

Tseng, W. S., and Streltzer, J., eds. 2001. *Culture and Psychotherapy: A Guide for Clinical Practice.* Washington, D.C.: American Psychiatric Press.

Tseng, W. S., and Wu, D. Y. H. 1985. *Chinese Culture and Mental Health.* Orlando, Fla.: Academic Press.

Tung, M. P. M. 1994. Symbolic meanings of the body in Chinese culture and somatization. *Culture, Medicine, and Psychiatry* 18:483–492.

Vaillant, G. E. 1971. Theoretical hierarchy of adaptive ego mechanisms. *Archive of General Psychiatry* 24:107–118.

———. 1986. Introduction: A brief history of empirical assessment of defense mechanisms. In *Empirical Studies of Ego Mechanisms of Defense,* ed. G. E. Vaillant, viii–xx. Washington, D.C.: American Psychiatric Press.

Varma, V. K. 1982. Present state of psychotherapy in India. *Indian Journal of Psychiatry* 24:209–226. (Reviewed in *Transcultural Psychiatric Research Review* 21 (4) (1984): 291.

Walsh, T. M. 1966. Responses on the famous sayings test of professional and nonprofessional personnel in a medical population. *Psychological Reports* 18:151–157.

Watts, A. W. 1957. *The Way of Zen.* New York: Mentor Books.

———. 1958. *Nature, Man and Woman.* New York: Vintage Books, 1991.

———. 1961. *Psychotherapy: East and West.* New York: Pantheon.

Wei Z. T. 1979. *Zhongguo sixiangshi* (History of Chinese thought). Taipei: Dalin Chubanshe.

Weiss, S. 1985. How culture influences the interpretation of the Oedipus myth. Reprinted in *The Oedipus Papers,* ed. G. Pollack and J. Ross. Madison, Wisc.: International Universities Press, 1988.

Williamson, M. 1992. The technique of self-psychological therapy and the Tao. *Australian Journal of Psychotherapy* 11 (2): 79–96.

Willis, R. 1993. Introduction. In *World Mythology,* ed. R. Willis, 10–16. New York: Henry Holt.

Wood, E. 1959. *Yoga.* Baltimore: Penguin Books, 1969.

Wright, A. F. 1953. Introduction. In *Studies in Chinese Thought,* 1–18. Chicago: University of Chicago Press.

———. 1959. *Buddhism in Chinese History.* Stanford, Calif.: Stanford University Press.

Wu, C. Y. 1997. Qigong: Chinese traditional psychotherapy. In *Chinese Mind and Therapy,* ed. W. S. Tseng, 372–379. Beijing: Beijing Medical University and China Xie-He Medical Joint Publishers (in Chinese).

Xiao, S. Y.; Young, D. S.; and Zhang, H. G. 1998. Taoistic cognitive psychotherapy for neurotic patients: A preliminary clinical trial. *Psychiatry and Clinical Neurosciences* 52 (Suppl.), S238–S241.

Xie, X. L.; Weinstein, L.; and Meredith, W. 1996. Hotline in China: One way to help Chinese people. *Psychological Reports* 78 (1): 90.

Xu, S. H. 1997. The concept of mind and body in Chinese traditional medicine and its implication for psychotherapy. In *Chinese Mind and Therapy,* ed. W. S. Tseng, 332–354. Beijing: Beijing Medical University and China Xie-He Medical Joint Publishers (in Chinese).

Xu, Y. X. 1997. Confucius' and Laozi's thought: The possible application in psychotherapy. In *Chinese Mind and Therapy,* ed. W. S. Tseng, 355–369. Beijing: Beijing Medical University and Xie-He Medical University Joint Publishers (in Chinese).

Yang H. R. 2001. *Yi jing dao du* (Introductory reading of the *Yi-Jing*). Beijing: Huawen Chubanshe.

Yang, J.; McCrae, R. R.; Costa, P. T., Jr.; Dai, X.; Yao, S.; Cai, T.; and Gao, B. 1999. Cross-cultural personality assessment in psychiatric populations: The NEO-PI-R in the People's Republic of China. *Psychological Assessment* 11:359–368.

Yang, K. S. 1986. Chinese personality and its change. In *The Psychology of the Chinese People,* ed. M. H. Bond, 106–170. Hong Kong: Oxford University Press.

Yang, K. S., and Bond, M. H. 1990. Exploring implicit personality theories with indigenous or imported constructs: The Chinese case. *Journal of Personality and Social Psychology* 58:1087–1095.

Young, D. S. 1997. Chinese mind and Chinese unique therapy. In *Chinese Mind and Therapy,* ed. W. S. Tseng, 22–38. Beijing: Beijing Medical University and Chinese Xie-He Medical University Joint Publishers (in Chinese).

Young, D. S.; Zhang, Y. L.; Xiao, S. Y.; Zhou, L.; and Zhu, J. F. N.d. Introduction of "Chinese Daoism Cognitive Therapy" (manuscript).

Zhai, S. T. 1995. Daojia sixiang yu xinlizhiliao (Daoist thought and psychotherapy). *Chinese Mental Health Journal* 9 (Suppl.), 63–64.

Zhang, J. X. 1997. Distinction between general trust and specific trust: Their unique patterns with personality trait domains, distinct roles in interpersonal situations, and different function in path models of trusting behavior. Doctoral dissertation, The Chinese University of Hong Kong.

Zhang, J. X., and Bond, M. H. 1998. Personality and filial piety among college students in two Chinese societies: The added value of indigenous constructs. *Journal of Cross-Cultural Psychology* 29:402–417.

Zhang, R. L.; Li, F. M.; Xu, Z. L.; and Feng, Y. M. 2000. Psychotherapy on negative emotions of coronary heart disease and its clinical implications. *Chinese Journal of Clinical Psychology* 8 (3): 139–142 (in Chinese).

Zhang Y.; Young, D. S.; Lee, S.; Li, L. J.; Zhang, H. G.; Xiao, Z. P.; Hao, W.; Feng, Y. M.; Zhou, H. X.; and Chang, D. F. 2002. Chinese Taoist cognitive psychotherapy in the treatment of generalized anxiety disorder in contemporary China. *Transcultural Psychiatry* 39:115–129.

Zheng, Y. P.; Xu, L. Y.; and Shen, Y. Q. 1986. Styles of verbal expression or emotional and physical experiences: A study of depressed patients and normal control in China. *Culture, Medicine and Psychiatry* 10:231–243.

Zuniga, M. E. 1992. Using metaphors in therapy: Dichos and Latio clients. *Social Work* 37 (91): 55–60.

Contributors

Suk Choo **Chang**, M.D.
Staff Psychiatrist, Department of Behavioral Health, Saint Mary's Hospital; and practicing psychiatrist, Waterbury, CT, U.S.A.

Fanny M. **Cheung**, Ph.D.
Professor and Chairperson, Department of Psychology, Chinese University of Hong Kong, Hong Kong, China; and Principal Investigator of the Chinese Personality Assessment Inventory Project.

Keisuke **Ebata**, M.D.
Former Superintendent, Tokyo Metropolitan Central Section Comprehensive Mental Health Center; Honorable Member, Japanese Cultural Psychiatry Association; President, Japanese Association of Psychiatric Rehabilitation; and practicing psychiatrist, Tokyo, Japan.

Yiqun **Gan**, Ph.D.
Associate Professor, Department of Psychology, Peking University, Beijing, China.

Jing **Hsu**, M.D.
Clinical Professor of Psychiatry, University of Hawai'i School of Medicine; and practicing psychiatrist, Honolulu, HI, U.S.A.

Sudhir **Kakar**, M.D.
Practicing psychoanalyst, Vikram Sarabhai Foundation, New Delhi, India.

Ryuzo **Kawahara**, M.D.
Professor and Chairman, Department of Neuropsychiatry, Faculty of Medicine, Totori University, Yonago, Japan.

Kwang-Iel **Kim**, M.D.
Professor Emeritus, Department of Neuropsychiatry, School of Medicine, Hanyang University, Seoul; former committee member, Transcultural Psychiatric Section, World Psychiatric Association; and practicing psychiatrist, Seoul, Korea.

Oksuk Mary **Kim**, M.D.
Clinical Professor of Psychiatry, University of Hawai'i School of Medicine; and practicing psychiatrist, Honolulu, HI, U.S.A.

S. Peter **Kim**, M.D., Ph.D., M.B.A.
Professor, Director of Child and Adolescent Forensic Psychiatry Program, Department of Psychiatry, University of Hawai'i School of Medicine, Honolulu, HI, U.S.A.

Kenji **Kitanishi**, M.D.
Professor, Department of Social Welfare, Japan Women's University; and Director, Morita Therapy Institute, Tokyo, Japan.

Osamu **Kitayama**, M.D.
Professor of Psychoanalysis, Graduate School of Human-Environment Studies, Kyushu University, Fukuoka, Japan.

Sing **Lee**, M.B., B.S., FRCPsych.
Professor, Department of Psychiatry, The Chinese University of Hong Kong, Hong Kong, China.

Poman **Lo**, Ph.D.
Former graduate student, Department of Psychology, The Chinese University of Hong Kong, Hong Kong, China.

Lü Qiuyun, M.D.
Professor of Psychiatry, Institute of Mental Health, Peking University, Beijing, China; and Chair, Psychotherapy and Counseling Committee of Chinese Association for Mental Health.

Masahisa **Nishizono**, M.D.
Professor Emeritus, Fukuoka University; President, Japan Psychoanalytic Society; and Director, Institute for Psychosocial Psychiatry and Psychoanalysis, Fukuoka City, Japan.

Keigo **Okonogi**, M.D. (deceased).
Professor, Tokyo International University Graduate School of Clinical Psychology; and former President, The Kodera Foundation for Psychoanalytic Study, Tokyo, Japan.

Rhee Dong-Shick, M.D.
Clinical Professor of Psychiatry, Hanyang University School of Medicine, Seoul, Korea; and Honorary President, The Korean Academy of Psychotherapists.

Wen-Shing **Tseng**, M.D.
Professor, Department of Psychiatry, University of Hawai'i School of Medicine, Honolulu, HI, U.S.A.; Guest Professor, Institute of Mental Health, Peking University, Beijing, China; and Honorable Adviser, Transcultural Psychiatric Section, World Psychiatric Association.

Yan Heqin, M.D.
Professor, Department of Psychiatry, Second Shanghai Medical University; and Honorable Director, Shanghai Mental Health Center, Shanghai, China.

Dersen **Young**, M.D.

Professor, Xiang-Ya Medical College, Central South University; Honorable Director, Mental Health Institute, Second Xiang-Ya Hospital, Changsha, Hunan, China; and former Vice-Chair, Chinese Psychiatric Society.

Liang **Zhou**, M. D.

Lecturer, Department of Social Medicine, College of Public Health, Central South University, Changsha, Hunan, China.

Index

About the Editors

Wen-Shing Tseng, M.D., is professor of psychiatry at the University of Hawai'i School of Medicine and honorable advisor of the Transcultural Psychiatric Section of the World Psychiatric Association. He is also guest professor at the Institute of Mental Health, Beijing University. He has authored and edited numerous books on culture and mental health.

Suk Choo Chang, M.D., is affiliated with the Department of Behavioral Health, Saint Mary's Hospital, and a practicing psychiatrist in Connecticut. Her publications include books related to Asian culture, psychology, and mental health.

Masahisa Nishizono, M.D., is professor emeritus at Fukuoka University and president of the Japan Psychoanalytic Society. Among his publications are works about Japanese psychiatry, Asian mental health, and psychotherapy.

Production Notes for Tseng/*Asian Culture and Psychotherapy*
Cover design by Chris Crochetiere, BW&A Books, Inc.
Text design and composition by Tseng Information Systems, Inc. using
Stone Serif and Stone Sans.
Printing and binding by The Maple-Vail Book Manufacturing Group
Printed on 60 lb. Sebago Eggshell, 420 ppi